Education Into the 21st Century:
Dangerous Terrain for Women?

Alison Mackinnon
Inga Elgqvist-Saltzman
Alison Prentice
(editors)

FALMER PRESS
· Taylor & Francis Group ·

UK   Falmer Press, 1 Gunpowder Square, London, EC4A 3DE
USA   Falmer Press, Taylor & Francis Inc., 1900 Frost Road, Suite 101,
          Bristol, PA 19007

First published in 1998

**A catalogue record for this book is available from the British
Library**

ISBN 0 7507 0656 2 cased
ISBN 0 7507 0657 0 paper

**Library of Congress Cataloging-in-Publication Data are
available on request**

Jacket design by Caroline Archer

Typeset in 10/12pt Garamond by
Graphicraft Typesetters Limited, Hong Kong

*Printed in Great Britain by Biddles Ltd., Guildford and King's Lynn
on paper which has a specified pH value on final paper manufacture
of not less than 7.5 and is therefore 'acid free'.*

*Every effort has been made to contact copyright holders for their
permission to reprint material in this book. The publishers would
be grateful to hear from any copyright holder who is not here
acknowledged and will undertake to rectify any errors or omissions
in future editions of this book.*

Contents

Contents

Acknowledgments

Books — not least conference anthologies — have their own histories of meetings between people and ideas, some joyful, others challenging. The circumstances supporting those meetings shape the final appearance of the work in print. This book is no exception. The editors are indebted to many people in different research communities and in various personal realms during the long process of the book's coming into being.

The unifying topic for the research that women from Australia, Canada, China and Scandinavia present here is gender and education — in the past, in our times and in the century to come. The writers work on different projects but come together in networks to pursue their common interest in linking feminist theory to educational theory, in relating educational reforms to women's realities, and in offering new perspectives on girls' and boys' education.

Some meetings which took place during the process of compiling this anthology have had particular significance. In December 1993 The Canadian History of Education Association in a joint meeting with the Australian and New Zealand History of Education Society offered the three editors of this volume the opportunity to present their work at a conference in Melbourne. In a session on early educated women in Australia, Canada and Sweden they reflected on the pattern of the life stories of women around the turn of the nineteenth century. Consideration of educational, vocational and familial expectations and frustrations inspired them to draw parallels with women's and girls' situation on the verge of the new century.

'Into the 21st Century: The Changing Face of Education' was the topic for a conference one and a half years later in Umeå in the northern part of Sweden. A developing research milieu on gender and education at the Department of Education at Umeå offered a forum where the contributors to this volume shared ideas and thoughts on educational theory, policy and practice and effects on women's lives and on the coming generation of girls and boys. The Swedish Council for Planning and Coordination of Research (particularly its programme for encouraging interdisciplinary feminist research) made it possible through a major grant to realize conference plans which had developed as an aftermath to the Melbourne conference and were finally crystallized on the shores in southern Australia. The faculty of Social Science, Umeå University, The Ontario Institute for Studies in Education, The Social Sciences and Humanities Research Council of Canada and the Faculty of Humanities and Social Sciences at the University of South Australia have all supported the Australian–Canadian–Swedish cooperation, facilitating research across continental boundaries.

Acknowledgments

Nearly a hundred women and men active in research and in practical educational work from all around the world met in June 1995 in Umeå, one of the northernmost Swedish universities. Researchers from Australia, Argentina, Canada, China, the UK, the USA and Scandinavia provided an international perspective on education and gender. Following the conference a two-day workshop focusing on current Swedish projects in the field was made possible through grants from the National Agency for Education in Sweden, and the Center for Women's Studies at Umeå. The midnight sun and the mountains of Lappland made a dramatic setting for the birth of the anthology based on the conference papers.

On their routes southwards from the conference — at Öland in southern Sweden — the three editors began the task of shaping the anthology. Editing such a book with contributions from all over the world, with editors living on different continents and a British publisher has been a daunting task even with the employment of electronic mail. We gratefully acknowledge the Swedish Council for Planning and Coordination of Research for supporting the final editorial meeting, this time on the southern shores of Australia, the home of the Australian editor, who has shouldered the main editorial burden. We thank the Faculty of Humanities and Social Sciences at the University of South Australia who funded the editorial assistance of Ingrid Day in finally putting the revised chapters together.

To the list of institutions who have supported our efforts we may finally add the Council for Studies of Higher Education, Stockholm, who in the last phase of the production offered the editors and some of the contributors the chance to meet again in Stockholm in August 1997 at a conference on the Gendered Nature of Higher Education. Finally, but certainly not least, a word of thanks to conference participants, particularly those of the Umeå conference, to contributors, translators, researchers and all the wonderful persons, too numerous to list here, who have read manuscripts and commented upon them and helped us to keep to time and space restraints.

The editors hope that this volume will help to sustain the conversation on the education of women and men as part of our desire for a better society in the century to come. Did we exceed the expectations of those who fought for educational reform for women a century ago? And are our achievements always unproblematic? One hundred years hence perhaps some scholars will come across this book in a dusty archive and wonder why the solutions so clear to them had to be so hard fought.

Alison Mackinnon, Inga Elgqvist-Saltzman, and Alison Prentice
Adelaide, Löttorp, and Victoria
January 1998

Introduction

Alison Mackinnon

This volume begins a conversation on the issue of gender and education as we approach the 21st century. We did not set out to survey the entire terrain: such a task would require a vast international project. Nevertheless, the questions we raise are significant for educators in societies as culturally diverse as Sweden, China and Great Britain. What did women in the late nineteenth and early twentieth century hope for in fighting for women's access to secondary and tertiary education, in entering the professions? Have we achieved those goals? Why, when we appear to make significant steps forward, do we encounter waves of resistance? And what do we mean by achieving our goals? Does the gaining of a degree in a male-dominated institution mean the same thing for a woman as for a man? Is the term 'an educated woman' a contradiction in terms, as Jane Martin provocatively suggests (Martin, 1985, 1991)? Is access a fitting measure of 'progress'? Does entry to a profession which requires long hours of commitment incompatible with the care of children constitute 'success'? And, worryingly, are we condemned to a cycle of advance and retreat, of constant justification of our presence of our continuing 'otherness'. Must we continue to be impertinent, as Kajsa Ohrlander asks?

While the production of this volume took place in assorted terrains, the material covered also spanned a period of over 100 years and a range of academic disciplines and perspectives. The participants spoke in different voices, indeed in different languages and academic vocabularies. Historian and philosopher, policy analyst and sociologist, educationist, practitioner and linguist from Sweden, Australia, Canada, Great Britain, China and Norway, from the United States and from Argentina listened to each other and were astonished to find that in spite of their varied cultures and circumstances many told similar stories. Those stories alarmed us all. Wherever women had made significant advances in education, and in the professions opened up by that education, they were encountering resistance, harassment, even violence. Further, men and women (to use for the moment an unfashionable categorization) often understood quite different versions of these narratives. Where women perceived an age-old dilemma of combining work and family, of dealing with the male culture of the workplace, of Sisyphus-like slow progress and retreat, many men appeared to see women bursting onto their territory in threatening numbers. Enough, they cried, women are doing better in schools, entering higher education in greater numbers, dominating primary school teaching. What about the boys?

Part 1

The collection is divided into three parts. Part I reaches back into the nine-teenth century to identify the hopes of early women educators, those women (and some men) who imagined a future where women and men would be equal citizens of a world made safe through shared responsibility, through shared access to the labour market and to the dignity of paid work. In reclaim-ing the past however, we often find the present. The past is not always a foreign country. There too, as Elgqvist-Saltzman demonstrates, there were dif-ferent positions as to the purpose and content of the education of women and girls. Should they be educated for the value of education in and of itself — or for their role as mothers and carers, as the primary educators of boys? Should they be prepared for vocations for which they were particularly suited? Linked to debates about the purpose of women's education was the issue of content. Should women study a male curriculum, thus proving their equality with men or should they explore an intellectual tradition rooted in their own experience? Was there a women's way of knowing, an intuitive, earth-rooted understand-ing which better expressed women's comprehension of the world as some novelists claimed (Mackinnon, this volume)? These notions of women's same-ness and difference, of their distinctive way of knowing or of the mind without sex exercised thinking women across the western world as they struggled for access to secondary and higher education.

Those women who a century ago undertook by choice or necessity the role of breadwinner (Prentice, this volume) trod unmarked winding tracks which often wound mysteriously around the straight roads laid out by men (Elgqvist-Saltzman, 1992). The obstacles they encountered, resistance, moral outrage, bureaucratic invisibility, unwelcome sexual attention — even violence, remain with us. But after a century in the public view feminists have named and codified many of the obstacles. Women have deemed unwelcome advances sexual or work place harassment. They have insisted that the keepers of statist-ics, of numbers of staff in universities for instance, or of student examinees, disaggregate the figures by sex, revealing the scarcity of women in senior positions, or the numbers of girls studying mathematics or physics. They have established 'beachheads' in state bureaucracies in order to develop and advance policies assisting women.

How were women to deal with the joys and burdens of childcare while claiming a voice in the public world? Many highly educated women in the past dealt with this dilemma by avoiding marriage and child-bearing, seeing a greater destiny in preparing future generations of girls and women for a different future (Mackinnon, 1997, Prentice, this volume). Others linked women's child rearing role to the argument for women's education. In feminist theory and in practice women have challenged the division of the world into binary opposi-tions such as public–private, nature–culture, recognizing that such a division is antithetical to life itself and results in the relegation of women to the private sphere, to the body. Women are to nature as men are to culture in Rosaldo and

Lamphere's now well-known formulation. Of course not all women agree on strategies to pursue — or indeed on analyses of the problem. Most recently some have questioned the strategic emphasis on women's disadvantage, turning the spotlight to male advantage (Eveline, 1994; see also Spurling, 1990).

Part 2

Is there a gap between feminist theory and educational practice as some have claimed? In this section we demonstrate both gendered educational practice, informed by theoretical understanding and the theorizing which arises from empirical work. The link between feminist theory and practice is a complex and dialectical one. Whilst educational practitioners frequently eschew the heights of philosophical and linguistic debate they are often attuned to current thinking and raise questions to challenge the theorists. In the major section of the collection we canvass a wide range of issues concerning relations between the sexes in schools and universities. We map current debates on girls' and boys' performance in schools, on the response to girls' access and on equality debates. We engage with the concern that women-are not progressing in university hierarchies in proportion to their numbers and expectations. And we construct theory as we go.

Attempts to change educational practice to meet goals of gender equality do not occur in a vacuum. National political cultures shape different approaches to change. Changing political and economic winds sweep through the terrain with all the devastation of a summer storm. Rebecca Coulter's analysis of the reshaping of education in Ontario, a case-study of the impact of policies based on economic rationalism, illustrates the fragility of equality measures when, as an unsympathetic bureaucrat declared, 'us guys in suits are back!'. To much of the western world countries such as Sweden and Norway have been a beacon of hope, of seemingly ideal gender equality legislation and practice. The political climate has assisted action research studies such as those of Hildur Ve and Britt Marie Berge, committed to the notion that boys should learn caring behaviours, girls assertiveness.

One of the important findings of their research was that although teachers and researchers collaborated closely to further social responsibility on the part of the boys, the idea that each pupil should develop self-reliance seemed to be very deeply embedded in the teachers' attitudes to crucial pedagogical values.

Does the introduction of more conservative policies always disadvantage girls? The British research reported by Gaby Weiner et al., raises interesting questions in relation to the introduction of a national curriculum and greater school assessment. Where fears had been held that girls would be disadvantaged the reverse appeared to be the case. The fact that girls seemed to narrow the gender gap in certain areas led to a moral panic over boys' disadvantage. Weiner's work reminds us of the importance of Lyn Yates' formulation that we must be flexible: while using liberal modernist arguments to challenge the establishment we can also draw on the complexities of post-modernism and deconstruct the category 'girls', asking always, which girls benefit, which group of girls lose out in any policy redirection (see also Joan Eveline, this volume).

Robin Burns and Victoria Foster bring us back to questions of the body in essays which view their questions through a post-modernist lens. Burns deconstructs the language of health and physical education in schools, revealing the problematic nature for educators of the female body. While nineteenth-century male educators claimed that education would destroy women's reproductive capacities, modern educators face the dilemma of treating girls' bodies like those of boys (should they play in the boys' football team, should they battle with the surf?) or of viewing the female body with dis-ease, as problematic and pathologized. Can the school provide challenging models of young healthy womenhood which counter media representations of (almost) anorexic girls, objects of the male gaze? Foster inserts the female body into the school setting and argues that there is no space for girls, that the female body itself is problematic and in danger in the public space of the school, that girls actively desiring education and 'space' represent a threat, no less than the new women of the late nineteenth- and early twentieth century (Mackinnon, see also Theobald, 1989). Foster proposes a liminal terrain, 'The space between', both physical and conceptual space between private and public spheres where girls can be free of unwanted hostility, and of the demands to care for others. Is this the space that women sought in earlier times in women's universities, that some seek now in single sex schools or in single sex classes? Participants at the Umeå conference were transfixed by a videotape shown by Australian Shirley Sampson which graphically showed girls claiming the benefits of single sex classes ('there were no boys to mess around and disrupt the lesson') while the boys deplored the loss of girls from their classes ('there was no-one to take notes').

Responding to a recent suggestion that a Sydney University College for men should admit women residents in order to interrupt the reproduction of a sexist, destructive masculinity, Ronald Conway asks, '. . . why should women be drafted to civilize those whose job it is to civilize themselves?' (Conway, 1997, see also Spurling, 1990). This question goes to the heart of a dilemma which spans the centuries: Do women have a different way of knowing/ learning which is at risk in the competitive environment of the university, an institution built on men's lives, men's patterns of knowledge? And should women bring that difference to bear to 'civilize' men? Kerstin Shands compares women's ways of working and thinking to Doppler effects, unfamiliar frequencies which cause distortion in the context of the academy. She draws on the work of Belenki et al., and of Jung to support her remedies for radical change: the making visible, even celebrating, of women's different way of operating in the world, calling on the university to embrace its 'shadow', the reverse of western, masculinist science. Shands' view is one that some feminists question, arguing that a focus on women's difference will relegate us to the private, the realm of nature, of the body and intuition, a position many have fought to escape. It also masks important differences between women. Yet Shands' discourse, and those who support a 'rationality of care' as equally vital for the democracies of the twenty-first century, is a persistent and insistent one (see Mackinnon and Ve, this volume and Martin, 1997).

The reality of women's 'otherness' in the university and the professions is underlined by two essays from radically different societies, Sweden and China. While substantive equality seems to exist in the fields which Benckert and Staberg describe, the fierce level of competition to advance, in the context of women's hopes for a family life, in effect creates two career paths. The division of university and household labour, ostensibly 'shared', in effect favours men's careers, in equality-conscious Sweden as in the People's Republic of China. In the latter, state policy encourages women's participation in education and the economy: as the slogan suggests, 'women hold up half the sky'. But as Grace Mak reveals, when individual lives are studied, statistical equalities give way to the familiar story of heavier domestic burdens for women, subtle preferment for men. A mismatch in public policy and private realities ensures that women's half of the sky is harder to support.

Part 3

Where do we go from here? Resistance is still essential. We must still be impertinent, assert our needs and desires, as Kajsa Ohrlander argues from a Swedish viewpoint. In spite of cries of 'what about the boys?', echoing across the globe, we must continue to support women's goals of an equal secondary and tertiary education, of full participation in the professions, rejecting false claims that we now have it all, indeed are disadvantaging men.

Feminist theory has advanced in complexity and women concerned with education, no less than others, have developed and built on that theory to find a way forward. We have a new understanding of the complexity of the situation, of the fact that there are many paths across the terrain and that we may need to advance on several fronts at once. Lyn Yates insists that we should both embrace the category 'girls' in contexts where it is politically useful, while at the same time deconstructing it where necessary to meet the needs of particular groups of girls who may be falsely represented (or under-represented) in that categorization (see also Bacchi, 1996). In her reflections on feminist theory Joan Eveline asks why we have not focused on men's advantage, preferring to highlight women's disadvantage. Confronting male advantage, indeed male resistance to change, will reveal hitherto hidden power structures and strategies, Eveline maintains. But the concept 'male advantage' also needs deconstruction, it is argued, as class and race fracture the category 'men'. In a subtle analysis of two approaches to Australian Aboriginal politics, Eveline not only reminds us of a significant gap in this collection, the omission of the complicating issue of race, but she teases out solutions similar to those of Yates. Sometimes we must use the modernist approaches of confrontation, at other times the more complex post-modern techniques of irony and hybridization.

Finally Eveline reminds us that we are not outsiders, that many of us are 'within the body of power'. From that position we can continue to challenge the institutions, to name the forces which restrain us.

Recognizing the privilege of our insider/outsider status we offer this collection — not as a bird's eye view of the field, but as a contribution to an ongoing dialogue. Much remains to discuss. Perhaps the pervasive nature of information technology will render education less hierarchical, more inclusive although the current literature on gender and information technology gives little cause for optimism. And some senior men, faced by the intolerable stresses of executive life in the restructuring/downsizing culture of western capitalism are speaking openly of the impossibility of combining public and private life (Harari, 1997). Will their voices be heeded as women's have not? If women cannot gain full access to citizenship through an education which values private as well as public life, reproductive as well as productive work, indeed which blurs those binary categories and unmasks the power which flows from such oppositions, then educational settings will continue to be difficult, even dangerous terrain for women.

References

BACCHI, C.L. (1996) *The Politics of Affirmative Action: 'Women', Equality and Category Politics*, London: Sage.

CONWAY, R. (1997) 'Why young men form so few deep and lasting friendships', Letter to the editor, *The Australian*, 12 February, p. 10.

ELGQVIST-SALTZMAN, I. (1992) 'Straight roads and winding tracks: Swedish educational policy from a gender perspective', *Gender and Education*, **4**, 1, 2.

EVELINE, J. (1994) 'The politics of advantage', *Australian Feminist Studies*, **19**.

FISKE, J. (1989) *Reading the Popular*, Boston: Unwin Hyman.

HARARI, F. (1997) 'The overwork ethic', *The Australian*, 13 February, p. 13.

MACKINNON, A. (1997) *Love and Freedom: Professional Women and the Reshaping of Personal Life*, Cambridge and Melbourne: Cambridge University Press.

MARTIN, J.R. (1985) *Reclaiming a Conversation*, New Haven: Yale University Press.

MARTIN, J.R. (1991) 'The contradiction and the challenge of the educated woman', *Women's Studies Quarterly*, **1**, 2.

MARTIN, J.R. (Spring, 1997) 'Bound for the Promised Land: The gendered character of higher education', *Duke Journal of Gender Law and Policy*, **4**, 1.

SPURLING, A. (1990) Report of the Women in Higher Education research project, Cambridge: King's College Research Centre.

THEOBALD, M. (1989) 'Discourse of danger: Gender and the history of elementary schooling in Australia, 1850–1980', *Historical Studies in Education/Revue l'Histoire de l'Education*, **1**, 1.

Part I

Back to the Future? Hopes Frustrated or Fulfilled?

Introduction

The challenges we face as we approach the 21st century have familiar faces. Fear of educated women and women moving out of their prescribed roles; women invading 'men's' carefully maintained boundaries; the difficulties of combining productive, paid work and family life (and the choice of strategies to use) and the purpose of women's education are issues which have all been canvassed for well over a century — and often for much longer. Educationalists are all too familiar with Rousseau's famous work on the education of Sophie.

The three chapters in this section glance backwards at these old questions, at attempts to resolve them — and at their tendency to recur just when we think they've been resolved.

Mackinnon focuses on literary responses to women moving out into the world at the end of the nineteenth century. Some new women writers envisaged not only an independent woman but a 'woman's way of knowing' — while the male responses often ridiculed the new woman.

Elgqvist-Saltzman shows that the possibilities of using two strategies were well and truly canvassed in the 1860s — the strategy of social justice — and that of woman's particular role as mother. These debates prefigure debates of sameness and difference which perplex educators today (Bacchi, 1990). Now, however, we are conscious of difference not only between men and women, but among different groups of women of different social/ethnic and religious backgrounds. Elgqvist-Saltzman's work also introduces the main dilemma explored in manifest ways throughout this book — how can women combine paid work and a satisfactory family role? For those who have no wish for family life, how do they avoid the inevitable assumptions attributed to all women?

Prentice takes up the theme of women's public and private conflicts and the continuing resistance of men to the 'threat' of women in power. She also asks an important question: Do we want a career which absorbs all of our energies — and more — or do we seek to reassert the value of the spiritual, the meaningful, and a terrain in which to find *balance* for both men and women?

1 Revisiting the *Fin de Siècle*: The Threat of the Educated Woman

Alison Mackinnon

What did it mean to be an educated woman at the end of the nineteenth century? What does it mean now? In this paper I draw on cultural history to revisit the end of the nineteenth century and explore representations and discourses which revolved around and defined the newly educated woman. I suggest that these images restrained her as surely as material constraints, disallowing the exploration of modes of knowing and being with results which still limit women today. No shrinking violet, the educated woman was a central actor on the historical stage in all Anglophone societies. An acquaintance with her can enrich our understanding not only of the power of education to transform lives but of the central place of relations between the sexes in social change.

Increasingly historical work categorizes the decades around the turn of the last century as a period preoccupied with relations between the sexes. Art historian Carol Duncan writes: 'already in the late nineteenth century, European high culture was disposed to regard the male–female relationship as the central problem of human existence' (Duncan, 1982). Discussing European *avant-garde* art in the decade before World War I, Duncan argues that the paintings speak not of universal aspirations but of the fantasies and fears of middle class men living in a changing world (Duncan, 1982, p. 294). American cultural historian Mary Louise Roberts claims that to understand a society's discourse on gender — messy and obsessive as it can be — is to understand a whole society. Roberts writes (of the post World War I decade in France): 'gender was central to how change was understood . . . Debates concerning gender identity became a primary way to embrace, resist or reconcile oneself to changes associated with war' (Roberts, 1994, p. ix). Yet the debates about gender struggle were already old, as Roberts herself notes: 'Spiralling divorce rates, a vociferous feminist movement, adultery, and crimes of passion testify to the instability of domestic ideology from the *fin de siècle* onwards' (Roberts, p. 11). Discussion surrounding the educated woman, the woman moving into universities and the professions, and espousing feminism, anticipated those post war concerns, highlighted the hopes, fears and anxieties of western societies as they moved into a century in which the old certainties of religion were giving way to a faith in science and technology.

The transgressions of 'advanced' or 'new' women attracted intense opprobrium. Advanced women — usually single, highly educated and economically independent — were blamed for a vast range of social evils. Ann Ardis, in a quotation which anticipates Roberts' view, cites an anonymous author of an 1889 *Westminster Review* article who claimed that 'the New Woman's attempt to transform herself from a relative creature into a woman of independent means are "intimately connected" with the stirrings and rumblings now perceivable in the social and industrial world, the "Bitter Cries" of the disinherited classes, the "Social Wreckage" which is becoming able to make itself unpleasantly prominent, the "Problems of Great Cities", the spread of Socialism and Nihilism'. Concluding by way of a Hans Christian Andersen fairy tale this author wrote 'the Ego [of Woman] is a mighty Gen[ii], and the acrid smoke of its ascent may disintegrate many precious superorganic structures' (Ardis, 1990, p. 1). Here is power indeed!

The linguistic turn in history, that rich cross-fertilization of literature and historical work, has drawn our attention to the importance of language, to the notion that the real is only apprehended in language (Newton, 1989). The system of meaning is placed at the heart of the investigation. Other forms of cultural representation can be similarly decoded to reveal subtle forms of domination. How, we ask, does the symbolic system of meaning reflect the material lives of women and men in a particular historical period? By examining the languages available to women we can see how they become expert at using the dominant discourse while at the same time attempting to supplant it with a language of their own. Similarly language betrays epistemological positions, ways of knowing. While some late nineteenth-century women questioned the wisdom of engaging with dominant rational thinking, others embraced it as the only way towards the full life of the mind and of access to the public domain. At the gateway to the 21st century we still retain that ambivalence: the question of 'women's way of knowing' has not been resolved (Belenky et al., 1986).

In *fin de siècle* literature and art, in popular culture, then as now, language used by and about women, images and representations of women, were telling social barometers. Women constantly threatened to disrupt the western rational discourse by inserting emotion, the body and the senses, even intuition into the hallowed places of learning. Supporters of women's education realized that the body must be denied if women were to be permitted entry. Women engaged in the struggle for sexual autonomy could not be seen to be associated with the struggle for educational advance for fear of tainting it. The project of educational emancipation could not accommodate sexual emancipation.

The threat of the educated women was contained by an insistent relegation of women to particular categories, to one pole of a binary position, a relegation many women strenuously rejected. One hundred years later while much has changed, much has stayed the same. We still struggle for our own voice and learn to operate within the dominant discursive regimes — of economic rationalism and corporate managerialism, for instance. We become 'ideologically bilingual', learning the necessary key words — 'quality', 'performance indicators', 'benchmarks' — taking from that discourse what might assist us in our demand for greater inclusion. Yet at a deeper level we have come a long way in unsettling the dominant ways of knowing. Theorists, feminists and others from a range of disciplines have questioned the objective, detached, 'God's eye' view, allowing space for a rich variety of voices and languages.

At the turn of the last century highly educated women with the potential to be economically and sexually independent caused extreme anxiety in western societies. Women were an enigma, represented by that archetypal symbol of the enigmatic — the sphinx. They were boundary crossers who threatened and destabilized the established categories of society. They challenged the relegation of women to the emotional, men to the rational. They invaded culture, not content with their embeddedness in nature. Some women glorified their natural strengths, pleading their special knowledge, their maternalism, as vital for public life. They were often neither married nor single — but inhabited that grey category lost to the demographers, the woman who lived with women. For a time a degree of openness flourished, competing discourses about possibilities were heard. But that openness did not last; a curtain descended in the early years of the new century.

The battery of weapons, ideological, 'scientific', cultural, linguistic which were brought to bear on these pioneers was formidable. Overall, the counter attacks attempted to contain women by returning them to the confines of a binary discourse. Women could be one thing or the other, not both. For example, Duncan interprets the male *avant-garde*'s potential to paint powerless, faceless nudes as a defence against 'the first significant feminist challenge in history', a reassertion of sexual dominance (Duncan, 1982, p. 308). Women had to be pushed back into the domain of nature. They could be guardians of the emotions, not of rational thought. Nor could they invent new inclusive categories. Educated women were frequently forced onto the defensive, to argue that they were not abnormal, deviant, asexual, that they were capable of bearing children, that they were not the cause of 'race suicide'; their education would make them good mothers. Unable to claim a language or a voice of their own, they were forced to operate within the discourses of the time (Smith-Rosenberg, 1985, p. 282 ff).

What was at risk? What caused such social unease? Underlying much of the hysteria was the threat to sexual boundaries — to the notion of heterosexuality, of monogamous marriage and the family. On these it seemed, the foundations of empire and of civilization depended. Roberts argued of post World War I France that the crossing of boundaries between sexes was emblematic of a profound breakdown of civilization. She quotes Pierre Drieu Rochelle: 'This civilisation no longer has clothes, no longer has churches, no longer has palaces, no longer has paintings, no longer has books, no longer has sexes.' Were sexes (finely achieved and differentiated) one of civilization's 'most highly valued cultural achievements' (Roberts, 1994, p. 3)? The discourses which Roberts identifies were not peculiar to post war France. As we have seen, they can be found emerging strongly in the voices surrounding the education, particularly the higher education, of women in the late nineteenth century. Their echoes reverberate in our lives.

It is revealing to revisit these crises of the late nineteenth century as many of the discourses of the past are still with us. As the last years of the nineteenth century were characterized by an immense fluidity and questioning of relations between the sexes so too the press, the literature, the popular culture of our time resonates with that instability. Forewarned, we can meet the echoes of the past with confidence.

In much of the culture of western society the 1890s were characterized by contradictory forces. It was a period of birth and of death, often described by cultural and literary historians as 'decadent' with Oscar Wilde's life and work emblematic of a wider sense of decay (Showalter, 1992). The pejorative use of the term 'decadent' is of course designed for men who lapse from a masculine standard. But the fear of un-masculine men was matched by an equally strong aversion in many quarters to the un-feminine woman. As the nineteenth century drew to a close images of decay, of uncharted and unacceptable boundary crossings, of the world falling apart, of the natural order turned on its head, permeated popular culture. Fears of imperial decline, of uncontrollable epidemics, added to the apocalyptic sense of the end of an era. In Australia images of ends and beginnings, of birth and death intermingled as Australia struggled towards Federation and an end to colonial status (Castle and Pringle, 1993).

Yet not all groups viewed this period through the lens of despair. The period 1880–1920 was marked by multiple constructions of the world. For many women the period was one of new beginnings — of the consolidation of the entrance of women into higher education and the professions, of the gaining of women's suffrage in Australia and New Zealand and the intensification of that demand in much of the rest of the industrializing world. Further, many women were seriously demanding acknowledgment of their sexuality and of their rights to control their fertility. The declining birth rate and a reluctance to marry amongst highly educated women attracted massive social anxiety and investigation (Mackinnon, 1997).

In English literature the assertion of women's independence, both economically and sexually, manifested itself in an explosion of New Women literature. Authors such as George Egerton, Olive Schreiner, Sarah Grand, Mona Caird, Rosa Praed, often influenced by works of Ibsen and Strindberg, explored a future for women in which economically independent women could live without men, could express their sexuality outside marriage and on their own terms, and could admit to primal instincts which challenged the ideology and morality of Victorian bourgeois life. While some women fought to be admitted to the bastions of western rational thought — the universities — others challenged the primacy of the way of thinking taught within university walls.

Mary Chavelita Dunne wrote in England in the 1890s under the pseudonym of George Egerton. Egerton explored new possibilities, attempted to rewrite male mythologies of women, often replacing them with her own mythology. 'Feeling' was the key to the 'enigma of women': 'We are contradictions, leading a dual life . . . our varying moods bound up with the physiological gamut of our being. We have been taught to shrink from the honest expression of our wants and feelings as violations of modesty, or at least of good taste. We are always battling with some bottom layer of real womanhood that we may not reveal; the primary impulses of our original destiny keep shooting out mimosa-like threads of natural feeling through the outside husk of our artificial selves, producing complex creatures' (Egerton, 1983).

The women in Egerton's short stories could succeed in a man's field, could even 'go out and win the bread and butter' while their husbands stayed at home but they had their own skills to contribute, such as 'an intuition that is almost second sight' (Egerton, 1993). Egerton valorized women's intuitive nature: 'All your elaborately reasoned codes for controlling morals or man do not weigh a jot with us against an impulse, an instinct'. Her picture of an unconventional lady professor, 'so like a clever-faced slight man' is softened by the professor's understanding of what to say to another inquiring woman: 'How she knew just the subjects that worked in me I knew not; some subtle intuitive sympathy, I suppose, enabled her to find it out' (Egerton, 1983).

As Lyn Pykett writes, Egerton's representation of the feminine tends to align itself with the nature side of the nature–culture dichotomy, her true womanly is 'women's witchcraft', 'the eternal wildness, the untamed primitive savage temperament that lurks in the mildest best woman . . . [which] may be concealed but is never eradicated by culture' (Egerton, 1983). 'Anticipating the version of the feminine celebrated by some late twentieth century theorists of the feminine, (such as Helene Cixous and Luce Irigaray)', Pykett argues, 'Egerton tends to represent woman as a pre-cultural primitive, bound to the mysteries and cycles of nature.' Woman is the sorceress who contains within herself the repressed past of a culture, 'who in the end is able to dream Nature', who 'incarnates the reinscription of the traces of paganism that triumphant Christianity repressed'. Close to nature, yet she is man's superior: 'her maternity lifts her above him every time' (Egerton, 1983). Egerton's work was a brave attempt to carve out a unique women's perspective, a precursor of women's ways of knowing. Her work was popular and inspiring. Highly educated women, however, striving to gain academic and professional acceptance, could not afford to risk adopting views which would consign them again to the realm of nature which they were at pains to escape.

An important theme for Egerton was the repression of women's sexuality. She directly challenged the repressions women suffered due to conventional morality. In one of her famous Keynotes (1983) short stories, 'Now Spring Has Come' she writes: 'Women repress and . . . repress, and then some day we stumble on the man who just satisfies our sexual and emotional nature, and then there is shipwreck of some sort' (*Keynotes*, p. 57). Egerton's dream is of free women who can rejoice in their sexuality. Clearly targeting the blue-stocking stereotype she rejects the 'desexualized half man, with a pride in the absence of sex feeling' as the outcome of centuries of patient repression. But the free woman does not devote her entire life to love: 'it will never be more than one note: true a grand note, in the harmony of union; but not the harmony' (Regeneration, p. 244). She has a full life with 'a new standard of woman's worth'. She must learn 'to worthen herself', to rise above 'ignorant innocence' by all-seeing knowledge, a knowledge forged through the emotions. Egerton's free woman is contrasted with the celibate scholar. In adopting this stereotype she adopts the male language used against the earliest university women.

In a recent rereading of Olive Schreiner's unfinished novel, *From Man to Man*, Ann Heilmann argues that 'while in the old (phallocentric) world view everything had its preordained if arbitrary place, the new (holistic, humanist, feminist) spirit of the age realizes the interconnectedness of all elements or organisms in the universe, forming one "great pulsating, always interacting whole"' (Heilmann, 1995, p. 35). Schreiner's vision of connectedness anticipates both the ecological Gaia thesis and feminist theory which refuses to separate public and private, structure and agency, nature and culture, body and mind. Work and love, thought and emotion would not be separated. In this Schreiner's work is consistent with Egerton's.

When one of the strong women of Egerton's stories reveals emotional strength, rejection of social conventions and passionate commitment to social action, the poet she loves exclaims: 'You look so strong, so capable — you are half a woman, it is wonderful — I begin to fear you!' Here is the crunch. Was the world ready for the strong new women represented in work such as Egerton's, women who claimed their sexuality, their intuitive sense of the world, while they claimed the right to a place in the public sphere?

As Ann Ardis has shown, many of the real challenges presented by new women were ultimately contained by its relegation to a literary form: the new woman in society became the new woman of literature. And that literature was subsequently marginalized in the literary canon, demoted by critics to a form of 'ideology' or polemic to be categorized, criticized and eventually forgotten.

The New Woman in Literature and Art confronted an opposing image — the Symbolists' *femme fatale*, the fatal woman of Dowson's poetry, of Rider Haggard's famous novel, *She*, and the predatory Salomes in the art of Aubrey Beardsley and Gustav Klimt. In the central character of Haggard's *She*, the mysterious African Queen Ayesha, we see the fearsome new woman through male eyes, displaced geographically to Africa. Ayesha, as Ardis points out, is the embodiment of one of the most potent and ambivalent figures of western mythology, a female who is both monstrous and desirable — deadlier than the male. Both Jung and Freud were to use her to illustrate the concept of the *anima*, the feminine force in mankind (Spurling, 1993). When the beautiful, imperious Ayesha displays her determination to return to England with the intrepid explorers, the narrator betrays exactly the fears voiced about the New Woman's entrance into the public sphere: 'it made me absolutely shudder to think what would be the result of her arrival there' he acknowledges (Haggard, 1991, p. 256).

What will happen if 'the passion that has kept her for so many centuries chained and comparatively harmless' is released and rechannelled into political activism? 'Witch-burning would not be too strong a term for Haggard's ritualistic destruction of both She's desire to "change the order of the world" and her physical being', claims Ardis (Ardis, 1990, p. 141). Ayesha's death symbolically retraces the evolutionary steps which brought her to her glorious peak: 'True enough — I faint even as I write it in the living presence of that terrible recollection — she *was* shrivelling up; the golden snake that had encircled her gracious form slipped over her hips and to the ground; smaller and smaller she grew; her skin changed colour, and in place of the perfect whiteness of its lustre it turned dirty brown and yellow, like an old piece of withered parchment. She felt at her head: the delicate hand was nothing but a claw now . . .'. 'Smaller she grew and smaller yet, till she was no larger than a baboon' (Haggard, 1991, pp. 293–4).

New Woman or Fatal Woman? — the consignment of women to this dualism served to contain them and to caricature them. Both were terrifying and bore little resemblance to the lives of most women of the time. A very limited array of images was available to those who wanted to depict woman in art, literature and popular culture. Lacking a category for the independent woman, observers either categorized her as witch or goddess or parodied, highlighted and trivialized her boundary-crossing potential.

The coexistence of the discourses of decadence on the one hand and of new beginnings for women on the other, were not unconnected. Much of the anxiety of the *fin de siècle* was caused precisely because of the boundary crossings of the period. Women and men were challenging the always precarious allocation to their appointed gender roles. Fears of colonial unrest, of the metropolis invaded by the margins, underpinned fears of racial decline. In this climate women who spearheaded educational advances for women and girls were forced onto the defensive, frequently having to argue in the terms of the dominant discourse. A common justification for women's education, for instance, was that educated women would be ideal 'mothers of the race'. The notion of education for motherhood accelerated in the early years of the twentieth century with unfortunate results for women's schooling (see Dyhouse, 1981, for example). The focus on motherhood overtook the attempt to claim women's sexuality as part of a whole self.

What relevance do these excursions into the past have for us? Many of the discourses of that period 'haunt present usage' (Smith-Rosenberg, 1989). A similar sense of dread, anxiety and doom pervades much popular culture of the late twentieth century. Fear of the 'breakdown' of the nuclear family (often attributed to 'selfish' women who initiate divorce or to single mothers), fear of women taking men's jobs, indeed of taking men's history, fills the press. A recent headline on changing patterns in the workplace commented misleadingly, 'Poor men slide, rich women rise' (*Australian*, 29 April, 1995). As girls complete secondary school in greater numbers than boys, and young women begin to equal young men in university courses, cries of 'disadvantage' for boys and men echo through the media. Yet throughout the western world concerned women wonder at the slow progress of women through the academic ranks, the pervasive sexual harassment and subtle discouragement widely reported (Castleman et al., 1995).

Popular films such as *Fatal Attraction* and *The Last Seduction* depict the economically and sexually independent women as predatory, dangerous, echoing the monstrous women of 100 years ago. There is a 'long-standing tradition of anti-feminist caricature' (Showalter, 1990, p. 14). Fears of race suicide, heard at the beginning of the century, have now amplified to a global scale. We hear racist cries that the developed nations will be outbred by the population-rich countries of the developing world (*Atlantic Monthly*, 1995). Women in developed countries are accused of having too few babies, women in the developing countries of having too many, thus dividing women along lines of race and reproductive capacity. Demographers speak cautiously of 'problems' when educated women have fewer children.

Are we again being forced onto the defensive: will our literature be relegated to the margins and lost to posterity? Is 'the feminist' the scapegoat of the 1990s as 'the New Woman' was in the 1890s? (Ardis, 1990, p. 174). The media encourages public brawls between feminists as illustrated by a long-running discussion in Australia of Helen Garner's (1995), *The First Stone*, a semi-fictionalized account of sexual harassment in university college. A new generation of feminists attempts to reclaim women's sexuality, suggesting, incorrectly, that older feminists rejected that aspect of self as they fought for 'male' privileges. Some say we lack feminist heroines. Showalter asks, 'Where are our Noras and our Heddas?' (Showalter, 1990, p. 15).

Yet amidst *fin de siècle* confusion important gains have been made. We have many positive models of independent women in public life. Women enthusiastically embrace higher education and public life. We assert our needs in national and international forums. We have claimed our voice in courses such as Women's Studies although its use is always precarious. And we are ideologically bilingual. We learn to speak the dominant language, even the language of economic rationalism where necessary. Counter discourses, such as that of social justice, while muted, still carry weight.

Egalitarian feminists in the late nineteenth century, such as Charlotte Gilman Perkins, Olive Schriener and Mona Caird, developed a strong vision of a caring society, where a nurturing communal spirit was the guiding moral force (Heilmann, 1995, p. 37). The notion of an ethic of care, of a rationality of care and connection (Belenky et al., 1986; Gilligan, 1982; Ruddick, 1989) is a persistent thread and still informs much feminist theory and policy making.

The question of women's ways of knowing has not disappeared: approaches to understanding, rooted in intuitivism and connectedness, venerated by pre-positivist philosophers such as Spinoza and Bergson, are increasingly validated and proffered as a way forward for both men and women (Shands, this volume). As sociologist Anthony Giddens sums up: 'The post-modern outlook sees a plurality of heterogeneous claims to knowledge' (Giddens, 1991, p. 2). Belenky and her co-authors suggest an integrated way of knowing, one which is precisely an integration of reason and emotion, of objective and subjective modes of knowing, a blending of one's intuition and the expertise of others (Belenky et al., pp. 131–7). 'All knowledge is constructed', they claim 'and the knower is an intimate part of the known' (p. 137). The empathy which comes with this position is signified by Simone Weil's term, 'attentive love' and by Sara Ruddick's 'maternal thinking' (p. 143).

Women have learned that knowing can come from sources other than the rational and procedural, that understanding our inner voices, our oppression, our grief, is also a form of deep knowing, proceeding not from some female essence but from our social position. As American theorist Donna Haraway claims: 'Feminism is about a critical vision consequent upon a critical positioning in unhomogeneous gendered social space' (Haraway, 1988, p. 589). Audre Lord famously wrote: 'for the master's tools will never dismantle the master's house' (Lord, 1984). Can we say with confidence that the mistress's tools are now in place and the dismantling can begin? Will there be an acknowledgment of the centrality of care, of the connectedness of public and private in courses of all types for both men and women? Will we build another house in the 21st century?

It was not until the 1920s that women artists in Australia, Grace Crowley and Thea Proctor for example, began to paint independent women, securely gazing from the canvas, active, engaged and in control of their lives (Hoorn, 1994) countering the faceless nudes of the early modernists. Through the female robots of films such as *Metropolis* the twentieth-century fear of technology out of control is displaced onto older fears about untrammelled female sexuality as a threat to social order (Donald, 1992). In late twentieth-century popular culture some women artists, cyberfeminists, appropriate these images, create their own hybrids, make 'monsters' in their own image, imagining themselves in 'subversive and liberating ways' (Bonner et al., 1992, p. 12). South Australian computer artists, VNS Matrix, parody and celebrate their own sexuality. Portraying an active sexuality they invent a form of predatory women. If women are to be monstrous, they imply, we will be dangerous on our own terms.

References

ARDIS, A.L. (1990) *New Women, New Novels: Feminism and Early Modernism*, New Brunswick and London: Rutgers University Press.

BACCHI, C.L. (1990) *Same Difference: feminism and sexual difference*, Sydney: Allen and Unwin.

BELENKY, M.F., McVICKER CLINCHY, B., RULE GOLDBERGER, N. and MATTUCK TARULE, J. (1986) *Women's Ways of Knowing: The Development of Self, Voice and Mind*, New York: Basic Books.

BONNER, F., GOODMAN, L., ALLEN, R., JANES, L. and KING, C. (1992) *Imagining Women: Cultural Representations and Gender*, Cambridge: Polity Press/Open University.

CASTLE, J. and PRINGLE, H. (1993) 'Sovereignty and sexual identity in political cartoons', in MAGAREY, S., ROWLEY, S. and SHERIDAN, S. (eds) *Debutante Nation*, St Leonards: Allen and Unwin.

CASTLEMAN, T., ALLEN, M., WRIGHT, P. and BASTERLICH, W. (1995) *Limited Access: Women's Disadvantage in Higher Education*: NTEU.

CONNELLY, M. and KENNEDY, P. (1994) 'Must it be the rest against the West?', *Atlantic Monthly*, December.

DONALD, J. (1992) *Sentimental Education*, London: Verso.

DUNCAN, C. (1982) 'Virility and domination in early twentieth-century Vanguard Painting', in BROUDE, N. and GARRARD, M. (eds) *Feminism and Art History: Questioning the Litany*, Cambridge: Harper and Row.

DYHOUSE, C. (1981) *Girls Growing Up in Late Victorian and Edwardian England*, London: Routledge and Kegan Paul.

EGERTON, C. (1983) *Keynotes and Discords*, London: Virago Press.

EGERTON, G. (1993) 'A cross line', in SHOWALTER, E. (eds) *Daughters of Decadence: Women Winters of the Fin-de-Siecle*, London: Virago Press.

GARNER, H. (1995) *The First Stone: Questions about Sex and Power*, Sydney: Picador.

GIDDENS, A. (1991) *The Consequences of Modernity*, Cambridge: Polity Press.

GILLIGAN, C. (1982) *In a Different Voice: Psychological Theory and Women's Development*, Cambridge, MA: Harvard University Press.

HARDING, S. and MERRILL, B.H. (1983) *Discovering Reality: Feminist Perspectives on Epistemology, Metaphysics, Methodology and Philosophy of Science*, Holland: Dordrecht.

HAGGARD, R.H. (1991) *She*, Oxford: Oxford University Press: The World's Classics.

HARAWAY, D. (1988) 'Situated knowledges: The science question in feminism and the privilege of partial perspectives', *Feminist Studies*, **14**, 3, pp. 575–99.

HEILMANN, A. (1995) 'Over that bridge built with our bodies the entire human race will pass': A rereading of Olive Schreiner's From Man to Man' (1926) in *The European Journal of Women's Studies*, **2**, 1, p. 35.

HOORN, J. (1994) *Strange Women: Essays in Art and Gender*, Melbourne: Melbourne University Press.

LORD, A. (1984) *Sister Outsider: Essays and Speeches by Audre Lord*, Freedom: The Crossing Press.

MACKINNON, A. (1997) *Love and Freedom: Professional Women and the Reshaping of Personal Life*, Cambridge and Melbourne: Cambridge University Press.

NEWTON, J. (1989) 'Family fortunes: "New history" and "the new historicism"', in *Radical History Review*, **43**.

PAGLIA, C. (1990) *Sexual Personae: Art and Decadence from Nefertiti to Emily Dickinson*, New Haven: Yale University Press.

PYKETT, L. (1992) *The Improper Feminine: The Women's Sensation Novel and the New Woman Writing*, London and New York: Routledge.

ROBERTS, M.L. (1994) *Civilization Without Sexes: Reconstructing Gender in Postwar France 1917–27*, Chicago and London: University of Chicago Press.

RUDDICK, S. (1989) *Maternal Thinking: Towards a Politics of Peace*, Boston: Beacon Press.

SHOWALTER, E. (1990) *Sexual Anarchy: Gender and Culture at the Fin de Siècle*, London: Virago.

SMITH-ROSENBERG, C. (1985) 'The new woman as androgyne: Social disorder and gender crisis', in *Disorderly Conduct: Visions of Gender in Victorian America*, New York and Oxford: Oxford University Press.

SMITH-ROSENBERG, C. (1989) 'The body politic', in WEED, E. (ed.) *Coming to Terms: Feminism, Theory, Politics*, New York and London: Routledge.

SPURLING, J. (1993) 'Utopian imperialist', *Times Literary Supplement*, 3 September.

2 'Why Are We Standing Still?' Reflections from History

Inga Elgqvist-Saltzman

> Only when the state gives its daughters some of the care it provides to its sons will there be hope for a solid and advanced intellectual training for women.

In 1859, when women in Sweden opened the first issue of a Swedish feminist journal, they were met with a plea for women's access to education and intellectual training. The journal was *Tidskrift for Hemmet (Home Journal)*, claiming the heritage of the feminist author Fredrika Bremer, who actively campaigned for the rights of women in the early and mid 1800s. The journal aimed to convey the debate in some parts of Europe and in the United States to women in Sweden, a country which at that time was backward with regard to family law and economic legislation for women. The *Home Journal* identified public responsibility for the education of girls and women as one of the most important contemporary controversies. The first issue opened with an article on 'The need for woman's intellectual education'.

How was the purpose and the aim of women's education defined almost one and a half centuries ago? A further look at the *Home Journal*'s articles on education during the decades around 1860 will be the point of departure for this paper. How were women's lives affected when educational opportunities opened up? The second part of the article explores the life stories of some women of later times, when Sweden became renowned for being the first country in the world where gender equality policies tried to change the roles of men as well as those of women. In the concluding section I link the early debate on gender and education in the *Home Journal* with issues and strategies today.

The Voice of the *Home Journal* in mid-1800s Sweden:

Education for Social Harmony

> Most content will she be, most content her family as well, if her education succeeds in developing her mental facilities, if it makes her into a useful member of society.

The *Home Journal's* first article (probably written by one of the two female editors, Sophie Leijonhufvud) claimed that harmony was lacking in the education of both sexes. In the case of women, there was perceived to be a great need for intellectual training while men were seen to need moral training. A harmoniously composed physical, ethical, and intellectual education was considered to be a goal for women as well as for men. Intellectual and moral training in combination would better equip women to fulfill their particular roles in the home and in society, and to succeed as educators of coming generations.

'Well, my Lady, this is a comprehensive educational system; you have to cultivate mothers who understand how to educate their children.' The motto for the first article was taken from *Education of Family-mothers or The Refinement of Mankind through Women's Education*, an influential 500-page volume by the French author Aimé Martin (1843), translated into Swedish and published in several editions. A quotation from the same book concluded the article: 'So ought the education of our daughters be accomplished. As for the education of men, why concern ourselves? It shall simply and naturally be brought through the virtues of women.'

The ideology of separateness — that the nature of women was different from that of men, that women had special gifts or unique talents, especially caring qualities — was expressed by Fredrika Bremer and Ellen Key, both influential Swedish authors of the time. Bremer's most important novel *Hertha*, published in 1856, advocated emancipation based on the equality of men and women but also on women's special maternal role in society. Key, somewhat later, preached a fundamental belief in the sanctity of motherhood. How was this perspective expressed in the journal?

Women's particular duty in family and society, claimed the editors of the *Home Journal*, is not separate but deeply intertwined and inseparable from the duty of men. We do not advocate the abandoning of the concept of true womanhood, they wrote, but we believe in a more true and free conception of it. Human beings, thinking and acting independently, are the goal.

Intellectual Education and Its Influence on the Character and Happiness of Women by feminist Emily Shireff, is another contemporary work the editors strongly recommended to their readers. It was suggested that the more serious part of girls' education should begin at 12 years of age. According to Shireff, suitable subjects for young girls' education included not only geometry, physics and the other sciences but also the rudiments of Latin and Greek.

Elin's Letter on Education

Mothers were the key target group for the *Home Journal*, and the encouragement of their self-education was an important goal of the journal. Mothers were encouraged to inspire their daughters to serious studies and vocational training. In a series 'Letters on Education' starting in 1861, some fictitious mothers and former classmates exchanged ideas about educating their daughters. The first letter by 'Alma' stressed the importance of making girls independent and reflective human beings in society, with the courage and strength of mind to meet changing fortunes. The second letter pays homage to the happiness of living in the countryside and being able to read from the great picture-book of nature. While the first two letters were written by well-to-do women, the third was assumed to be from the poor teacher Elin who, after many years of engagement, married a subordinate civil servant of a government office in Stockholm and 'entered his poor home with empty but work-willing hands'.

The letter describes her hard work to keep the home functioning with six children, among them four girls, and to give even the girls a proper education adapted to their particular abilities and talents. Her husband's salary as a civil servant could not cover the expenses of sending the girls to private schools. Elin drew on her brothers and her whole circle of acquaintances to educate her daughters in different subjects (including sciences) and to stimulate the most gifted to become teachers. She described how she arranged study trips to libraries and the Academy of Science. Sometimes the father and the two sons, who were able to attend state-supported grammar schools, joined in and the whole family took part in educational excursions led by the mother.

The *Home Journal* had as a subtitle 'Journal for Women'. Men appear as husbands, sons and representatives of the state in articles and reports from government authorities. However the name Olof Eneroth appeared at the end of several of the educational articles. An industrious writer and debater in school matters, Eneroth agitated for women to take an interest in the development of the Swedish elementary school, which had become compulsory in 1842, but was in a period of crisis in the 1850s. In another article (1862) he suggested that women could play an important role in environmental improvement. Eneroth, himself a skilled landscape gardener, wanted to see more women gardening around the homes and schools. Under the provocative title, 'Human development even for women', he argued for women's equal access to the most prestigious subjects at that time: the classics, Greek, and Latin (*Home Journal*, 1867).

Eneroth, the only son of a widowed, self-educated woman elementary teacher, was a reform-minded man, who also advocated women's access to higher education. He shared a strong belief in women's ability to take advantage of a reformed education system and to help turn it into 'a more human educational system for both men and women' (Eneroth, 1870).

Very few articles in the *Home Journal* feature women's access to higher education. The journal's task was said to be to till the soil and to slowly change the prejudices against women's education. At this time many took it for granted that women entering institutions of higher education were exceptions; those who could not devote their lives to the roles of women as wives and mothers. In a series of articles on 'Women's need for higher education' in a Stockholm daily newspaper (November, 1869) a male writer argued that it was in the best interests of males to have educated wives and mothers who could be good conversation partners and collaborators, and also provide them with sons who would get a better start on their education. Educated wives and mothers would bring fortune to the whole family. The education of unmarried women working outside the home, however, seemed to be a more difficult matter to handle. The writer was willing to recognize some exceptions, but assured the reader that there was little cause to fear that the number of women willing to study and complete their degrees at the universities would ever be particularly great!

In Sweden as well as in other countries in the mid 1800s, demographic and structural changes were causing a great 'surplus' of women in all age groups and the question of women's maintenance was becoming a significant issue (Qvist, 1960). A woman's right to receive education in her own right as an individual and not just as a mother or daughter was never questioned in the *Home Journal*. The quote 'Women need Work and Work needs Women', taken from the English pamphlet by Barbara Smith (1857) was used by the editors of the *Home Journal* to claim an education for self-supporting women. The teaching profession had been opened for women in 1860. At that time teacher training colleges for elementary teaching which initially included only men, became colleges also for women. The same year a training institute for educating teachers for girls' schools was erected. In 1873 Swedish universities were opened for women. The lengthy debate leading up to the state gradually assuming full responsibility for girls' secondary education can be followed in the *Home Journal*. However, public grammar schools were not fully opened to girls until 1927 and it was not until the greater reforms after World War II that girls and boys had equal access to all forms of schooling (Johansson and Florin, 1994).

Teacher, Woman and Citizen in the early 1900s

Ruth

Ruth, born around the turn of the century, graduated in 1929 to become a teacher in Swedish elementary school. Her life-line parallels the modelling of the modern welfare state of Sweden (Elgqvist-Saltzman, 1993, 1994a). Her story is the story of a gifted young girl who found her own winding track to the Rostad teacher training college at Kalmar at a time when girls' schooling was very dependent on the family and private economy. It is a story of women models and supporters; a mother who never had the opportunity to use her nurse's training in paid employment, and a grandmother with frustrated educational ambitions for her son and a small legacy. It was also a story about stimulating women teachers along the way. Ruth was the first woman student at Rostad engaged to be married while a student. Her husband was a young engineer, trained to handle the new technical invention of the time, the radio; he was also the nephew of the female head of the teacher training college. At a time of population crisis, (Myrdal, 1934) they planned and brought up four children following recipes for the rational management of household and childcare. Ruth was determined to combine 'women's two roles' (Myrdal and Klein, 1956). After completing teacher training (one of the few educational fields available for her at that time) Ruth succeeded in getting a teaching job. This was achieved during a time of severe economic crisis, a time when married women teachers were informed that they were taking the bread out of the mouths of men teachers (Holm, 1991).

Ruth and her classmates attained equality in terms of equal pay, equal housing and equal teaching opportunity for women teachers. A series of rules and ordinances prohibiting dismissal on the grounds of childbirth and the right to retain one's salary and position during periods of childbearing were some of the family-friendly measures of redesigned family policy, which started to develop in the 1930s and became important ingredients of the welfare state. Ruth and her colleagues also experienced the transformation of the small poor schools (where most began their teaching careers) into big, modern and well-equipped educational institutions. They lived, indeed, through an era of educational reform, a period which also transformed formerly class- and sex-bound educational tracks into a highly uniform educational system. The motto was 'the same education for all' (Andrae-Thelin and Elgqvist-Saltzman, 1990).

Like many of her classmates Ruth was actively engaged in welfare politics. For a time she was chair of Kalmar's council. She was in many respects a pioneer, as an early advocate of state-supported childcare for professional women and her involvement in forming a women's section of the liberal party. Ruth was representative of the modern woman who believed in progress and in rational ways of solving the age-old dilemma of work and family. A companionate marriage and good house-helpers helped her to realize her career ambitions. The work of several women, in fact, was behind her successful combination of a full-time teacher's job, raising four children and an active political life. As she pointed out: 'I have had a loyal family'.

Looking in the rearview mirror the 80-year old Ruth said: 'How can it be that women — as far as political influence is concerned — are getting nowhere; *why are we standing still on the same old spot while all the society around us is developing?*' Confronted with the new equality problems that her daughters and daughters-in-law were facing, Ruth was reluctant to give an unconditionally positive assessment of women's progress in relation to work and family. When the same question about the changing conditions of equality over a 50-year perspective was put to a generation of younger women teachers, they were generally more optimistic. We will now turn to Karin and her story.

Education, Work and Family in the mid-1900s

Karin

Karin graduated from secondary school in 1967, and belonged to a generation of women for whom new opportunities had opened up in terms of education, well-paid jobs, and sexual freedom. When writing her life story in the early 1980s she was a university graduate in her late 30s, and a teacher at an alternative high school in the centre of Sweden. At her own school she had initiated feminist studies and was involved in the women's movement of the 1970s. She was married with one daughter.

Karin was unusually outspoken concerning hidden conflicts; verbalizing what many women in her cohort were more vague about:

> I feel that since I had children, I have been constantly cruising between women's liberation and the demands of working life on one hand, and the responsibility for home and family, on the other. I have never quite managed to join the two halves I split into when my child was born. They are two separate lives. The reason is, I think, the way society is organized. Nothing interesting occurs in the domestic world, all the interesting things happen in professional life. (Andersson and Elgqvist-Saltzman, 1984).

Karin deliberately chose to work part-time, a solution that gained ground for many women in the 1960s and 1970s. The impact of part-time work on her own career was described as follows: 'I have a lower status now'. It was, according to Karin, 'a painful experience to . . . form part of a system maintaining inequality. The children are indoctrinated to regard their mothers as moderate work power, and society deprecates part-time workers.' Karin, living at a time and in a society where good child care and paid parental leave are provided, expressed her worries concerning a society where children and adults live in separate worlds.

Karin's story was told as part of an educational project aiming to study how the reforms of higher education were affecting the lives and living conditions of women representing different social strata and regions graduating from secondary school in the 1950s and 60s (Elgqvist-Saltzman, 1994b). The women's life patterns, the researchers found, followed an 'in and out pattern' in education and work, which was linked to their reproductive responsibilities. Women's opportunities to take advantage of educational programmes, to pursue their educational plans, and to use their education seemed to be dependent on what was happening in their 'private sector'. Most women investigated had chosen typically 'female professions', only a few of them held leading positions, and only a few were politically active.

Many women reported that the main problems were related to the difficulties of combining career and family. The problems concerned attitudes and feelings more than hindrances of a more practical nature. Karin's solution to the problem was that both parents should decrease their working hours in productive work, in order to share the responsibility for small children and she persuaded her own husband, also a high-school teacher, to work part-time for certain periods. This solution to the work/family dilemma was very much in line with offical Swedish equality efforts, which since 1968 have gone in two directions: strengthening women's position in the labour market as well as men's position in the home (Dahlström, 1971). The *Parental Leave Insurance Act* implemented in 1974 made it possible for both men and women to take time out from work with a high level of compensation to take care of their infants.

However most families preferred a situation where the mother stayed at home during the child's first year. The parental insurance scheme's potential to challenge 'the entire structure and function of society' has been pointed to (Widerberg, 1991) but questions have also been raised as to whether the state has any real commitment to honouring its pact with woman (Eduards et al., 1985; Eduards, 1992). The supposition that men and women are able to share work and care tasks equally is problematic since men have the 'freedom to voluntarily choose involvement in both or either sphere; women generally do not'.

Straight Roads and Winding Tracks in the late 1900s

Karin's difficulties of combining education, work and family challenge educational policy. Has the reform policy, in its endeavour to adopt higher education to the labour market, overlooked other aspects of human life?

The planning policy of the 1960s and 1970s was characteristic of what has been called a 'technical' model of educational planning (Pusey, 1976). Education was discussed in terms of input and output with stress on flow through to the labour market. The planners staked out straight roads to be followed in the educational system with an imagined 'average' student in mind. Extensive reforms of primary and secondary levels of schooling during the decades after World War II, were followed by far reaching higher education reforms in the 1970s. A broad occupational orientation was imposed upon undergraduate studies, organized to meet the projected need of trained manpower for the labour market. The concept of higher education was extended to include vocational colleges such as the colleges of teaching and nursing.

The high visibility of labour market considerations in reform work subsequently influenced the research models adopted. Success in terms of educational and vocational careers was often determined in terms of incomes and position in the labour market. Women became a problematic element in many ways. In mobility studies constructed around a quantitative paradigm it was much easier to place men in the social structure according to occupation than women. The close ties between policy and research in Sweden could easily lead to a 'perspective from above' from which women's choices of the 'wrong study programmes' were alarming. High hopes for equal distribution of men and women in all educational areas had become an important part of the equality endeavours in the 1980s. Measures were taken to change women's educational choices and to attract them to the male-dominated science and technology streams in an effort to discourage their concentration in traditionally women-dominated fields such as teaching and nursing. The increasing number of women in higher education was considered more of a problem than a resource: women became gravel in the machinery (Elgqvist-Saltzman, 1988, 1992).

As Bacchi (1996) has recently pointed out, making 'women' the problem has had the effect of diverting attention from the processes which are problematic and from those defining the nature of the 'problem'. In my own research, from which Karin's and Ruth's stories have been taken as examples, the notion of women as the problem in education has been in focus. A life-line methodology, allowing a broader perspective on vocational and educational careers was helful in challenging the male norm (Bjerén and Elgqvist-Saltzman, 1994). Within this methodology, the visibility of the reproductive duties helped to reveal women's choices and routes through education as complex and rational decisions and encouraged new questions concerning the content of the educational experience during different phases of life (Elgqvist-Saltzman, 1994c). What kind of competence do women and men acquire in connection with reproductive duties? How in a life-long perspective is particular competence taken into consideration?

Linking Past and Present to Challenge the Future

Feminist researchers of today often meet with accusations that women's educational history is an elite history without general interest. The broad interest of the *Home Journal* in educational matters and the educational needs of girls and women from all social strata does not support this view.

Closed doors and the lack of state support were the big concerns in the educational debate in the mid-nineteenth century. Doors that were previously closed (at all levels and in all areas) are today open to women, and equality projects aim at an equal distribution of women and men in all educational levels and institutions. The Swedish goal of equality gives women and men the same obligations and rights in relation to work, family and citizenship. But statistics tell another story. Sweden still has a very sex-segregated education and labour sector (compare Berge, Staberg and Shands, this volume). At a managerial level, the picture of missing women is one of contemporary concern, with a comparative study of women and men in managerial positions in Australia and Sweden revealing great differences in gender equality theory and ideology, but surprisingly small differences in reality (Eveline, 1994). The dearth of women in leading positions in higher education and research is currently one of the Swedish Government's great worries. A recent governmental report on the lack of senior women academics was entitled 'The will to know, the will to understand'; a title which could very well have been found in the *Home Journal* in the 1860s. Propositions from the Government concerning higher education promise to increase the number of women professors in Swedish universities.

During this century, women have marched into secondary and higher education at such a pace that today they outnumber men among university graduates. Evaluations show that girls and women perform as well as men and the notion of women's intellectual inferiority, so real to educational planners in the past century, has been dismissed. Educated women have proved to be 'useful members' of their society, as the *Home Journal* suggested.

Today women's access to higher education and research provides possibilities for using women's experiences far in advance of those conceivable to the editors of the *Home Journal* one and a half centuries ago. On the brink of a new century feminists are now facing the problem of constructing a new political agenda which offers women full rights as citizens. The early debate on gender and education found in the *Home Journal* has interesting links to debates on gender and education of today. When facing the notion of women's particular duty in society as an obstacle to women's access to education, the journal brought up questions and challenged old concepts. It also claimed that women's and men's duties in family and society were deeply intertwined and required changes in the content of education of both sexes. In this volume, Ve and Berge report action research in the Nordic countries aiming to make schools more 'gender sensitive'. (Compare Berge and Ve, this volume.) The debate in the *Home Journal* can be linked to Jane Martin's extensive writings on the missing three c's (care, concern and connection) in modern schooling, and the necessity to change the whole educational landscape for the sake of women as well as men (1985, 1994).

The straight roads in education laid out during a period of social engineering are today being questioned. A new labour market situation and new demands in society have also forced men to winding tracks in education and work. In a 'post modern', culturally diverse society a competitive 'masculine' career system may no longer be relevant. Women's social skills and communicative resources, which have remained unused in the meritocratic-career model may be more appreciated in a post modern form of social organization (Häyrynen, 1994).

The complex interface between education, work and family was a recurrent theme in the women's life stories above. We have met different strategies for refuting the notion that women's closer connection with reproductive duties would make it more difficult for them to combine the roles of parents, professionals and citizens. Ruth believed in rational solutions to the family/ work dilemma. Karin's generation enjoyed open doors in education and work, but experienced hidden obstacles due to growing expectations and demands, not least on parents, and different notions of children's place and space in a society on the move.

Since the Myrdal's alarm over a population crisis in the 1930s, family friendly measures have been important in the Swedish welfare state. The hard economic reality of the 1990s, with a growing number of people outside the regulated labour market, has resulted in less social security and a declining birth rate. Now that many have less confidence in the welfare state the family and equality between men and women continue to be important issues in the Swedish debate.

A newspaper headline in a Stockholm paper proclaiming 'The place for real and true equality' attracted my attention the day I was going to put an end to this essay. The woman writer claimed that the family is the place where true equality has to be built; a family where fathers are parents on the same terms as mothers. Such a family will be the point of departure for a reformed school system and a labour market with shorter working days for both men and women with small children (Zetterström, 1997). Mothers' education for the benefit of children was a great concern when the *Home Journal* appeared in the mid-1800s. Will fathers' re-education be the challenge for the century to come?

References

ANDRAE-THELIN, A. and ELGQVIST-SALTZMAN, I. (1990) 'Sweden', in KELLY, G.P. (ed.), *International Handbook of Women's Education*, New York: Greenwood Press, pp. 349–70.

ANDERSSON, Y. and ELGQVIST-SALTZMAN, I. (1984) *Högskoleutbildning, Yrkeskarriär och Familjemönster* (Higher Education, Career and Family Pattern), Umeå: Department of Education.

BACCHI, C.L. (1996) *The Politics of Affirmative Action*, London: Sage.

BENGTSSON, M. (1996) 'Time, place, gender and identity: Perceptions of parental identification, parental dominance and authority in young adults before and after the "gender-revolution" of the 1970s', *Feminism and Psychology*, December.

BJERÉN, G. and ELGQVIST-SALTZMAN, I. (1994) *Gender and Education*, Aldershot: Avebury.

BREMER, F. (1856) *Hertha*, London: Hall.

DAHLSTRÖM, E. (1971) *The Changing Roles of Men and Women*, Boston: Beacon Press.

EDUARDS, M.L. (1992) 'Against the rules of the games', in EDUARDS, M.L., ELGQVIST-SALTZMAN, I., LUNDGREN, E., SJOBLAD, C., SUNDIN, E. and WIKANDER, U. (eds) *Rethinking Change: Current Swedish Feminist Research*, Uppsala: HSFR.

EDUARDS, M.L., HALSAA, B. and SKJEIE, H. (1985) 'Equality: how equal? Public equality policies in the Nordic countries', in HAAVIO-MANILA, E. et al. (eds) *Unfinished Democracy: Women in Nordic Politics*, Oxford: Pergamon Press.

ELGQVIST-SALTZMAN, I. (1988) 'Educational reforms — Woman's life patterns: A Swedish case study', *Higher Education*, **17**, pp. 491–504.

ELGQVIST-SALTZMAN, I. (1992) 'Gravel in the machinery or the hub of the wheel?', in EDUARDS, M.L., ELGQVIST-SALTZMAN, I., LUNDGREN, E., SJÖBLAD, C., SUNDIN, E. and WIKANDER, U. *Rethinking Change: Current Swedish Feminist Research*, Uppsala, Sweden: HSFR.

ELGQVIST-SALTZMAN, I. (1993) *Lärrinna, Kvinna, Människa* (Teacher, Woman and Human Being), Stockholm: Carlssons.

ELGQVIST-SALTZMAN, I. (1994a) 'Teacher, woman and human being', in BJERÉN, G. and ELGQVIST-SALTZMAN, I. op. cit., pp. 115–32.

ELGQVIST-SALTZMAN, I. (1994b) 'Straight roads and winding tracks', in BJERÉN, G. and ELGQVIST-SALTZMAN, I. op. cit., pp. 7–16.

ELGQVIST-SALTZMAN, I. (1994c) 'Declines and green hills: Competence development in a life perspective', in BJERÉN, G. and ELGQVIST-SALTZMAN, I. op. cit., pp. 133–56.

ENEROTH, O. (1863, 1866, 1867, 1869) *Om Folkskolan i Sverige I–1V* (Elementary school in Sweden), Stockholm: Norstedt and Söner.

ENEROTH, O. (1862, 1865, 1867) Articles in the *Home Journal.*

ENEROTH, O. (1870) *Tankar i Afseende på Högskolans Inrättande* (Thoughts on a New University).

EVELINE, J. (1994) '*The politics of advantage: Managing work and care in Australia and Sweden*', Murdoch University.

GUSTAFSSON, G. (1991) 'Women's subordination in formally gender neutral welfare states like Sweden', Xvth World Congress of the International Political Science Association, July 21–5, Buenos Aires, Argentina.

HÄYRYNEN, Y.P. (1994) 'Creative trajectories of female intellectuals', in BJEREN, G. and ELGQVIST-SALTZMAN, I. (eds) *Gender and Education*, Aldershot: Avebury.

HEARN, J. (1987) *The Gender of Oppression: Men, Masculinity and the Critique of Marxism*, Brighton: Wheatsheaf Press.

HOLM, R. (1991) 'Rut's bok', *Reports from the Rostad-project*, Umeå University, Department of Education.

JOHANSSON, U. and FLORIN, C. (1994) 'Order in the (middle) class! Culture, class and gender in the Swedish state grammar school 1850–1914', *Historical Studies in Education/Revue d'Histoire de l'Education*, **6**, 1.

MARTIN, A. (1843) *Familje-mödrars Uppfostran eller Menniskoslägtets Förädling Genom Qvinnan*, WESTERBERG, L. (Trans.), Stockholm: CA Bagges Förlag.

MARTIN, J.R. (1985) *Reclaiming a Conversation: The Ideal of the Educated Woman*, Yale: Yale University Press.

MARTIN, J.R. (1994) *Changing the Educational Landscape*, London: Routledge.

MYRDAL, A. and G. (1934) *Kris i Befolkningsfrågan* (Crisis in the Population Issue), Stockholm: Bonniers.

MYRDAL, A. and KLEIN, V. (1956) *Women's Two Roles*, London: Routledge and Kegan Paul.

PUSEY, M. (1976) *Dynamics of Bureaucracy: A Case Analysis in Education*, Sydney: John Wiley and Sons.

QVIST, G. (1960) *Kvinnofrågan i Sverige 1809–46* (Women's Question in Sweden), Göteborg: Kvinnohistoriskt arkiv.

SCHMUCK, P. (1987) *Women Educators: Employees of Schools in Western Countries*, Albany: State University of New York Press.

SHIREFF, E. (1858) *Intellectual Education and its influence on the character and happiness of women*, London: J.W. Parker.

SOU (1995:110) *Viljan att Veta och Viljan att Förstå* (The Will to Know, the Will to Understand), Stockholm: Utbildningsdeparetementet.

Stockholms Dagblad (1869) 15, 16, 17 November.

Tidskrift för Hemmet tillegnad den svenska Qvinnan. Stockholm: Flodins boktryckeri, 1859–1885.

WIDERBERG, K. (1991) 'Reforms for women — On male terms', *International Journal of Sociology of Law*, **19**, 1, pp. 27–44.

WIKANDER, U. (1992) 'International women's congresses, 1878–1914', in EDUARDS, M.L. et al. (eds) *Rethinking Change: Current Swedish Feminist Research*, Uppsala: HSFR.

ZETTERSTRÖM, M. (1997) *Plasten for Sann och äkta jämlikhet (The Place for True and Real Equality)*, Svenska: Dagbladet.

3 Mapping Canadian Women's Teaching Work: Challenging the Stereotypes

Alison Prentice

In 1893 Elizabeth Binmore published an essay on Montreal women teachers in the *Educational Record of the Province of Quebec*. Explicitly refusing to use the epithet 'lady teacher' on the grounds that such a term suggested leisure rather than labour, Binmore identified herself as a 'female teacher' and called for better salaries and principalships for women working in Montreal schools. She clearly hoped that organized teachers of both sexes would cooperate in seeking justice for Quebec's teaching women (cited in Prentice, 1975). Elizabeth Binmore's plea impressed me when I first encountered it and it impresses me still. It must have taken courage, in a period before women had the vote or were easily accepted on most platforms, to state her case so publicly. Even more impressive was Elizabeth Binmore's willingness to attack the stereotype of the 'lady teacher'. Montreal's female teachers were respectable women. But, Binmore made it clear, they also needed decent wages in order to live.

Elizabeth Binmore was one of countless women who have given over portions of their lives to the educational endeavour. What may we learn about their experience? Canadian studies suggest that women's movement into public educational space has frequently caused pain as well as pleasure to both women and men. Concern about the woman teacher, moreover, has characterized all levels of public schooling from elementary to university, and continued from the nineteenth century to the present. Like Elizabeth Binmore, women in education have struggled both to understand and resist the forces that have been marshalled to contain, stereotype, or subordinate them. They have also worked hard to develop teaching lives that made sense, given their circumstances and needs.

Women in State Schools: Central Canada

Canadian women have always taught. Increasingly, we are aware of First Nations women's educational roles in both traditional and contemporary settings (Cruikshank et al., 1991); and we know that non-aboriginal women settlers were also involved from the earliest days in various kinds of educational work. But what first intrigued Canadian historians of women who were interested in teachers was the apparently dramatic shift from predominantly male to predominantly female teaching forces in state schools in the second half of the nineteenth century (Prentice, 1975; Prentice, 1990). We wanted, especially, to understand the structures of inequality that seemed connected to this shift. The earliest research, which focused largely although not exclusively on the central Canadian provinces of Ontario and Quebec, discovered that nineteenth-century rural communities tended to hire women teachers 'for half the price' that men cost, while urban school boards engaged them to fill the lower paid positions in schools headed by principals who were invariably male. At the same time, the ideologues who promoted the development of state schooling began to argue that women had a special capacity for subordinate roles in education, along with special nurturing abilities suited to the instruction of younger children and older girls. Less often stated was the concomitant view — that women were by definition *unsuited* to play leadership roles in public education or to teach adolescent boys.

Statements of women's disability were initially muted but, as women moved into co-educational secondary teaching, the volume rose (Gelman, 1990). The question of women's right to administrative roles came up at once when, following the provincial law of 1871 mandating their presence, girls were admitted to the Toronto High School in 1871. The committee investigating complaints against the new 'Lady Superintendent', Mrs Howe, resolved that Howe 'must subject herself to the rector in reference to the management of the school'; within a year the position of 'Lady Superintendent' had disappeared. The new 'Head Female Teacher' was clearly not in a supervisory position herself, but firmly under the control of Toronto High School's male principal.

Three decades later, so many women were engaged in secondary teaching in Ontario their numbers alone were seen as a threat (Gelman, 1990). Male educators worried about the 'feminization' of adolescent boys who missed out on tutelage by men. Clearly some felt that the very manhood of Ontario's youth was at stake. The work of John Abbott (1986) has exposed the extraordinary unease felt by turn-of-the-century Ontario school inspectors on this score. Their writings, he suggests, 'exude a pungent aroma of fear', the fear that failure to recruit young men to the teaching profession 'entailed the subversion of patriarchal civilization'. To be a school inspector in the early 1900s was, Abbott's research demonstrates, to be part of a brotherhood that jealously guarded its rights and powers against female encroachment. Decades later, as Cecilia Reynolds' research has revealed, women teachers still felt the stigma associated with female ambition and were often reluctant to move into the principal's office, let alone the inspector's chair (Reynolds, 1990a).

If the prejudice against women teaching older boys or taking administrative posts was potent, equally powerful was the bias against married women teaching. Earlier private school and academy teachers had frequently been married women (Errington, 1995) and the bias developed only gradually. But by the twentieth century an unwritten marriage bar was in place in most parts of Canada, as it was in many other western countries. A married woman was perhaps too knowledgeable; like Mrs Howe, she might expect to wield authority. Although Canadian historians have not examined the marriage bar for all periods or places, they have explored mid-twentieth century Ontario reactions to its removal. As World War II and post-war teacher shortages began to alter the rules, many men and quite a few women remained dubious about the wisdom of allowing married women into the classroom (Gaskell, 1989, Reynolds, 1990b).

Marital status is only one of many factors that we need to explore in our quest to understand women teachers' lives and the prejudices they have encountered over the years. Collaborative research on rural Ontario and Quebec demonstrated that poor, country places were often the first to develop strongly female teaching forces. But by comparing the ages, ethnicity, marital status, and social class backgrounds of male and female teachers by region, we were able to show that the reasons for this were complex; although gender was clearly a powerful force, other factors were also important as communities made decisions about who should teach in their local schools. Where immigrant men were available, for example, fewer women teachers were hired. Poor, resource frontier settlements were more likely to engage young women than wealthier, older communities, presumably because they could not afford the wages of men (Danylewycz, Light and Prentice, 1983). We also established that early rural women teachers rarely idealized their roles, leaving this task to the male administrators who needed to account for the growing numbers of women working in state schools. Indeed, what emerged from the sources most clearly was women's sense of grievance. Poor wages, difficult working conditions, and heavy work loads were what typically motivated country schoolmistresses to put pen to paper at least (Danylewycz and Prentice, 1986).

Nor was it only rural schoolmistresses who gave voice to such concerns, as Elizabeth Binmore's 1893 plea for justice demonstrates. Binmore was representative of urban women teachers, who tended to be older and more career-oriented than their rural counterparts (Danylewycz and Prentice, 1984); she was also among the activists who formed women teachers' associations in Montreal and Toronto at the turn of the century (Prentice, 1985; Smaller, 1991; Heap and Prentice, 1993). They took their complaints to the press and, in one extraordinary incident, directly to the prime minister in an attempt to win justice for themselves and their sister teachers. French Catholic *institutrices* cooperated with English-Protestant schoolmistresses and both groups with suffragists and other politically-oriented women; in Toronto they sought cooperation from the labour movement, suggesting that Elizabeth Binmore was not alone in trying to reconstitute the image of the teacher as respectable worker rather than leisured lady. Much of their work was consciousness-raising, as they attempted to educate not only the public but each other about the realities of their circumstances. Eventually, organizations similar to those in Toronto and Montreal sprang up in other centres and, in Ontario, local groups amalgamated to form the provincial Federation of Women Teachers' Associations shortly after the end of World War I. The FWTAO, as Rebecca Coulter tells us in her contribution to this volume, has only recently yielded to pressure to amalgamate with its male counterpart, after more than seven decades of existence as a unique force in Canadian education and gender politics.

Expanding the View: Other Regions and Individual Teachers' Lives

Studies of western and eastern Canada have added further complexity to the story of women teachers and state schooling. In British Columbia, in contrast to Ontario and Quebec, the shift towards a predominantly female teaching force began in towns and spread only slowly to rural areas (Barman, 1990). Working conditions and social environments remained so difficult for some isolated young women teachers that the province created, for a brief period in the late 1920s and early 1930s, the special position of 'Rural Teachers' Welfare Officer (Women)'. Lottie Bowron's job was created when a young female teacher committed suicide; while it lasted, Bowron travelled countless miles in her efforts to help British Columbia's teaching women (Wilson, 1991). Although the prairie provinces did not create such a service, their women teachers often had much to contend with too and their histories are gradually being documented (Kojder, 1977; Poelzer, 1990; Kinnear, 1995). Historians have also begun to explore the religious and imperialist dimensions of English-speaking Protestant teachers' work, examining for example the story of British women teachers who were drawn to western Canada by the Anglican Fellowship of the Maple Leaf (Lyons, 1984; Barber, 1991).

Drawing on a rich body of sources to study shifting gender boundaries in teaching in nineteenth-century Nova Scotia, Janet Guildford (1992) renews the argument for recognizing the unique character of each region and against simplifying dichotomies. Nova Scotia women teachers, in her view, were motivated both by their need to earn a living *and* their belief in women's special powers to govern the young. Historians have also published some fascinating accounts of individual Nova Scotia women teachers' careers. Annie Leake, whose story was unearthed by Marilyn Färdig Whitely, began as a domestic servant, acquired an education, and then carved out a career as a model school teacher and principal, for 10 years in Nova Scotia and a further 10 in Newfoundland. Abandoning this educational work when family illness required it, Leake eventually managed a home for Chinese prostitutes in British Columbia before returning to the east coast to marry an old love who was now a widower. Her memoirs recorded few regrets. She recalled difficulties, but perseverance rewarded; injustices in salary and workload, but gratitude for the opportunity to use her talents, fulfil her Christian mission, and earn her living (Whitely, 1992).

A rather different story is told by Dianne Hallman about her less career-oriented mother, Margaret Johnston Miller, who taught in Nova Scotia rural schools from 1935 until her marriage in 1941. Miller's memories of teaching were also largely positive; like so many, she felt grateful to have any job at all during the 1930s. If she remembered ill-equipped schools and low pay, she also recalled reasonable equity with respect to men's and women's salaries in rural Nova Scotia, and communities in which teachers were admired and children cooperative. Margaret Johnston left the classroom for good when she married, but did not believe that the marriage bar had been very rigidly enforced in her community, in the 1940s at least. Indeed, many of her woman friends had continued teaching after marriage, she recalled (Hallman, 1992).

Intriguing stories are also emerging about individual teachers in other provinces. Afua Cooper's account of Mary Bibb is particularly evocative. Information about this black woman teacher and abolitionist proved elusive, but the very gaps in Bibb's story are meaningful, emblematic as they are of our failure to honour or even record and remember black women's teaching work. In restoring Mary Bibb to our consciousness, Cooper performs an important task. Her subject's heroism emerges as the heroism of a woman who had to cope with racial as well as gender prejudice, not to mention the stresses of migration. A trained teacher with considerable American experience, she came to Ontario (then Canada West) with her missionary husband before the American Civil War, devoting herself to the schooling of black children, when state support for such an endeavour was almost non-existent. When necessity required it she turned to dressmaking and, possibly, storekeeping to keep body and soul together. Yet she was clearly revered in her own community for her educational work (Cooper, 1991 and 1994). Mary Bibb's story is useful to us because, like Margaret Miller's and even Annie Leake's, it reminds us that there were positive as well as negative aspects to most women's teaching careers and that, although their school work was important to them, it was rarely the only work that women teachers did.

Beyond State Schools: Academy, College and University Teachers

What of the women teachers who carried on outside state school systems? In Canada, Roman Catholic teaching sisters have inhabited both public and private educational worlds and some have been powerful figures (Fahmy-Eid and Dumont, 1983; Smyth, 1991, 1997; del C Bruno-Joffré, 1993). Occasionally private and ladies' academy teachers also exercised considerable autonomy in their work (Errington, 1995; Selles, 1996). Some of these women were involved in higher education and insisted on women's claim to the scholarly life. Increasingly, they saw this as occurring not just in colleges set apart for women, but in men's universities.

Mary Electa Adams was such a woman (Prentice, 1989). A renowned educator in her time, Adams followed her vocational path with several goals in mind: to be financially independent and make a home for herself and her sister; to both provide and advance the cause of higher education for women; and to achieve the control over her own work that she thought her due. Many of Adams' dreams came true. Certainly, by the 1880s, most English-Canadian universities had admitted women, although their presence was frequently an uneasy one (LaPierre, 1990). And early women graduates often became teachers. In addition, some pursued graduate studies and, of these, quite a few looked forward to teaching careers in higher education.

The universities only slowly accepted their services, however. The Canadian physicist, Elizabeth Laird, is an example of the exclusions women typically suffered. Despite leading her University of Toronto mathematics and physics class three years in a row, when she graduated in 1896 she was denied the scholarship that should have given her the opportunity to begin graduate work in Europe. Passed over in favour of a man, Laird headed for the women's colleges of the United States, acquiring a doctorate from Bryn Mawr and, eventually, the leadership of a thriving physics department at Mount Holyoke, a position she retained for nearly three decades (Prentice, 1996). In contrast, some of Laird's contemporaries were able to achieve university teaching careers in Canada with the advent of household science faculties. Elizabeth Laird's own sister, Annie, chose this path, as did the University of Toronto's first woman full professor, Clara Benson, both entering university teaching and research through the university's Lillian Massey School of Household Science prior to World War I. As time went on, women would find or create similar vital enclaves in fields like social work and nursing. And they would gradually creep into other faculties as well, albeit very haltingly.

For the prejudice against women in higher education remained powerful. When the University of Toronto built a state-of-the-art athletic, cultural and social facility in the 1920s, for example, women were not permitted to enter it. Female faculty were thus effectively barred from the meetings and other events that took place within its walls and thus from important aspects of university life. A different problem faced the historian Margaret Ormsby when she took up her first university teaching post at McMaster University, in Hamilton, Ontario, in the early years of Wold War II. Informed that the university had no offices for women instructors, she found that her work space was to be a table in the ladies' washroom. Ormsby was subsequently able to carve out a career at the University of British Columbia that was marked by major honours, but she had few female colleagues in her field. Of Canadian universities, only two in the west, UBC and Saskatchewan, showed any inclination to welcome women into the history professoriate (Prentice, 1991 and 1997b). Interestingly, despite Elizabeth Laird's rejection, women physicists may have fared slightly better, along with other women in the sciences. We have only begun to look at the gendering of the academic disciplines in Canada, but evidence from the University of Toronto during the interwar years is suggestive. As the research university expanded, there were more jobs for women in scientific than in other fields. They usually found positions as demonstrators, research and teaching assistants, or secretaries, but some were able to make it into the professorial ranks (Prentice, 1991, 1996 and 1997a).

The Chilly Climate

The situation was rarely easy for women academics, whatever their discipline. Judith Fingard has documented the chilly climate endured by the few women faculty employed at Nova Scotia's Dalhousie University, in the decades before 1950. Many gave their services for little or no pay for years, Fingard found (Fingard, 1984/85). Mary Kinnear, who interviewed women who taught at the University of Manitoba prior to the 1970s, also discovered that her subjects rarely felt genuinely included there; most maintained a low profile in order to survive. Although many were grateful to have university jobs, others resented their subordinate status (Kinnear, 1995). According to Kinnear, women faculty reported very little in the way of female associative life at Manitoba and women who worked at other universities have made similar claims. Yet there is evidence that some women involved in university teaching before our own era had support groups, although not necessarily all female ones, at least at certain key points in their careers. Departmental or topically oriented clubs, university women's clubs, the Federation of University Women and its international counterpart were clearly vital organizations for many early women academics (Prentice, 1997a and b).

Some female academics found support in close, informal friendships with their women associates (Prentice, 1997a) and, despite strong prohibitions against their doing so, some were sustained by marriage. At Toronto's University College, the dean of women and English instructor, Mossie May Waddington, married a Trinity College professor of classics in the early 1920s; at least two other Toronto faculty women (in astronomy and biology) were married by the 1940s and a woman mathematician retained her job, although she married shortly after the war. But Toronto also provides instances of women who were forced to leave the university when they married: in the 1930s, for example, Gladys Wookey in English, and Irene Biss and Adelaide McDonald in political science. The University of Toronto physicist, Elizabeth Allin, recalled that firing married women was a major way the university 'got rid of' many of its female faculty during the Great Depression (Prentice, 1991 and 1997a; Ainley Gostonyi 1996).

Kinnear ties the marriage bar to professionalism. Professionals were supposed to give everything to their work, leaving family and 'personal' tasks to others (Kinnear, 1995). One might add to this interpretation the increasing value of young, unmarried women's work as assistants, in the development of male academics' professional careers. Men usually had wives at home; increasingly, they had secretarial, teaching, and technical help at work as well. Women scholars rarely enjoyed such support; they were supposed to be the supporters. Prior to the 1970s, therefore, academically oriented women experienced pressures on three fronts. First, there was the pressure to accept the male professor/female assistant model and remain subordinate — and unmarried. Then, there was the pressure to give it all up and marry. Finally, there were the pressures, if one did marry and keep one's university job, of juggling many roles at once. That Mossie May Waddington Kirkwood, who had children, experienced some difficulties doing so is reflected in the spread of her publications. Her thesis was published in 1919; a booklet dealing with the problems of women in higher education came out in 1938; her third book, on the philosopher Santayana, had to wait until her full retirement over 30 years later. Despite the difficulties she must have encountered, Kirkwood stuck to her vocation as a teacher and a scholar. Her 1938 pamphlet contains a powerful statement on women's need for and right to have meaningful work (cited, Prentice, 1989).

The Recent Past and the Future

If I conclude this account of research on Canadian women teachers a few decades before our own times, it is because my expertise does not extend to the recent past, except as I have experienced it. I have done so as a secondary school teacher who left teaching to raise children and was drawn into university work with the university expansions of the 1960s and 1970s. Marriage and child-rearing delayed my final degree and introduction to university teaching, but with all their ups and downs, marriage and child-rearing also gave balance to life and a measure of stability. I have also been fortunate in the women's and mixed gender groups that have supported my scholarly endeavours. And, although juggling family and scholarly responsibilities has often been a struggle, I have only rarely felt outright hostility to my work.

My younger colleagues have had more to contend with. In 1989, they experienced the anguish all university women felt when 14 female engineering students at the University of Montreal were massacred by a man who, denied entry to their programme, believed that they — and all feminists — were his enemies. On a less dramatic scale, they have had to deal with routine harassment and overt hostility to women's and feminist studies, and sometimes hostility to themselves as women instructors (Chilly Collective, 1995). They are also increasingly burdened, as Rebecca Coulter notes in her essay for this volume, with workloads that a combination of university cutbacks, demanding students and colleagues, and their own idealism have created. Nor are the solutions women have found to their problems in the academy easy ones. Some have given up partnerships or parenting that could not be combined with scholarly or teaching lives; others have sacrificed their academic work in order to keep families, or body and soul, together. Some women, finding themselves excluded from the academy, continue their scholarly work in their 'spare' time, while they work at other jobs. Others, who have made it into the academy, have decided, like Elizabeth Binmore did, to make political organizing and administration their highest priorities, because there is so much important political work that needs to be done.

What we need now and in the future is research that explores the multi-faceted lives of women teachers, in the past and the present, along with the connections and dissonances in their spiritual, domestic, personal, educational and scholarly vocations that both inform and disrupt female educational workers' careers. We also need strong affirmation of *all* the different paths that women educators and scholarly workers choose, fall into, or have thrust upon them. We must continue the struggles that Mary Electa Adams and Elizabeth

Binmore began and Mossie May Kirkwood continued: for women's right to meaningful work, equitable remuneration, and fulfilling personal and spiritual lives that may (or may not) include partners, children and community.

This means changing schools and universities to accommodate women workers' needs. It also means changing our images of the 'good teacher' and the 'brilliant professor', especially if these images suggest the need to sacrifice everything to one's professional work. Our task is to seek balance, more flexible working conditions, and a world that welcomes women's work as teachers and scholars, whether or not they are full-time employees of schools or universities. This may mean encouraging individuals, especially men, who are employed full-time, to ease off and make space for others. It may also mean expanding our models to include women like Annie Leake, Margaret Miller and Mary Bibb. As they knew and their lives demonstrated, there is more to life — and education — than work in schools and universities.

References

ABBOTT, J. (1986) 'Accomplishing "a man's task": Rural women teachers, male culture and the school inspectorate in turn-of-the-century Ontario', *Ontario History*, **78**, 4, pp. 313–30, Reprinted in HEAP, R. and PRENTICE, A. (eds) (1991) *Gender and Education in Ontario*, Toronto: Canadian Scholars' Press.

AINLEY GOSTONYI, M. (1996) 'Marriage and scientific work in twentieth-century Canada: The Berkeleys in marine biology and the Hoggs in astronomy', in PYCIOR, H.M., SLACK, N.G. and ABIR-AM, P.G. (eds) *Creative Couples in the Sciences*, New Brunswick, New Jersey: Rutgers University Press.

BARBER, M. (1991) 'The fellowship of the maple leaf teachers', in FERGUSON, B. (ed.) *The Anglican Church and the World of Western Canada, 1820–1970*, Regina: Canadian Plains Research Centre, University of Regina.

BARMAN, J. (1990) 'Birds of passage or early professionals? Teachers in late nineteenth-century British Columbia', *Historical Studies in Education/Revue d'Histoire de l'Education*, **2**, 1, pp. 17–36.

BURNET, J. (1981) 'Minorities I have belonged to', *Canadian Ethnic Studies*, **XIII**, 1, pp. 24–36.

(THE) CHILLY COLLECTIVE (1995) *Breaking Anonymity: The Chilly Climate for Women Faculty*, Waterloo, Ontario: Wilfrid Laurier University Press.

COOPER, A. (1991) 'The search for Mary Bibb, black woman teacher in nineteenth-century Canada West', *Ontario History*, **83**, 1, pp. 39–54.

COOPER, A. (1994) 'Black women and work in nineteenth-century Canada West: Black woman teacher Mary Bibb', in BRISTOW, P., BRAND, D., CARTY, L., COOPER, A., HAMILTON, S. and SHADD, A. (eds) *'We're Rooted Here and They Can't Pull Us Up': Essays in African Canadian Women's History*, Toronto: University of Toronto Press.

CRUIKSHANK, J., SIDNEY, A., SMITH, K. and NED, A. (1991) *Life Lived Like a Story: Life Stories of Three Yukon Elder*, Vancouver: University of British Columbia Press.

DANYLEWYCZ, M. (1987) *Taking the Veil: An Alternative to Marriage, Motherhood and Spinsterhood in Quebec, 1840–1920*, Toronto: McClelland and Stewart.

DANYLEWYCZ, M., LIGHT, B. and PRENTICE, A. (1983) 'The evolution of the sexual division of labour in teaching: A nineteenth-century Ontario and Quebec case study', *Histoire Sociale/Social History*, **XVI**, 31, pp. 81–109, Reprinted in GASKELL, J. and McLAREN[A. (eds) (1987) *Women and Education: A Canadian Perspective*, Calgary: Detselig, pp. 33–60.

DANYLEWYCZ, M. and PRENTICE, A. (1984) 'Teachers, gender and bureaucratizing school systems in 19th century Montreal and Toronto', *History of Education Quarterly*, **24**, pp. 75–100.

DANYLEWYCZ, M. and PRENTICE, A. (1986) 'Teachers' work: Changing patterns and perceptions in the emerging school systems of nineteenth and early twentieth century Central Canada', *Labour/le Travail*, **17**, pp. 59–80, Reprinted in PRENTICE, A. and THEOBALD, M.R. (eds) (1991) *Women Who Taught: Perspectives on the History of Women and Teaching*, Toronto: University of Toronto Press.

DEL C. BRUNO-JOFFRÉ, R. (1993) 'The Oblate Sisters, a Manitoba Order: Reconstructing early years, 1914–15', in R. DEL C. BRUNO-JOFFRÉ (ed.) *Issues in the History of Education in Manitoba: From the Construction of the Common Schools to the Politics of Voices*, Lewiston, NY: The Edwin Mellon Press.

ERRINGTON, J. (1995) *Wives and Mothers, School Mistresses and Scullery Maids: Working Women in Upper Canada, 1790–1840*, Montreal and Kingston: McGill: Queen's University Press.

FAHMY-EID, N. and DUMONT, M. (1983) *Maîtresses de Maison, Maîtresses d'Ecole: Femmes, Famille et Education dans l'Histoire du Québec*, Montréal: Boréal Express.

FINGARD, J. (1984/85) 'Gender and inequality at Dalhousie: Faculty women before 1950', *Dalhousie Review*, **64**, pp. 687–703.

GASKELL, S. (1989) 'The problems and professionalism of women elementary public school teachers in Ontario, 1944–54', Ed.D Thesis: University of Toronto.

GELMAN, S. (1990) 'The "Feminization" of the high schools? Women secondary school teachers in Toronto 1871–1930', *Historical Studies in Education/Revue d'Histoire de l'Education*, **2**, 1, pp. 119–48, Reprinted in HEAP, R. and PRENTICE, A. (eds) (1991) *Gender and Education in Ontario*, Toronto: Canadian Scholars Press.

GUILDFORD, J. (1992) '"Separate spheres": The feminization of teaching in Nova Scotia, 1838–80', *Acadiensis*, **22**, 1, pp. 44–64, Reprinted in GUILDFORD, J. and MORTON, S. (eds) (1994) *Separate Spheres: Women's Worlds in the 19th Century Maritimes*, Fredericton: Acadiensis Press.

HALLMAN, D. (1992) '"A thing of the past": Teaching in one-room schools in rural Nova Scotia, 1935–41', *Historical Studies in Education/Revue d'Histoire de l'Education*, **4**, 1, pp. 113–32.

HEAP, R. and PRENTICE, A. (1993) '"The outlook for old age is not hopeful": The struggle of female teachers over pensions in Quebec, 1880–1914', *Histoire Sociale/Social History*, **XXVI**, pp. 67–94.

KINNEAR, M. (1995) *In Subordination: Professional Women 1870–1970*, Montreal and Kingston: McGill: Queen's University Press.

KOJDER, A.M. (1977) 'The Saskatoon Women Teachers' Association: A demand for recognition', *Saskatchewan History*, pp. 63–74, Reprinted in JONES, D.C., SHENAN, N.M. and STAMP, M. (eds) (1979) *Shaping the Schools of the Canadian West*, Calgary: Detselig.

LAPIERRE, J. (1990) 'The academic life of Canadian Coeds, 1880–1900', *Historical Studies in Education/Revue d'Histoire de l'Education*, **2**, 2, pp. 225–45, Reprinted in HEAP, R. and PRENTICE, A. (eds) (1991) *Gender and Education in Ontario*, Toronto: Canadian Scholars' Press.

Lyons, J.E. (1984) 'For St George and Canada: The fellowship of the maple leaf and education on the prairies, 1919–29', in Wilson, J.D. (ed.) *An Imperfect Past: Education and Society in Canadian History*, Vancouver: Faculty of Education, University of British Columbia.

Poelzer, I. (1990) *Saskatchewan Women Teachers 1905–20: Their Contributions*. Saskatoon: Lindenblatt and Hamonic.

Prentice, A. (1975) 'The feminization of teaching in British North America and Canada, 1845–1975', *Histoire Sociale/Social History*, **VIII**, pp. 5–20, Reprinted in Mann Trofimenkoff, S. and Prentice, A. (eds) (1977) *The Neglected Majority: Essays in Canadian Women's History*, Toronto: McClelland and Stewart.

Prentice, A. (1985) 'Themes in the early history of the Women Teachers' Association of Toronto', in Bourne, P. (ed.) *Women's Paid and Unpaid Work*, Toronto: New Hogtown Press.

Prentice, A. (1989) 'Scholarly passion: Two persons who caught it', *Historical Studies in Education/Revue d'Histoire de l'Education*, **1**, 1, pp. 7–27, Reprinted in Prentice, A. and Theobald, M.R. (eds) (1991) *Women Who Taught: Perspectives on the History of Women and Teaching*, Toronto: University of Toronto Press.

Prentice, A. (1990) 'Multiple realities: The history of women teachers in Canada', in Forman, F., O'Brien, M., Haddad, J., Hallman, D. and Masters, P. (eds) *Feminism and Education: A Canadian Perspective*, Toronto: Centre for Women's Studies in Education, Ontario Institute for Studies in Education.

Prentice, A. (1991) 'Bluestockings, feminists, or women workers? A preliminary look at women's early employment at the University of Toronto', *Journal of the Canadian Historical Association*, NS 2, pp. 231–61.

Prentice, A. (1996) 'The early history of women in university physics: A Toronto case study', *Physics in Canada*, **52**, 2, pp. 94–100.

Prentice, A. (1997a) 'Elizabeth Allin: Physicist', in Dickin, J. and Cameron, E. (eds) *Great Dames*, Toronto: University of Toronto Press.

Prentice, A. (1997b) 'Laying siege to the history professoriate', in Boutilier, B. and Prentice, A. (eds) *Creating Historical Memory: English-Canadian Women and the Work of History*, Vancouver: University of British Columbia Press.

Reynolds, C. (1990a) 'Hegemony and hierarchy: Becoming a teacher in Toronto, 1930–80', *Historical Studies in Education/Revue d'Histoire de l'Education*, **2**, 1, pp. 95–118.

Reynolds, C. (1990b) 'Too limiting a liberation: Discourse and actuality in the case of married women teachers', in Forman, F., O'Brien, M., Haddad, J., Hallman, D. and Masters, P. (eds) *Feminism and Education: A Canadian Perspective*, Toronto: Ontario Institute for Studies in Education, Centre for Women's Studies in Education.

Selles, J.M. (1996) *Methodists and Women's Education in Ontario, 1836–1925*, Montreal and Kingston: McGill Queen's University Press.

Smaller, H. (1991) '"A Room of One's Own": The early years of the Toronto Women Teachers Association', in Heap, R. and Prentice, A. (eds) *Gender and Education in Ontario*, Canadian Scholars Press.

Smyth, E. (1991) '"A noble proof of excellence": The culture and curriculum of a nineteenth century Ontario convent academy', in Heap, R. and Prentice, A. (eds) *Gender and Education in Ontario*, Toronto: Canadian Scholars' Press.

Smyth, E. (1997) '"Writing teaches us our mysteries": Women religious recording and writing history', in Boutilier, B. and Prentice, A. *Creating Historical Memory: English-Canadian Women and the Work of History*, Vancouver: University of British Columbia Press.

WHITELY, M.F. (1992) 'Annie Leake's occupation: Development of a teaching career, 1858–86', *Historical Studies in Education/Revue d'Histoire de l'Education*, **1**, 4, pp. 97–112.

WILSON, J.D. (1991) '"I am ready to be of assistance when I can": Lottie Bowron and rural women teachers in British Columbia', in PRENTICE, A. and THEOBALD, M.R. (eds) *Women Who Taught: Perspectives on the History of Women and Teaching*, Toronto: University of Toronto Press.

Part II

Feminist Strategies for Change

Introduction

From stories of the past we turn to analyses and strategies of recent times, tracking ways in which women have sought to bring educational provision closer to their needs. We look variously at schools, at universities and at broader education systems. We move from classroom interactions and learning environments to the impact of global markets. Overall we find that while women have made considerable gains, current economic thinking does not auger well for an assault on the final bastions of male privilege.

Hildur Ve and Britt-Marie Berge focus on action research in Scandinavian classrooms. Reflecting gender equity policies in that region, classroom research teaching boys to be more caring and girls to be more autonomous has received official backing. Yet even here interesting questions emerge. The teacher/researchers' own values intervene bringing into the classroom previously internalized gender expectations, even, Ve argues, newer global values of individualism which contrast with previous Norwegian collectivist values.

Similarly gendered expectations of girls' and womens' bodies — the need to be 'attractive', to reproduce — underlie and subvert well-meaning health and physical education programmes, as Robin Burns points out. Girls' bodies, indeed their presence, are also a 'problem' in schools in Victoria Foster's essay. Where can girls feel at ease in school systems, Foster asks, without appearing to threaten boys? Do they need a special space?

Coulter and Weiner et al. move the focus to system-wide change, looking particularly at the impact of conservative policies on girls' education and women's educational work respectively. Weiner sees opportunities for girls in the British national curriculum initiatives but fears that schools will be increasingly blamed for boys' and men's inabilities to find employment in a restructuring global economy. Coulter's focus on Canada at the present time continues elements of Prentice's work, particularly the dispensable nature of women's employment in times of economic stringency. Coulter, like Weiner, wonders if schools (and teachers) are becoming scapegoats for the broader problems of post-industrial society. These pieces are central to our thesis overall, that old patterns re-emerge, that steps forward for women may be too threatening when global economic shifts disrupt decades-long patterns of work and gender relations.

Sylvia Benckert and Else-Marie Staberg, and Grace Mak also pick up on a continuing dilemma — the difficulty for highly educated women with families of combining career and care. From very different parts of the globe — Sweden and China — countries with official gender equity programmes (albeit very differently expressed) are unable to solve the inequities posed by women's 'double burden' and deeply internalized gendered identity structures.

Even within universities Kerstin Shands suggests, women have not made sufficient headway *in their own terms* either in curriculum content or in their physical presence at senior levels. In a vein similar to that argued by American philosopher Jane Martin, Shands proposes an 'acculturalist' rather than an 'assimilationist' perspective (Martin, 1997). Academic frequencies, she argues, must become modulated to hear women's voices, not to insist that women speak like men.

4 Education for Change: Action Research for Increased Gender Equality

Hildur Ve

A Feminist Critique of New Trends within the Norwegian Educational System: Introduction

Are the values of care, concern and connection of central importance in our school system? And if they are, what about the future? Who will be the bearers of these values — girls, boys or both together?

These questions are pertinent in relation both to the present educational situation and to future trends within western societies. With changes within the Norwegian educational system as my point of departure I present an action research project aimed at increasing gender equality in grades 1–3 (7–9 years) in primary school where the values of care, concern and connection have played an important part (Martin, 1985). In the final section I discuss the tendency to individualism in our school system, arguing that we need both to acknowledge it and oppose it.

Looking to the Future

Looking ahead and attempting to make forecasts about the situation of women and men in the next century, it seems crucial to focus on the group of 'knowledge workers'. This is the group that some social scientists predict will become more numerous and influential than were other dominant groups such as farmers until the middle of the twentieth century, and industrial workers in the last decades (Drucker, 1994; Hobsbawm, 1994). The 'knowledge workers' comprise many different types of workers. Typically, they have a considerable amount of formal schooling and/or administrative-technological education and are continuously upgrading their knowledge. They are specialists in their fields, and their knowledge is the decisive or central force of production — not machines. Therefore they have greater power than industrial workers ever had.

In *The Age of Extremes* Eric Hobsbawm questions the fate of the welfare state in countries where industrial workers are a minority of less than 25 per cent (in the US less than 15 per cent) of the population (Hobsbawm, 1994).

Will the new group of 'knowledge workers' develop welfare state solidarity, as the industrial workers did? Some social scientists predict that rather than supporting a tax based social security system based on citizen's rights, new voluntary organizations will emerge (Druckert, 1994).

If these predictions are fulfilled, an area of higher education that has been dominated by girls and women in the last part of this century (i.e. education preparing students for work in welfare state jobs) may be reduced. In Sweden, clear signs of such a tendency are already appearing, with a potential outcome being that girls and women, despite higher educational achievement, may face diminished employment avenues. The following discussion looks at the latest research data on girls' achievements in the Norwegian school system.

Are Girls the Winners in the Norwegian Educational System?

In 1996 Ivar Frønes published an article entitled: 'Revolution without rebellion: Gender, generation and social change in Norway in the 80s' (my translation, Frønes, 1996). The conclusion of the article (based on both data and theory) was that girls now did better than boys at all levels, in all subject areas, within our educational system. This was identified as the most important change in our country in the twentieth century. Frønes defined the girls as 'winners', adding that the trend is likely to accelerate where there is severe competition at point of entry (e.g. medicine). However, the picture is much more complicated than Frønes suggests.

Firstly, in those subjects within higher education most popular among girls such as nursing, teaching and social work, far fewer places are available than within the typical 'boys' subjects' such as engineering. The competition for places is therefore severe. Secondly, even if women do better in school, within the job market men are still most often awarded the jobs with the highest amount of power, prestige and salaries. Thirdly, while unemployment has traditionally been higher for men than for women, in Sweden and in many other European countries it is now higher for women than for men. This trend has been explained by the reduction of welfare state jobs.

Many social scientists maintain that the policy of gender equality within the educational system (introduced in Norway in 1973) must be the reason for the girls' success, arguing that an equality policy for boys is needed. But at the same time as Frønes wrote his article, Gunn Imsen published a research-based evaluation of the way that gender equality policy has been effected in Norway (Imsen, 1996). Imsen finds that although generally both school leaders and teachers approve of the aims of the policy, in practice very little has been done. She finds no evidence that girls are treated differently to boys by female teachers, an argument that has frequently been mounted. The recent success of girls compared to boys in the school system cannot, therefore, be explained by girls being given preferential treatment.

Changes within the Norwegian Educational System

To a great extent recent changes have been inspired and influenced by the sociological perspective called *Rational Choice Theory* (Coleman, 1990; Hernes and Knudsen, 1976). Some of the basic elements in the Coleman/Hernes conception of sociology and of education are exchange theory, human capital, the instrumental actor and strategic choice.

In 1988 an important public document entitled *With Insight and Resolution* (Hernes et al., 1988) was published, presenting many of the ideas now being implemented in the Norwegian educational system. Here the authors maintained that 'the country does not get enough competency out of the talents of its population'. In another section they argue that in order to secure continuing growth of Norway's gross national product (a condition for continuance of the state welfare system) Norway as a nation must be able to compete with other industrial nations of the world: 'What we produce must be comparable with what others produce'. They argue that Norwegians must place more emphasis on teaching basic knowledge (i.e. the Norwegian and English languages, physics and mathematics) and perhaps introduce a grading system at primary school level.

Although the document contains many both humanistic and progressive ideas, it considers the school system to be an instrument in creating a higher GNP, essentially an instrument to getting a good job. The authors are clearly influenced by trends in western economies toward increasing significance of the knowledge workers. They also emphasize the types of competencies that enhance productive capacity, but do not mention the types of competencies needed within paid (and unpaid) carework, an occupation often cited as important by girls and women when asked about their work.

Critique of the Changes from a Progressive Perspective and a Gender Perspective

Alfred Oftedal Telhaug provocatively and convincingly compared the school of the first part of this century with that after 1930, predicting the Norwegian school scenario once reforms have been effected (Telhaug, 1992). While labelling the first type 'The old fashioned school' and maintaining that this was a school for masculine culture, he argues that the school after 1930 became increasingly dominated by social-democratic perspectives and progressive ideals. Telhaug asks: 'A pedagogy that continuously asks about the needs and reactions of the child, isn't that more an expression of women's culture and feminine values than a pedagogy that has as its main worry society's, and especially business', claims on the school?' He maintains that the school should give care in addition to knowledge.

He also maintains that the women-friendly school is challenged by claims from society's industrial and economic sectors who insist on quality, competence, productivity, excellence, and especially efficiency, competition, staying power and 'giving one's best'. Despite his perspective, Telhaug's analyses of what is happening in the Norwegian educational system are quite similar to mine, which I shall enlarge upon after discussing the emergence of Norwegian feminist ideas.

Towards the end of the 1970s Bjørg Aase Sørensen developed two concepts of rationality that were to impact significantly on Norwegian gender discourse: technical limited rationality — and responsible rationality (Sørensen, 1982). The former comprised the rationality developed within commodity production and was thought to have had a stronger impact on men's thought patterns than on those of women. Important subdimensions are technical, economic and bureaucratic rationality (Ve, 1990). The social relations inherent in this rationality may be described as individualistic: 'Everybody must fend for him — or her — self'.

The latter type of responsible rationality may be understood as an extension of Max Weber's concept of value rationality, which draws on the work experiences of both paid and unpaid dependent persons. An important subdimension of this rationality is the ability to identify with the interests of dependent persons. For Norwegian feminist sociologists, in analyses of various types of care work (e.g. mothering, nursing, social work, teaching), the concept of responsible rationality, or care work rationality, proved very productive (Wærness, 1982; Ve, 1983). An important subdimension is that of combining the concepts of responsibility or care with rationality, making it possible to perceive care work as more than simply warm feelings and supportive attitudes. Care work is hard work that warrants consideration in terms of its aims, and planning about appropriate means. A third subdimension is the understanding and interpretation of women's actions according to their own premises, rather than according to male value standards.

In analyses of the educational system the two concepts of technical limited rationality and responsible rationality serve to highlight variations between boys' and girls' approaches to school and the school's differentiated treatment of the two groups of children (Ve, 1983). They also provide a basis for categorizing the underlying values in the new Norwegian educational reforms (Ve, 1994).

After the introduction of post modern theory within feminist discourse in Norway, the two concepts of rationality were criticized for being both universalist and essentialist, perhaps leading to an exaggeration of likenesses and oversight of differences. When using these concepts, feminist sociologists may not have sufficiently explained how the differences that we write about are statistical ones; therefore the post modern critique has made us more aware of how we present our theories and data. Recently, however, post modern perspectives themselves have been criticized for being just as context-bound as are the grand narratives (Bauman, 1992). Feminists like Dorothy Smith, using as her point of departure George Herbert Mead's understanding of the social aspects of human interaction, refer to various weak points in, for example, Foucault's theoretical deconstruction of the subject (Smith, 1996). And many Norwegian feminists continue to find the two rationality concepts productive and doubt that by using them as analytical tools we distort our understanding of reality. In particular, they have served as tools for analysing the negative aspects for women of our new educational policies.

The action research project described here has been influenced to a large degree by the Norwegian feminist discourse on responsible rationality and critique of the school system, but also by various other research data on differences between girls and boys in school. My intention is to present a picture of how school work may function as a possibility for furthering coop-eration and growth. I also discuss some aspects of school work that may help to develop boys' social abilities.

An Action Research Project on Gender Equality in 7–9-year-olds

In the autumn of 1986 I was asked to lead a research team given the task of developing an atmosphere of gender equality in first grade (7-year-olds) class-rooms from the first week of school. The team comprised another researcher and some consultants from the school administration. We soon realized that in order to achieve our ambitious aim, we should have to work closely with teachers who shared these aims.

We sent invitations to all teachers (in the county of Hordaland) who were to start as class teachers in the first grade in the autumn of 1987. Fourteen teachers, two men and 12 women indicated interest and were included in the research team. During our first seminars in the spring of 1987 we discussed our aims and methods. We had long and thoughtful discussions about the mean-ing of the concepts of equality, equity and equal worth. Indeed, during the four years that the team worked together we never really came to a joint conclusion about which concept to prioritize. However, we agreed that one important condition for equality between the sexes is that men must begin to share with women the responsibility for dependent person care work. Women must also take a greater part both in technological development and in the general decision-making processes in society.

Both teachers and researchers agreed that 'an atmosphere of equality between girls and boys' cannot be created through verbal attempts at attitude change only. We increasingly focused on ideas that had to do with teaching girls and boys greater respect and understanding for each other by giving them opportunities to experience ways in which both groups may master the same challenges. In other words, we decided that it would be important for girls to experience mastery of the same activities as boys while the boys observe — and vice versa.

The whole team agreed to use pedagogical methods that built upon John Dewey's theories of learning by doing. Many of the teachers had experience in group work and activity pedagogics. The administrators from the director's office also had experience with giving courses in project pedagogies. Several teachers informed us about a special activity-oriented method where many *different* group activities take place in the classroom at the same time. Since it is impossible for the teacher to closely supervise all the groups, the children learn to organize themselves.

Slowly we developed our plans for creating an 'equality atmosphere' in the classrooms. We decided that one day per week should be 'project' day. Each teacher was to divide the class into single sex groups. The idea was developed with reference to research — and also to some of the teachers' experiences — which suggested that if one organizes practical tasks with mixed groups, very often the boys will occupy those parts of the task that they enjoy carrying out and delegate the other parts to the girls. (An example of this is a group of pupils that are to prepare a meal. The boys will take part in or take over the cooking, while the washing up will be delegated to the girls.)

The five groups were to work with different tasks to be circulated between the groups so that in the course of five weeks all groups had carried out all the tasks. Then the next step would be for the research team to further develop the tasks and include new and more challenging situations.

For the researchers this model seemed to be almost impossibly complicated. I must admit that in the beginning I could not envisage how a teacher of a class of first graders might be able to organize the pupils in this way without it all becoming hopelessly chaotic. This was the first time of many when the researchers realized that without the participation of the teachers in a democratically organized team, the whole project would have been of a much less creative and challenging character. Having had the chance to observe several of the classes in the first part of the project it became obvious that the researchers had underestimated both the teachers' organizing abilities, and the children's — truly amazing — willingness to seriously accept such arrangements (Ve, 1991).

Challenges

Of course we had many problems coming to terms with each other, and we had to resolve many conflicts. We decided at the outset that one of the activities on the 'project day' should involve the use of tools such as hammers, saws and screwdrivers. We decided that another should be about solving technical problems, like changing light bulbs and fuses, and using technical Lego. On the other hand we found it productive for the boys to experience sewing and knitting. Likewise, learning how to cook, set a table and do the dishes were considered very appropriate equality activities. We found it very difficult to develop care work pedagogies. Finally we agreed that probably the best way was to do what girls always have done, i.e. learn how to take care of babies by playing with dolls. Each teacher would obtain some dolls, dolls' clothes, doll beds. We decided that the training and learning about caring for small children would have to be carried out by playing with these dolls. At the end of each project day the children were to report in their 'log books' about what they had been doing.

In addition to the 'project day' we also decided that during ordinary school work the teachers should keep in mind that they must give as much attention to the girls as to the boys. Especially important was the rule that in all types of discussions the teacher should not allow boys to 'steal' the word from girls, which much research indicates is a usual pattern. We also agreed that teachers should introduce as many typical girls' as typical boys' activities in physical education. They should also encourage the girls to really learn how to play football (soccer).

In terms of ensuring cooperation between teachers, researchers and administrators, we decided that for the rest of the research period we should continue our discussions three times each semester in seminars of two or three days.

Something then happened that was to constitute a very great challenge to the action research team. In order to create some kind of evaluative measures of effects, the school director of the county of Hordaland who had initiated the research asked us to include control classes into the research design. We realized that in order to measure the effects, if any, of the methods that we were to introduce, we should have to design some means of testing what we were doing.

It became obvious that the idea of control classes might seriously alter the project because of the inflexibility that this new research design imposed upon us. As our work developed we often wanted to make changes regarding our various methods. We realized that action research does not imply the type of static research situation that corresponds with the control classes and tests intended to capture the same dimensions at the start and at the end of the project period. We did not abandon the tests and control classes, but we introduced other methods such as interviewing the teachers and observing project classrooms.

Care Work Pedagogies

I shall give an example of a situation which demonstrates the need for flexibility in action research where the aim is to change a system, not — as in traditional research — only to observe it. The example illustrates participatory democracy, so important for action research. In the autumn of 1987 (when the teachers had worked for a couple of months with their respective classes) during a seminar some declared that they could not go on with the part of the project that included boys playing with dolls in order to learn care work for babies. They described how aggressively the boys handled the dolls — kicking them around and throwing them on the floor. The teachers felt that this method could only serve to alienate the boys from care work, and to make the girls shocked and unhappy at the boys' behaviour. The teachers thought that to continue with this method would have a negative impact on the work for greater gender equality.

For the researchers this was a serious setback. For my own part, having worked with the theoretical concept of responsible rationality, the idea of developing an atmosphere in which the boys experienced empathy and learned how to take care of babies was a central part of the project. Again we engaged in heated discussions. Many of the teachers had experienced similarly negative situations. Then one of the teachers described a method that she had developed in her own class that seemed to work well both for the girls and the boys. She had found a pattern for the making of 'cloth dolls', and had let the pupils make their own dolls, doll clothes and doll bed. She had found that the boys enjoyed this task very much, and had become attached to their dolls to the same — or even to a greater — degree than the girls. Afterwards, the researchers had several opportunities to observe the boys' groups playing with their dolls (which in our eyes did not look very much like dolls), and we were struck by the obvious care that the boys demonstrated, and their pride in the various types of doll's' equipment that they had made.

After some discussion a number of the teachers agreed to try this method, and the team decided to continue with the care work activity and to allow for greater flexibility on the part of the teachers in developing individual approaches.

Results

Our different types of data — tests, observations and teacher interviews — all indicate that we had accomplished some changes towards greater gender equality in the classrooms. The teacher interviews constitute the most interesting and illuminating data. They agree that the project has had a very important outcome for girls in that they have learned to speak with more confidence and to stand up for their views against the boys. Many of them have really learned to like using traditionally male tools and are proud of their skills. Although in the beginning some of the girls had argued that the technical tasks were not suitable for girls, they learned to enjoy them and technical Lego became very popular. In the beginning a number of boys remarked that the various tasks were not suitable for boys, but they soon learned to enjoy most of them, and became very enthusiastic about cooking.

The teachers often indicated that the boys accepted the girls as equals. One important exception concerned playing soccer, which often resulted in bitter remarks from the girls that the boys only passed the ball to other boys.

In the third grade (9-year-olds) the teachers introduced a new element to the care work activity. They invited mothers with babies to come to their classrooms and arranged beforehand that the pupils should be allowed to change diapers and carry out other types of tasks. The group carried out an interview with the mother about care work for babies. Some of the teachers were quite amazed at the impact this experience had on many of the boys. The teachers found that in the third grade the children's ability to discuss equality between girls and boys among many of the girls had become quite reflective and that they were able to verbalize their views in various ways. The teachers also reported the boys' remarks about situations where their parents showed little understanding of what the boys had learned. One boy told of his mother having asked him to call his sister in order that she might set the table. 'As if I couldn't do it just as well as her!'

All the teachers maintain that through taking part in this project they have developed a much deeper insight and understanding of what gender equality in the classroom implies, all expressing, independently something like 'You have to have an idea about gender equality at the back of your head all the time'. Furthermore they report about changes in their own behaviour generally, for example, regarding the use of unfamiliar tools. Taking part in the project has forced them to do many things they have not tried before and this has enhanced their own self-image. The teachers also found themselves much more engaged in social questions about gender equality.

Many of our own experiences and insights parallel those of the teachers in relation to changes in the researchers' own understanding of gender equality in the classroom. We feel that action research, especially its aspect of participatory democracy, has caused the teachers to reflect upon gender equality to an extent that is unusual, and that this type of research model is very effective in challenging traditional attitudes.

Discussion

One of the founders of action research, Kurt Lewin, once observed that to understand a social system, you have to change it (Lewin, 1948). One of our most important insights was that even when the teachers struggled valiantly to change the patterns both for girls and boys, they found it more 'easy' or 'natural' to work with methods concerning the situation of the girls. In one part of the research project the team was joined by a Norwegian psychologist, Mette Gulbrandsen, who has extensive experience with gender research. She was able to clarify the thoughts of the researchers by commenting that what we tried to accomplish regarding the girls was working within the general trend of the Norwegian culture where most people find it important that girls learn more about technology and about standing up for themselves against the boys. However, we felt that our efforts to 'change' the boys, especially when trying to enhance their capacity for empathy, was working against the tide.

Speaking as a sociologist, I summarize my experiences by saying that we discovered that we were challenging the deep structure of our culture, a very important part of which is the increasing tendency to move from collectivism towards individualism. Much of our work with the girls had to do with enhancing their self-worth and their ability to argue their opinions. This may be interpreted as a method for increasing individualism. Regarding our work with the boys, even if the teachers were enthusiastic about their learning empathy and care work, when summing up the results from the research, what they particularly emphasized was the increase in the pupils' self-reliance, in relation to both girls and boys. Although it was obvious to the researchers that boys have great abilities for care work, and for adopting the values of care, concern and connection, for teachers in our educational system the value of autonomy is of greater importance.

In some ways this insight corresponds to data from a research project carried out by Mette Gulbrandsen (1994). Among other things she finds that the teachers delegate the social responsibility for creating a good atmosphere among the sexes to the girls. Had the teachers helped the girls to illuminate or interpret the 'nurturance trap' (see Berge, this volume), they might also help the girls to be able to reflect upon the consequences for their own identity of this trap. But Gulbrandsen argues that our individually oriented cultural code makes it difficult to analyse social relationships in the classroom.

Girls are most often delegated social responsibility. However, it can be argued that social responsibility in itself is a basic necessity in human society and that the human being is a *social* creature who becomes human through interaction with other people (Mead, 1934). We quote the famous words of the English poet John Donne that 'no man is an island'. However, this is certainly not accepted as important within mainstream Norwegian thought. For example, in one of the latest Norwegian works on socialization by sociologist Ivar Frønes, the value of individualism is very prominent (Frønes, 1994) and he argues that: 'The individual is the nucleus of European culture. Solidarity and justice is understood with basis in the free, independent individual'. From a somewhat different perspective, the Coleman/Hernes ideas regarding the human being as an instrumental actor making strategic choices is very different from the understanding presented by Mead (Mead op.cit). For feminists, in relation to the educational system, the future task is to both argue the necessity of the values of care, concern and connection and to illuminate the ways in which the responsibility for supporting these values are delegated to girls. It is likely that a change will also make the boys more socially responsible, serving them well in that it will also make them more mature as people. Data from our research project indicates that it is possible to teach boys to care, but as has been argued in the first part of this paper, the educational system of the future may not move in this direction. With this understanding in mind, as feminists we shall have to strive to strengthen the girls' autonomy and continue our insistence on the values of care, concern and connection. We must advance over the terrain on both fronts at once.

References

BAUMAN, Z. (1992) *Intimations of Post Modernity*, London: Routledge.
COLEMAN, J.S. (1990) *Foundations of Social Theory*, Cambridge, Mass: Belknap of Harvard University Press.

DRUCKER, P.F. (1994) 'The age of social transformation', in *The Atlantic Monthly*, November.

FRØNES, I. (1994) *De Likeverdige: Om Sosialisering og de Jevnaldrendes Betydnin*, (Equals: On Socialisation and the Importance of Peers), Oslo: Universitetsforlaget.

FRØNES, I. (1996) 'Revolusjon uten opprør: Kjønn, generasjon og sosial endring i Norge i 80årene', (Revolution without rebellion: Gender, generation and social change in the 80s), in *Tidsskrift for Samfunnsforskning*, **1**.

GULBRANDSEN, L.M. (1994) 'Blant hester og gorillaer i skolegården: Utvikling i en kjønnet kultur', (Among horses and gorillas in the school playground: Development in a gendered culture), in *Psyke og Logos*, **1**.

HERNES, G. and KNUDSEN, K. (1976) *Utdanning og Ulikhet*: NOU.

HERNES, G. (1988) *Med Viten og Vilje (With Insight and Resolution)*: NOU 28.

HOBSBAWM, E. (1994) *Age of Extremes*, Great Britain: Abacus.

IMSEN, G. (1996) *Mot økt Likestilling*, Rapport 11, Institute of Pedagogy, Norway: NTNU.

LEWIN, K. (1948) *Resolving Social Conflicts: selected papers on group dynamics*, New York: Harper Row.

MARTIN, J.R. (1985) *Reclaiming a Conversation: The Ideal of the Educated Woman*, Yale: Yale University Press.

MEAD, G.H. (1934) *Mind, Self, and Society*, Chicago: The University of Chicago Press.

SMITH, D.E. (1996) 'Telling the truth after Postmodernism', in *Symbolic Interaction*, **19**, 3.

SØRENSEN, B.A. (1982) 'Ansvarsrasjonalitet', in HOLTER, H. (ed.) *Kvinner i Fellesskap*, Oslo: Universitetsforlaget.

TELHAUG, A.O. (1992) 'Det kvinnevennlige utdaningssystemet' (The women-friendly educational system), in ANNFELT, T. and IMSEN, G. (eds) *Utdanningskultur og Kjønn*, (Educational Culture and Gender) Center for Women's Studies: University of Trondheim, AVH, Series number 3.

TIMASCHEFF, N. (1967) *Sociological Theory: Its Nature and Growth*, New York: Random House.

VE, H. (1983) 'Likhetsidealer i velferdsstatens skole', in HAAVELSRUD, M. and HARTVIGSEN, H.H. (eds) *Utdanning og Likhetsidealer*, Oslo: Aschehoug.

VE, H. (1990) 'Kvinners kunskap — Forutsetning for en ny fremtid' (Women's knowledge — Preconditions for a new future), in HALSAA, B. and VIESTAD, E. (eds) *I Pose og Sekk*, Oslo: Emilia forlag.

VE, H. (1991) 'Children and teachers in exceptional learning situations', in RADFORD, J. (ed.) *Talent, Teaching and Achievement*, London: Kingsley.

VE, H. (1994) 'On gender and equality in schools in late modernity', in REISBY, K. and SCHNACK, K. (eds) (1995) *What Can Curriculum Studies and Pedagogy Learn from Sociology To-day? Studies in Educational Theory and Curriculum*, **16**, Royal Danish School of Educational Studies.

WÆRNESS, K. (1982) *Kvinneperspektiver på Sosialpolitikken*, Oslo: Universitetsforlaget.

5   Fear of 'Disorder'? Resistance to and Fear of Female Advantage

Britt-Marie Berge

'She's a real nuisance!' This is the description by a teacher of a girl, who (according to the teacher) behaves badly. The teacher also gives examples of situations when this girl claims space in the classroom. Some colleagues support and stress the teacher's opinion because they too are very disturbed by girls who struggle to gain advantage in the classroom. Who is this teacher? Who are the supporting teachers? My guess is that many readers would assume that the teacher is male, but in fact it is a female teacher working with some female colleagues with gender equity pedagogy in a compulsory school in northern Sweden. Why do these teachers seemingly act against their own intent to give girls more space in the classroom?

This chapter aims to describe how the contextually dominant symbols of femininity and masculinity (for gender symbols see, for example, Harding, 1986) work to subvert gender equity pedagogy. I describe the process with examples from my own research where five female and four male teachers, during a three-year period tried to educate 6–13-year-old girls and boys in gender equity. Our presupposition was that when teachers try to break existing gender power relations there would be moments of resistance among the pupils — especially the boys. Although this assumption was confirmed, during the research period we also became painfully aware how strongly we ourselves were affected by the dominant gender symbols and how teachers and researchers, more or less consciously, on some occasions tried to normalize the situation. To 'normalize' a situation is to act in ways that fulfil the meaning of femininity and masculinity in sympathy with the dominant discourse (Walkerdine, 1986; Bordo, 1990; Burns, 1998).

Foucauldian concepts can be used to describe and interpret such situations. In this framework 'power' comes from below. It is neither a structure nor an ability possessed by just a few people. Power is a complex strategic situation within society and it is exercised from innumerable positions in asymmetric and mobile relations in a type of web (see also Middleton, 1993, p. 49). Neither the class/caste or groups who control the affairs of the state nor those who make the most important economic decisions can control the whole web of power relations in society because where there are power relations, there is also resistance. But since power relations are mobile, groups will change, split and new groups will be created. These unstable, floating and split power relations pervade people's minds and bodies (Foucault, 1976, 1980).

Is it possible to change unequal power relations, even if they infiltrate our own bodies? According to the Focauldian framework it is the strategic codification of these positions of resistance that promotes change (*ibid.*, p. 117ff). In order to not underestimate our own fear of 'disorder', I will present some moments of resistance towards girls and boys who position themselves differently from the prescriptions of the dominant discourse in this particular Swedish context. If we codify and learn from these situations there is potential for change towards gender equity in education.

Context

I begin with a short discussion of the Swedish context in which this project was carried out, first with some information about women and men in Sweden, and then about the local context.

Women and Men in Sweden

Compared with other countries, state feminism in Sweden is very advanced. Sweden has, for example, the most generous parental allowance system in the western world. On childbirth parents receive a parental allowance for a total of 450 days. Each parent can use half — that is, 225 — of these days. Each parent can also transfer her or his days to the other parent, with the exception of 30 days that must be used by the mother and 30 days (the so-called 'Daddy-month') that must be used by the father. During this month the parent who stays at home receives 85 per cent of the wages. During the remaining 390 days the compensation is 90 days with SEK 60, the so-called guarantee level, and the rest with 75 per cent of the wages. The temporary cash benefit can be transferred from the parents to any other person who stays at home from work to take care of the child. In 1990 the temporary cash benefit increased to 120 days per child (under 12 years) a year. In 1994 72 per cent of the persons who used the child-birth allowance were women and only 28 per cent were men, whereas men accounted for 36 per cent of the temporary cash benefit and women for 64 per cent. However, this is a time of great change in Sweden. Since entering the European Union the social democratic government is trying to reorganize the economy and to cutback state subsidies. The 1996 payments for the 'daddy'- and 'mummy-month' fell from 90 per cent to 85 per cent of the wages with cash benefits for the remaining 300 days falling from 80 per cent to 75 per cent. The family allowances fell from SEK 750 to SEK 640 for each child.

Sweden has one of the world's highest employment rates among women. In 1995 80 per cent of the women, compared with 85 per cent of the men, were in the labour force. But Swedish women do not work as much full-time as Swedish men. Forty five per cent of the women worked full-time, 25 per cent long part-time, 4 per cent short part-time and 5 per cent were unemployed. Seventy-one per cent of the men worked full-time, 5 per cent long part-time, 2 per cent short part-time and 7 per cent were unemployed. The influence and power at the top level of politics became equal after the latest election. In 1994 50 per cent of all top officials in the ministries and 43 per cent of all members of parliament committees were women (Statistics Sweden, 1996, p. 36ff).

But there are contradictions. Sweden has one of the world's most sex-segregated labour markets. Using Swedish statistics we can map the structural sex/gender differences. It is obvious that segregation and hierarchy permeate paid and unpaid work as well as higher education in Sweden. The fact that women in Sweden work part-time to a higher degree than men suggests that women are, to a much higher degree than men, responsible for the unpaid work in the private sphere. A cross-national study in seven countries (the United States, Canada, Great Britain, Australia, Sweden, Norway and Japan) confirms that Sweden and Norway have two of the largest gender gaps in workplace authority. The relatively large gender gap in workplace authority in the social democratic Scandinavian countries can be explained as a by-product of the relatively low priority given to the liberal goals of individual competition and achievement compared with more communal benefits. A women's movement embedded in a social democratic political culture such as Sweden's would be expected to be less concerned with labour market mechanisms and more with state interventions, directly providing services and resources promoting women's welfare, e.g. parental leave, maternal health care, child care services and child allowances (Wright et al., 1995).

The Gender Equity Project — The Local Context

The particular school in this study is situated in a district with about 8,500 inhabitants in the local authority of Umeå, a university and administrative town in the north of Sweden. In the district, as well as in the whole local authority, there is a young population with an average age of 35 years. A majority of the inhabitants (almost 70 per cent) live in small self-contained houses. Eighty seven per cent of the population have gainful employment. The men in the district on average earn slightly more than the men in the whole local authority and the women on average earn slightly less than the women in the whole local authority. Thirty five per cent of the population work in the district, 61 per cent in Umeå city and the rest (4 per cent) in other local authorities. In the district 40 per cent of the jobs can be found in the industrial sector, 30 per cent in the public sector and only 12 jobs in agriculture and forestry. (The latest description from the district.) The absolute majority of the pupils in this school come from white middle-class and lower middle-class families. The handful of black children in the project classes were, with one exception, adopted.

The participants in the project were two female researchers, five female and four male teachers and about 120 pupils from the junior and intermediate levels of a compulsory school. It is often assumed in the dominant discourse of the western world that women must act like men in order to be active and adequate citizens (Pateman, 1988, p. 14), however in this project we have acted against this notion of citizenship by referring to the following Swedish definition of gender equity:

> . . . equal rights:
> • to have work that provides economic independence;
> • to care for children and the home;
> • to participate in political, union, and other activities in the society.

The statistical profile implies that there is an equitable distribution of women and men in all areas (including the area of education) of society and positions of power. If there are more than 60 per cent of men in a group, it is male-dominated. The qualitative aspect implies that the knowledge, experiences, and values of both women and men are used to enrich and affect development in all areas of society, including education. (Statistics Sweden, 1995, p. 4).

Some would argue that this concept is just another liberal slogan of 'equal rights' needing only a minimum of change. We do not agree. We believe that this concept, if pursued seriously, involves confronting the structure of gender inequity. Gender equity, according to our interpretation, includes not only programmes to help girls/women 'catch up' with boys/men. Rather, the aim must be to promote respect and consideration for women's experiences and women's work as well as to help boys claim their rights concerning, for example, caring for children and the home. This also suggests the importance of developing teaching styles and educational content encouraging girls and boys to acquire powerful knowledge in order to become active citizens working for gender equity (Ladson-Billings, 1994).

The researchers' tasks have been to function as discussion partners and, after planning the work with the teachers, to carry out different kinds of gender sensitive classroom 'evaluations' in the form of classroom observations and group interviews along with different kinds of individual written documents. The aim of these classroom evaluations was to bring the pupils' experiences and perspectives into our discussions (Berge, 1996b).

Moments of Resistance

What happens when teachers consciously try to change unequal power relations between the sexes? This analysis presents the voice of the researcher interpreting observations, interviews, and written documents from teachers and pupils. When interpreting the data one needs to consider that teachers work within a field of tensions where they try to supplant the dominant discourse at the same time as they work within and often use the language and

symbols from the available dominant discourse. They are supposed to deconstruct the 'order' and at the same time invent a new 'more equal order'. I will
provide some examples of moments when the normalizing and regulative
aspects of dominant discourses operate in the bodies and minds of the teachers
and researchers to subvert our explicit ambitions to fulfil equity pedagogy in
the classrooms.

Fear of 'Disorder'-moments of Resistance to Demanding Girls

I now present two cases illustrating some teachers' reactions to demanding girls.
      When one of the teachers at the junior level told me her life story she
often returned to the fact that she was the elder sister brought up to take
responsibility for her younger brothers. She often said that the boys in the
classroom reminded her of her helpless, irritating but charming younger
brothers. Even when she said that the boys had to take care of themselves, I
observed that she acted as a caring elder sister towards them. She was more
accommodating with demanding boys than with demanding girls. I observed
her both neglecting demanding girls: 'Try to do it yourself!', and claiming
caring duties and empathy from the girls: 'Don't laugh, you know how easily
boys can be disturbed!' I consider that she educated girls to behave like strong,
sensitive, problem-solving elder sisters at the same time as she treated boys as
helpless, irritating but charming younger brothers. She also declared that she
did not like demanding girls; neither 'weak' girls demanding help nor clever
but 'egocentric' girls. She called one of the 'egocentric' girls a 'real nuisance'.
      A somewhat similar situation occurred in a 'calm' classroom at the inter-
mediate level. By observing the class I tried to find out if the calm climate
could be explained by the fact that the gender relations were normalized
according to boys' norms. This did not seem to be the case. The female
teacher always seemed to have the situation in hand, firmly controlling the
room and trying to give both boys and girls equal space. But in the interviews
and in the written documents some girls expressed discomfort and disappointment with this teacher. They claimed that she was not feminist enough when
the researchers were absent and that she in fact rejected the girls' demands
and was more receptive to the boys' demands. The girls' opinion was also that
the teacher was more lenient with the boys than with the girls. In an interview
the teacher declared that she wanted to attain equity in the classroom by
illuminating similarities between the sexes in her teaching. The girls complained that she did not care about actual differences and that in reality she
treated the pupils unequally. 'You should place a hidden camera in the classroom', they said in a group interview. An example of clearly favouring the
boys was reported by both girls and boys during single-sex group interviews.
In a group interview the boys said that they felt insecure about the teacher's
gender equity ambitions. The girls felt more accepted by the male teachers.

The two male teachers described these girls in words like spontaneous, unfeigned, clever and marvellous. However, the female teacher interpreted their behaviour as manipulative in relation to the male teachers and the researchers saying that the girls just wanted to be the centre of attention. According to the girls and to the best of my knowledge these girls did not get any genuine feedback from the teacher before they entered the upper level. The teacher never hesitated to continuously present her view of egocentric demanding girls wanting to distinguish themselves.

When we discussed these and other similar cases all female teachers, with the exception of the female teacher who defined herself as a feminist, supported and confirmed each other's response to the above scenarios and mentioned 'demanding girls'. This does not mean that the male teachers never complained about these girls' behaviour. But, according to my diary of our discussions the female teachers were more provoked by these girls than the other teachers. The paradox is that these teachers tried to support the girls in single-sex classes, but when the girls used their knowledge in co-ed classes they seemed to become a threat towards the teachers themselves. In gender-mixed teacher discussions, the female teachers also disagreed more often than they agreed with the teacher who defined herself as a feminist (cf. similar experiences in Kenway et al., 1993, p. 72).

Fear of 'Disorder'-moments of Falling into the Maternal Nurturance Trap

In order to avoid misinterpretations of this subheading I would like to point out that maternal nurturance or the caring rationality (Ve, 1995) should not be avoided *per se*. One of our most important aims was to educate boys in caring duties. What should be avoided, however, is that only women or girls take on the burden of nurturance towards boys and men. We start this discussion by highlighting my own first experience in a classroom at the intermediate level where, according to the teachers, at this point of time the girls had the advantage in the classroom. During my first observations in this classroom I felt sorry for the boys since I felt that the girls' domination in the classroom was unfair to them. I, a female researcher, fell in the nurturance trap in this particular situation. It was not until afterwards, rereading my written observations, that I realized that both subject content and teaching styles were adjusted and normalized to fit the boys.

Two more cases will be presented to illustrate how the nurturance trap for the female is one aspect of the ways in which the normalization and regulative aspects of dominant discourses operate to subvert spearheading equity pedagogy. The first is from the same classroom at the intermediate level where the 'clever' girls were pulled and pushed into the nurturance trap by the male teacher. The second case is from a parallel classroom where the female teacher was pulled and pushed into the same trap.

During one observation the subject was Swedish and the pupils were organized in small gender mixed reading groups. The task was to train oral reading ability. Compared with the boys the girls in this class were outstanding readers. The reading groups were spread all over the building. In these reading groups the girls took responsibility for both the boys' reading and their behaviour. During these situations the boys giggled, elbowed and nudged each other while the girls became more and more irritated by the boys' bad behaviour and poor oral reading. When I asked the teacher why he had chosen this particular content he replied that all pupils need to practise oral reading. In this case 'pupils' needs' were in reality the boys' needs. I asked him why the girls did not get more challenging assignments in Swedish. The teacher promised to think about it, but he was hesitant about giving the pupils different assignments, even if this was obviously already the case. Nor did he see any harm in training the pupils (read the girls) to support each other.

This approach could not be observed in the classroom dominated by a handful of clever boys who loved to compete. In this classroom the female teacher attempted to educate the children in solidarity and empathy. She therefore wanted to avoid competitive tasks. But during the first two classroom observations, announced in advance, she performed some smaller competitions. She declared that these were isolated cases. She said that she did not know why she had done it. But these competitions obviously occurred when she lost control of the boys. The teacher dealt with the situations by letting the boys compete. Although she was aware of her male colleague's argument for training pupils to support each other, she never suggested that the clever boys in her classroom should take care of the less talented girls. She thought that the boys would never accept such an approach.

These three cases say something about normalizing tendencies. When we presented the researchers' analysis of these and similar situations to the teachers, we often became involved in heated discussions. After or during our discussions we frequently realized that our focus was on the boys' needs. We had spent almost all the time talking about different boys' needs and we had almost forgotten different girls' needs. Even if our group was aware of the normalization tendencies and realized that boys' demands to be taken care of is a direct product of the gendered public/private segregation, and even if we discussed the need for change, there moments of both conscious and unconscious resistance to changing concrete classroom situations. Back in the classrooms the teachers also often encountered different obstacles, the most frequent being that the whole thing receded to the background due to 'more demanding tasks', 'not the right time' and other unexpected circumstances.

Fear of 'Disorder'-moments of Resistance to Compliant Masculinity

Until now I have described reactions towards the girls. I now discuss reactions towards the boys. In the project we struggled to educate both boys and girls with three goals for gender equity: sharing rights, responsibilities and opportunities within paid work, domestic work and politics. The teachers were required to affirm more contextual symbolic female aspects to masculinity such as listening to each other without competing, learning how to exchange perspectives, how to be more empathetic, and how to solve conflicts by reasoning. The male teachers and the boys at the intermediate level spent some days on camp in single-sex groups to discuss emotions, sexuality and coexistence. The teachers at the intermediate level also decided to let one of the male teachers educate both boys and girls in single-sex groups in home economics in order to give them a male role model in a 'female' subject. They also dealt with different activities such as Swedish, library work, and sports in so-called godfather and godmother groups. For the older boys this meant each taking responsibility for one boy at the junior level, with the younger boys gaining an older boy as a caring role model.

However when the aims of the project seemed to be fulfilled it sometimes appeared to frighten the teachers, particularly in relation to the boys in the classroom with clever visible girls and more compliant boys. When the male form teacher wanted to discuss his anxiety about how his boys, almost teenagers, had become outsiders and were neither accepted by the girls nor the boys in the two parallel classes, it was difficult to challenge the construction of masculinity which seems to be highly valued among pupils and adults in the district. To be a good sportsman is an important goal in constructing masculinity in this school. This small district has two competing football teams. The impact of this focus on sports can be illustrated by the experiences of one of the female teachers. She grew up in the district and it was altogether impossible for her to have boyfriends in the competing football team. The teachers agreed that boys with high status, admired by both boys and girls, are often clever sportsmen. The majority of the dominant and most competitive boys were included in that group.

I invited the Danish feminist researcher Anne-Mette Kruse to our group. Kruse has worked with teachers in single-sex boys' groups. The teachers challenged and discussed with the boys the fact that those boys who were not interested in sports were often harassed. They also discussed the fact that boys who were interested and good at sports dominated not only the sporting situations but almost every situation in school (Kruse, 1992). In the Danish school they tried to bring out other qualities of masculinity by discussing real cases. In respect to Kruse's visit, as well as on other occasions, I asked if the avoidance of sport was perhaps due merely to the fact that these boys were not good at 'boys' sports' or even disliked sports and competitions. The teachers did not agree. Instead they said that these boys did not have the same teacher in sport as the other boys; that three parallel classes is one too many and that some of these boys actually play football. But the most common explanation was their 'childish behaviour'. They changed the focus of the problem from the children who avoided these boys to the boys who were avoided. The discussions also turned quickly from the negative towards the positive effects of sports activities. There was never any discussion with the boys involved that actually scrutinized and challenged the constructions of masculinity in more concrete terms. No serious attempts were made to integrate these boys into the fellowship of the others. The problem was defined by the teachers as merely a question of childish behaviour caused by slow biological maturity. They believed that they could not therefore do very much about it and the problem could thus be avoided. The construction of masculinity in terms of a clever competitive sportsman was never really challenged.

Moments of Equity?

What is the lesson to be learnt from this Swedish project? In this chapter I have analysed moments when normalizing and regulative aspects of the dominant discourse operate to subvert attempts at introducing equity pedagogy. Even so, I argue strongly in favour of developing education for equity in schools. We have learnt how important it is to be aware of the ways in which gender relations offer resistance to change including our own bodies and minds. Work for change must therefore include an awareness of our practices and an attempt to change them. This knowledge can be painful but it is the origin from which changes can grow and different ways of thinking and acting can be discovered.

So, what about the author herself? In what way has the process influenced her? I have argued in favour of the importance of learning from the pupils themselves by interpreting from which positions girls and boys are talking, writing or acting in different situations. I have also described moments when we did not agree on the interpretations. By challenging each other's interpretations we have had to exchange perspectives and, thus, our experiences have hopefully become more nuanced.

I have therefore asked myself the following question: Is it a step forward that the majority of the teachers consider girls to be active, manipulative and skilled in managing power? Or is it a backlash, a sign of a normalizing process, with hidden symbolic and individual unequal power relations? Since this whole project aims at bridging gaps not only between girls and boys but also between researchers and teachers, I have exerted myself to avoid binary oppositions. My answer is therefore: yes and no! I have identified the teachers as contributing to unequal normalizing processes and the teachers have, in our discussions of the same events, identified the girls as manipulating subjects fighting for their own good. What does a combination between these two views give? Moments of equity will perhaps arise when we have the courage to integrate both opportunities and obstacles. Thus we can regard existing normalizing processes as realistic obstacles, but also codify the potential in the girls' actions when they are being 'manipulative'. During this process I have also realized that fighting for gender equity is a never ending struggle. It has to be done in every situation in every relation. During this never ending journey there will always be moments of backlash but also moments of opportunities of gender equity in the classrooms.

References

BERGE, B.-M. in cooperation with the teaching team at Storsjoskolan (1995) 'Equity pedagogy: A description of one year collaborative work within an action research project', in ARNESEN, A.L. (ed.) *Gender and Equality as Quality in School and Teacher Education*, Oslo: Nordic Council of Ministers.

BERGE, B.-M. (April, 1996a) 'Education for change: A Swedish case-study on gender equity pedagogy', Paper presented to 6th Interdisciplinary Congress on Women, Adelaide, Australia.

BERGE, B.-M. (1996b) 'Jämställdhetspedagogik på Storsjöskolan i Holmsund: Ett aktionsforskningsprojekt/Equity Pedagogy at Storsjöskolan in Holmsund — An action research project', Arbetsrapporter från Pedagogiska institutionen, Umeå universitet, Number 15.

BORDO, S. (1990) 'Reading the slender body', in JACOBUS, M., KELLER, E., FOX, E. and SHUTTLEWORTH, S. (eds) *Body/Politics: Women and the Discourses of Science*, New York: Routledge.

BURNS, R. (1998) 'Engendering health: Feminist issues in school health and psychical education in Australia', in MACKINNON, A. et al. (eds) *Education into the Twenty-first Century: Dangerous Terrain for Women?*, London: Falmer Press.

CODE, L. (1993) 'Taking subjectivity into account', in ALCOFF, L. and POTTER, E. (eds) *Feminist Epistemologies*, London: Routledge.

EPSTEIN, D. (1993) *Changing Classroom Cultures Anti-racism, Politics and Schools*, Trenham Books.

FOUCAULT, M. (1976) *Sexualitetnes Historia 1: Viljan att Veta/Histoire de la Sexualité 1: La Volonté de Savoir*, Södertälje: Gidlunds.

HARDING, S. (1986) *The Science Question in Feminism*, USA: Cornell University Press.

KENWAY, J., WILLIS, S., BLACKMORE, J. and RENNIE, L. (1993) 'Learning from girls: What can girls teach feminist teachers?', in YATES, L. (ed.) *Feminism and Education*, Melbourne Studies in Education: La Trobe University Press.

KRUSE, A.-M. (1992) '. . . We have learnt not to sit back, twiddle our thumbs and let them take over: Single-sex settings and the development of a pedagogy for girls and a pedagogy for boys in Danish schools', *Gender and Education*, 4, 1, 2.

LADSON-BILLINGS, G. (1994) *The Dreamkeepers, Successful Teachers of African American Children*, San Francisco: Jossey-Bass Publishers.

LUKE, C. and GORE, J. (eds) (1992) *Feminisms and Critical Pedagogy*, London: Routledge.

MIDDLETON, S. (1993) *Educating Feminists: Life Histories and Pedagogy*, New York, Teachers' College: Columbia University.

PATEMAN, C. (1988) *The Sexual Contract*, Cambridge, UK: Polity Press.

PROPOSITION 1993/94:147 Delad makt delat ansvar. /Shared power shared responsibility, Government bill.

PROPOSITION 1994/95:164 Jämställdhet mellan kvinnor och män inom utbildningsområdet. /Equality between men and women within education, Government bill.

STATISTICS SWEDEN (1995/1996) *Women and Men in Sweden — Equality between the Sexes*, Facts and figures.

VE, H. (1995) 'On gender and equality in schools in late modernity', in REISBY, K. and SCHNACK, K. (eds) *What Can Curriculum Studies and Pedagogy Learn from Sociology To-day? Didaktiske Studier*, **16**, Royal Danish School of Educational Studies.

WALKERDINE, V. (1992) 'Progressive pedagogy and political struggle', in *Screen*, 1986, **27**, 5, in LUKE, C. and GORE, J. (eds) *Feminisms and Critical Pedagogy*, London: Routledge.

WEEDON C. (1987) *Feminist Practice and Poststructuralist Theory*, Oxford: Basil Blackwell.

WRIGHT, E.O., BAXTER, J. and BIRKELUND GUNN, E. (1995) 'The gender gap in workplace authority: A cross national study', *American Sociological Review*, **60**.

6   Dis/ease: Discourses in Australian Health and Physical Education

Robin Burns

Teenage girls to be told: get fit or put health at risk.
The Age, 11 March, 1995, page 9.

This headline suggests a popularized image of teenage girls today. I argue here that it also represents a major discourse which can, in itself, put girls and young women at risk. That discourse is about the body, fitness, health and female subjectivity and in it the female body is problematized in ways which are health-compromising: a 'health-ist' discourse. Schools may reinforce or challenge the discourse, directly through physical and health education programmes, and also through the whole school context. This paper explores the ramifications of the health-ist discourse for young female subjectivity, and asks if feminist educators can develop a practice of health and physical education that interrogates 'healthism'.

During my participation as researcher-evaluator in an innovative primary school health education project (Health in Primary Schools, known as HIPS), I became aware how soon girls become self-conscious and concerned about their bodies, especially their weight, and the ways that teachers saw the attainment of particular body characteristics as a goal in their health and fitness programmes. Teachers were asked to rate the perceived importance to children's health of various health and physical education activities, and were tested on their knowledge of some basic biomedical aspects of nutrition and fitness. Their basic dietary knowledge reflected current orthodoxy in Australia (the national food and nutrition guidelines), but they were weak on knowledge of factors contributing to weight and its loss, and on aerobic fitness. Their practice focused on introducing new physical activities with their class and cooking lessons, rather than on biology, sexuality or specifically targeted activities for girls. More cooperative games and more self-esteem activities were undertaken by teachers in the project schools than in matched schools (Burns, 1991; Sheehan and Burns, 1993).

This finding can be seen as a demonstration that schools are dependent institutions, passing on community beliefs and attitudes about health, fitness, nutrition and body size together with elements of 1980s biomedical orthodoxy in the way they link fitness, diet and health. One problem with this is that this very knowledge, and the discourses within which it is couched, reinforces negative messages about female subjectivity and female embodiment. I will investigate this through examination of the particular contents of these discourses, and argue that they contain messages about the female body which reinforce an ideal of young femininity that is limiting, disempowering and potentially life-threatening. Pedagogy and content in nutrition and physical education create at best ambivalences for girls, even to produce the prescribed 'health' outcomes.

Health and Physical Education: How Have Girls Been Addressed?

Using the Australian state of Victoria as my main example, the history of health education shows that health and fitness were central, and medically legitimated. Harvey Sutton, a key person in the development of school medical services and of public health, promoted sound nutrition and regular, vigorous exercise in schools as the way to health. Doctors visited schools as part of this programme, and hygiene, temperance and virtue were considered close and teachable allies in the search for health (St Leger, 1991). Clearly, a medical discourse was dominant in the approach to health education, subsuming a moral discourse. Not only were the physical and moral characteristics of the young nation being shaped in this way, however, but another discourse, also promoted by doctors, carried the concerns into the socio-political realm with a 'nationalist hygiene' discourse (Powles, 1987). Sutton, for example, wrote:

> What we want is not, of course, to create a race with great brute force, but a healthy people with a constant efficiency and endurance that will enable us to use our special abilities to the utmost. (Sutton, 1933, p. 76)

It is the content, rather than the three types of discourse, that persists in health and physical education curricula today. Looking at major content areas, nutrition has always found a ready place in the primary school health curriculum, and for girls in secondary schools in the most feminized subjects, home/domestic science and biology, injecting science into traditional female fields of competence. Food for healthy bodies is the emphasis, understanding bodies in a biomedical sense, with a recent emphasis on personal decision making in relation to food. Individual agency has become important, but the desired outcome of this is still a socially, morally and medically approved body-state. Personal hygiene, that other favourite theme in health education, emphasizes appearance, justified in health terms. Research is lacking on the content and impact of this subject on boys and girls. Expectations of personal appearance differ for boys and girls, (e.g. Carroll et al., 1986; Macintyre and West, 1991) so that it might be assumed that girls will be more receptive to the messages, especially if they are reinforced in other subjects they take.

Thus medical-scientific discourse runs through the major themes in school health education, including the newer areas of sex, and substance use. Females are more exposed to this discourse, especially in secondary schools, because of gendered patterns of subject choice. A social discourse is also evident, insofar as health is considered a national resource, and a way of evaluating worth: a worthwhile nation has a healthy 'social body', so one's contribution to the nation and public acceptability can be assessed by one's physical health. This is seen in the idealized images of physique and performance of young people: for men, in war, and for women, in motherhood (Powles, 1987; Scraton, 1990). The images translate into stereotyped versions of masculinity and femininity. Health and female beauty became appropriated — perhaps re-appropriated, following the pre-World War II nationalist hygiene discourse — to project an image of a modern nation (Johnson, 1993, pp. 141–7). In this we read a medical message from the young female body (its 'health') but translate it into a social one, which emphasizes desirability and value through conformity to a notion of beauty. External appearance becomes a signifier of health, and through this of moral and social worth.

The justification used for physical activity also combines medical and social discourses, especially in the English schools from which Australian education evolved. Team sports, a dominant approach, were associated historically with male single-sex schools, and with the development of values and skills as well as with physical development. The values included inter-group competition, loyalty and cooperation with one's own group (team), and leadership skills befitting those who were to become the 'leaders of men'. Drill, another paradigm for physical education, emphasizes obedience and following, qualities particularly applicable to hierarchically organized social formations (Mangan, 1981).

The development of physical activities for girls has been different (Okely, 1978). It is based on a construction of the female body which emphasizes limited and different female physical capabilities, and a notion of appropriateness rooted in concern with the expression of female sexuality through physical activity and public display of the female body (Scraton, 1990, pp. 15–17; 25–8). Competitive activities flourished especially in girls' boarding schools, and the egalitarian concerns of some early headmistresses played a role in offering team sports to girls. It was presented as a health issue, since physical activity had been denied to girls as a harmful threat to their reproductive capacity. It was also considered unseemly. However, in the confines of the all-female environment of the girls' boarding school in particular, sport

> . . . represented freedom in a very real sense, the freedom to abandon feminine decorum and run about in (relatively) light clothing in the open air, with other girls, for personal enjoyment rather than in the service of some abstract ideal or concrete person. (Auchmuty, 1992, p. 60)

The second theme in the development of physical activities for girls and women is that of gymnastics. Early feminists advocated these activities as part of the bid to free the female body from physical and social confines, exemplified in female clothing. Swedish gymnastics, which emphasizes neatness and precision, was favoured for girls. There was concern with developing an 'attractive' body, as well as a healthy one — within the terms of woman's reproductive role.

Scraton (1990) argues that a gendered discourse which emphasizes female differences, biologically and socially, is found throughout the development of physical education. It is particularly evident at puberty and beyond, where it becomes more confining, with lowered expectations of girls' participation in physical activity. It is, she maintains, a discourse of femininity. In this, both social and medical discourses can be discerned in an interplay of notions of female sexuality, reproductive capacity and health. The physical status of the young female body is both a sign of her femininity, and of her capacity to express that through giving birth to a healthy child.

Physical education has therefore been part of the process of forming and inscribing stereotyped gendered identities, with an emphasis on the body for females and on participation in the public world of government, armies, and jobs for males. Health is for performance of expected social roles. Organized physical activity for girls became potentially subversive, but kept in check especially in the state schools by a medical, moral and social discourse which reinforces stereotyped sex roles, possibly more inflexibly for boys. It is in the details of the body-text created for girls that health, and wider implications, will be read.

Health and Physical Education Now: Has It Changed?

There are three new themes in health education in the past 15 years: prevention, personal skill development, and health in a social context. All three themes echo the 'new' public health, which emphasizes that health is a positive concept based on physical, mental and social well being, not just the absence of disease. In addition to sick care, providers should promote health through preventive programmes. New strategies are required, including new public policies, to facilitate healthy decision-making, as well as new approaches to education. It is predominantly a social discourse, which recognizes an intimate relationship between social status and health status. Gender is mostly recognized in terms of gendered health disadvantages (Ottawa Charter, 1986).

Prevention through Schools

Schools have a role in this version of public health as agencies for transmitting information and skills, in particular ways:

> If teaching does not motivate constructive health behaviours then the learning remains ineffectual; simply telling people why over-eating or smoking, are destructive to health, is of little use *unless it motivates self-control.* (Victoria Advisory Committee Report, 1980, p. 6) [my emphasis]

This perpetuates the moralistic discourse, with social overtones, insofar as there is an outside arbiter of moral correctness. The emphasis on individual behaviour easily translates into individualism.

Prevention need not be moralistic or individualistic. However, when language like that quoted above is used, individual responsibility appears to require individual action, in which the individual is the only one who can maintain her good health. Since females are more likely to engage in health-promoting behaviour than males (Newell-Withrow, 1986; Dean, 1989; Palank, 1991), a preventive approach to health could build on female proclivities and may even legitimate them. However, if the assumption is that individuals, both male and female, do not have these skills or orientations, and have to be taught them, it may disempower females since their reality is initially ignored. And control is a consistent theme in male discourses of the female body (Ussher, 1989), so that *self*-control can be interpreted by females as an additional burden, that of self-censorship. This can lead to guilt, attached generally to one's physical entity (e.g. Wolf, 1990). The goal of self-acceptance, which personal development stresses, is complex, especially when dealing with female acceptance of their body.

The Development of Health-related Skills

The development of skills is a major goal of contemporary health education, from motor skills like tooth brushing to human relations and decision making. Victoria has now drawn together six curriculum areas: health, physical education, traffic safety, outdoor education, textiles and clothing, and home economics, and called it 'personal development'. Conceptually, these areas are linked through their 'common concern for choice and action in personal life', and concern 'with fulfilment and wellbeing in everyday life' (Office of Schools Administration, 1989). There is some content overlap between several areas, and choice and action skills are common to all.

One interpretation of skills for deciding and acting emphasizes personal empowerment through the ability to decide and act in everyday life, seen particularly in fields like drug education, where skills to resist group pressures are a major concern. The Victorian health education statement notes that:

> Learning in health education is concerned with developing understanding, skills and attitudes related to personal and community health and wellbeing.
> (Office of School Administration, 1989, p. 46)

The second interpretation is more narrow, and individually oriented: individuals should learn how to look after themselves. It attempts to empower the individual to take care of themselves, and resonates with the demand for competency-based education.

Skill development, especially in the area of mixed social relationships, is of interest to girls who are considered more relationship oriented, and therefore subject to different pressures in decision-making than boys (Gilligan, 1982). Outcomes may depend on how the issues are handled in the classroom. Since boys are less interested in health and body matters, more 'masculine' approaches in order to involve them may de-legitimate 'female' ones in mixed classrooms. And where does care for the sexed young body enter in to these programmes? If the male body is taken as the norm, difficulties may arise for young females to recognize and deal with their needs. If the discourse is predominantly a social one, then it is possible that female bodies become relegated to the medical sphere.

Social Orientations

The Victorian Framework document most clearly enunciates a social context for personal development. It is most well developed within the health education statement:

> Health education may be defined as a combination of learning experiences which affect the way students think, feel and act in relation to their wellbeing, and that of others . . . It values critical thinking about personal and community wellbeing and active interaction between school, home and community. (Office of Schools Administration, 1989, p. 45)

But how is the social context developed discursively, including the siting of female concerns? In the HIPS project, very few teachers developed topics and lessons which incorporated any social aspects of health.

Turning to physical education, competitive team sports are still the most common activities. Physical education, perceptual-motor skill development and now, 'fitness' or aerobic activities, are added according to changing fashions. Girls are less enthusiastically involved in sports and physical activity as they enter puberty, and until recently, this has received tacit approval, based in teachers' perceptions and expectations of girls. It is currently viewed as both a health and an equal opportunity issue, and is linked to issues of self-esteem (Department of Employment, Education and Training, 1988, p. 7; Oldenhove, 1989). The stress is on increasing participation and options, with a focus on school environments as well as programmes (Scraton, 1990; The HIPS Project, 1992; Yates, 1993).

Two aspects of physical education are of concern here: the way in which exercise is linked to fitness and this in turn to health, and the ways in which girls and physical activity are problematized.

Health and Fitness

Health and fitness are combined into a unitary concept incorporating various activities, and one normative task of schools is to promote 'health-and-fitness'.

The underlying discourse is medical, involving diagnosis and treatment, and invokes the legitimating power of medicine. Many schools in Victoria still base their health and physical education on this medical model, barely tempered with a social overlay. The notion of a 'health-promoting school' which is being propagated by some health educators involves a radical, collective approach, but it coexists with predominantly individual, and medicalized ones (Goltz, Colquhoun and Sheehan, 1997).

Medical discourse pathologizes the body, since it focuses on disease rather than health and bodies are the site of disease. Thus, bodies have to be worked on in order to achieve health, one way being through health and fitness programmes. There are contradictions within this, since medical indicators suggest that in general adolescents are the healthiest — or least sick — members of society (Rickwood and d'Espaignet, 1996). A medical model for health promotion focuses on prevention, which requires diagnosis of those aspects which are more likely to become pathological, both in the individual's body and behaviour. The social, health promotion model is concerned with health maintenance as well as disease prevention; we can point to other sites such as legislative and policy change. Regarding individuals, lifestyles receive the greatest attention. But physical entities behave, and post-modern lifestyles are concerned with surfaces and external appearances. In both models, fitness becomes a signifier of health, a way in which we know our own state and that of others. And as Glassner (1989) powerfully argues, in a post-modern world the external is the guide to the internal and so we 'know' we are fit — and acceptable, since the ill are allowed a specific sick role but are separated and isolated (Gilman, 1988) — by how we appear.

The image of the slim, controlled body becomes a yardstick for the female state of health. Schools transmit this through linking physical activity and health. The whole 'look good, feel better' slogan for huffing, puffing, striving children, links health and fitness in specific ways and locates this on the body surface. The process is seen in the use of 'fitness testing' and bodily goals which stress surface characteristics rather than skill achievement. Physical education programmes become geared to these goals through the application of a health and fitness discourse, labelled 'healthism', and spiced with an element of moral panic:

> Concern for the general level of Australian children's health and fitness is widespread and has been well documented in recent years. Statistics on children's cholesterol levels, obesity, poor nutritional intake, and lack of regular exercise appear regularly in daily newspapers and television news items. (Went and Sheehan, 1991, p. 4)

A 1993 Australian Schools Council paper names adolescent behaviour as a focal point for school programmes, and defines adolescent behaviour under four major headings: health and fitness; smoking, alcohol and drugs; sexuality, and suicide and attempted suicide (Compulsory Years of Schooling, Schools

Council, 1993, pp. 24–6). Concern about health and fitness is backed up by disparate statistics. It is as if adolescence is pathological and this gives authorities the right to promote a particular version of health.

The 'Problem' of Girls and Physical Education

The mixed medical and social discourse stigmatizes girls and young women in particular and focuses on their negative physical and performance characteristics. Girls are unhealthy, unfit and inactive; this suggests that girls' bodies themselves constitute a dangerous terrain, for themselves and for society, through the whole medical discourse of personal lifestyle and future, costly disease outcomes. As Wolf (1990) suggests, there is a *physical* price for women's entry into the public arena, and one which when carried to extremes, may be as life threatening as the overtly dangerous and suicidal *behaviour* of young men (Patience, 1992).

The inducements to engage in more physical activity, the images held out and the view of the female body require scrutiny as they may reinforce not only stereotypical femininity but practices which are unhealthy, such as excessive dieting and exercise, and low self-esteem. How the programmes are presented is also important: even the clothing allowed affects girls' comfort in participating. Calls for more health and fitness education, without dramatically rethinking what is offered, why, and its possible consequences, seems potentially damaging to girls and young women.

This danger stems from those discourses which stereotype femininity, embody it and then pathologize the female body. One end-point of this inscription today is the so-called epidemic of eating disorders amongst young women. Young women talk about their bodies negatively, anxiously, exhibiting ongoing concerns to appear acceptable, which is interpreted in external bodily terms. Eating disorders can be seen, at least symbolically, as ways in which the negative female body and female self are internalized and both physically and emotionally starved to create a lessened presence, and a statement of zones of control and being controlled, which some interpret as a resistance to or ambiguity concerning entry into the dangerous terrain of adulthood (Brumberg, 1988). The anorexic young woman is a powerful symbol of the young female position, physically and emotionally, and suggests that the means to discursively construct and locate the self contain the possibility for such denigration.

Insofar as the health-ist discourse incorporates medical, social and moral discourses which pathologize and disempower women, it provides the means for young women to construct a negative, gendered and embodied identity. Recent feminist writers have emphasized the advantage of a post-structuralist approach in providing 'discursive space in which the individual woman is able to resist her subject positioning (a specific fixing of identity and meaning)' (Weiner, 1994, p. 65). For this to happen, however, critique and alternative positions need, to be available, as suggested by educators who stress the importance of curriculum in addressing issues of gender and inequality (Kenway, 1993; Weiner, 1994 and Yates, 1993).

I argue that health is an important area for feminist educators to deconstruct. Both the construction of health, and its engendering, are infused with medical and cultural representations of disease. As shown above, these underpin the concern to use schools to promote health. This health-ist discourse has taken gendered health issues, and used medical language without the benefit of current and accurate information, which has important gender and power implications.

Healthy Young Female Bodies?

Do we know what a healthy young female is? Fifty years ago, articulated in the language of the eugenicists, it was physical, mental and physiological fitness to reproduce. Thanks to the World Health Organization (WHO) it is now, officially, the achievement of complete physical, mental and social well-being regardless of age or gender.

In the case of young women and girls, it is argued that the inclusion of the social and mental health is important since they are potentially the most phys-ically well group in society. The exceptions to this include those with genetic or chronic disorders or those for whom puberty or the mere possession of female sex organs poses particular risks: early childbearing, sexual abuse, physical abuse, sexually transmitted diseases, genital mutilation. Social posi-tion is a powerful predictor of health experiences, affecting resources to sur-vive and the physical and emotional quality of that survival; females are more likely to live in poverty than males. And insofar as girls and young women carry particular burdens related to their biological sex and their gender, their mental and social well being may also be threatened.

I argue that one threat comes from the way in which the female body is inscribed, and the health and fitness discourses which are incorporated into health education and physical education. For Australia, there is a relative absence of data on young women's health, especially morbidity as opposed to mortality. They consult medical practitioners more often, though this may be related to contraception and related issues of sexual health, and to the com-mon ascription that females are more willing and able to express symptoms and request help than males. The issues for young female health that attract the interest of public health, human rights and women's health lobbies are reproductive health and sexuality, emotional and mental health, violence against women, and the health effects of sex role stereotyping, including unemploy-ment. It is tempting to conclude from this that it is young women's sexuality which leads to their health problems, including the ways in which being a young woman — as the National Women's Health Policy (1989) puts it, make one particularly vulnerable 'at the stage of assuming the adult role' (p. 45), again emphasizing the dangerous terrain that adulthood can become for young women. Apart from specific physical consequences: pelvic inflammatory disease, the human papilloma virus (HPV, considered a precursor to cervical cancer), pregnancy (a disease?!) and physical injury, self-induced or by others, most health issues are then allocated to the non-physical realm: body image, vulnerability to stress, anxiety and depression, and low self esteem. From the emotional, back not to the physical but the behavioural, we then find concern with risky behaviours such as substance use, eating, low levels of physical activity and non-assertiveness.

Does the foregoing imply that possession of a female body is the basis for pathology? That it is inscribed in ways that label female sexuality, female behaviour and female emotions abnormal? And that, therefore, presented constantly with both structured positions and stereotyped roles, as well as evaluations of one's body and one's self that suggest inferior difference, the experience of *dis*-ease is readily translated into one of actual *disease*?

The extent to which this process of inscribing disease on the young female can be demonstrated, I argue, is in the ways in which body image is problematized and nutrition and fitness issues advocated. Perhaps the most guarded yet explicit statement about body image is found in the Australian National Women's Health Policy (1989):

> Promotion of a desirable body image for women, and its effects on adolescents in particular, is of serious concern. Redman et al. (1987) identified worry about weight and its link with social worth (given current stereotypes) as having illness status.
>
> A recent study has indicated that many teenage girls, particularly those with low self-esteem, hold similar attitudes to their body weight and shape as anorexic and bulimic patients. (p. 56)

This approaches what might be called a feminist medical discourse. It acknowledges that the problems, while located in the attitudes of young women, are linked to social stereotypes of women including desirable physical attributes. Feminist writers suggest that the desire for a slim body size is related to what appears to be socially desirable, and also to the invisibility of women so that many young, pubescent women in particular solve their own lived experience of the contradiction of being there, and feeling 'too much' there, by trying to reduce the space they occupy. This appears to be a psychosomatic process, where perceptions and feelings lead to actions which have physical consequences: they feel too fat so they starve, purge and exercise. What is pathologized, however, is not the desired image but the experienced image, the feelings not their social origins, the behaviour and its physical consequences which can be life-threatening, but not the behaviour and its physical base of predatory masculinity which requires controlled females for its satisfaction, up to and sometimes including violent sexual assault.

It is not just, or even, the medical accounts that construct young female bodies as overweight: overweight and obesity is more prevalent in men than women and it increases with age (Australian Institute of Health, 1990, p. 83). Medicine has certain pathologized obesity and linked it to adult serious chronic diseases. There are many steps, however, between a plump girl and a diabetic 45-year-old. Future health and illness are certainly cited as medical and social reasons for dealing with eating behaviours and nutrition in young people. However, an aesthetic of body size and build, and a discourse of social accept-ability and even morality, is drawn on by worried youth, and for young women, small size, shape and self are interwoven to determine who is, and who is not, a desirable, worthwhile female, as shown in case studies of so-called 'dis-ordered eaters' (Probyn, 1988; Steiner-Adair, 1991).

The aim of being desirable is to be acceptable to the opposite sex, to be desired rather than desiring. Thus female body shape and size can be an index of acceptable female sexuality. The female sex organs are also pathologized, however: medically, as the source of major health problems for young women, socially as the cause of behaviour which is problematic or leads to problems. The use of substances, too, is considered at the intersection of disease, prob-lem behaviour and potential victimization. Young men, at worst, will get STDs, fight, or kill themselves on the road; young women will get, but more likely be seen to transmit, STDs, disgrace themselves and perhaps get raped. It is not a symmetrical youth health discourse, nor one of youthful identity-formation.

There is another dimension to health discourses and their engendering: the meaning of illness. Gilman (1988) argues that illness evokes our primitive fear of chaos, which is represented in culture by disease. The fear is projected outwards to preserve our own internal order, onto 'an-Other who has already shown his or her vulnerability by having collapsed' (p. 1). Culture provides groups already more easily categorized as other, and therefore more readily at risk, and gender is one basis for this construction (p. 4). The Other accepts the stigmatization if they have internalized group norms about wholeness and its disruption because they fear the dominant group and wish to emulate it, and their own victimization is less chaotic than challenging dominance (p. 5). While his invocation of psychoanalysis in order to support this depiction may not be acceptable to some feminists, especially the prominence given to the Oedipal situation in the formation of an identity, Gilman nevertheless pro-vides a basis for change in order to break the effects of female acceptance of their bodies as pathological simply because they are female.

Conclusion

The foregoing traces ways in which young female embodiment — a social, cultural and historical phenomenon (Morgan and Scott, 1993, p. 6) — is problematized. Health and physical education resonate with medical, moral and social discourses which stereotype and pathologize that embodiment. And while there is an emancipatory potential in more recent approaches in these fields of education, they easily slip into a post-modern discourse of health and fitness, fitness as indicated by body characteristics as indicators of health, may pose health threats to girls and young women. Thus contemporary approaches to health and physical education can be read as messages about body and self — with the promise of 'more intentional selfhood' for women (Glassner, 1989, p. 185).

There are alternative approaches which, as Scraton (1990) has demonstrated, are derived from the major feminist educational approaches. However, either girls have to be bullied and seduced to become more active (and what more effective way than by appealing to their desire to be slim, attractive and desired?), with special efforts such as specifically allocated playground space, or they have to be offered alternative physical activities that better fit their needs and interests. The alternatives suggest that not only is a feminist project which seeks to transcend the category of gender extremely difficult, but that it may simply offer a new terrain which contains paradoxically a danger to women's health more directly injurious than the former ones. Girls in the football team, a girls' football team, or jazz ballet?

References

Auchmuty, R. (1992) *A World of Girls*, London: The Women's Press.

Australian Institute of Health (1990) *Australia's Health 1990*, Canberra: AGPS.

Brumberg, J. (1988) *Fasting Girls*, Cambridge, MA: Harvard University Press.

Burns, R. (1991) 'How health promotion works: The roles of teacher, school and community factors', Melbourne: Monash University (unpublished MPH research report).

Carroll, D., Gleeson, C., Risby, B. and Dugdale, A.E. (1986) 'Body build and the desire for slenderness in young people', *Australian Paediatric Journal*, **22**, pp. 121–5.

Compulsory Years of Schooling Project, National Board of Employment, Education and Training, Schools Council (1993) *In the Middle: Schooling for Young Adolescents*, Project Paper No. 7, Canberra: AGPS.

Dean, K. (1989) 'Self-care components of lifestyles: The importance of gender, attitudes and the social situation', *Social Science and Medicine*, **29**, pp. 137–52.

Department of Employment, Education and Training (1988) *Girls in Schools: Report on the National Policy for the Education of Girls in Australian Schools*, Canberra: AGPS.

Gilligan, C. (1982) *In a Different Voice*, Cambridge, MA: Harvard University Press.

Gilman, S. (1988) *Disease and Representation*, Ithaca and London: Cornell University Press.

Glassner, B. (1989) 'Fitness and the postmodern self', *Journal of Health and Social Behavior*, **30**, June, pp. 180–91.

Goltz, K., Colquhoun, D. and Sheehan, M. (1997) 'Broadening school health education: Towards the health promoting school', in Colquhoun, D., Goltz, K. and Sheehan, M. (eds) *The Health Promoting School*, Marrickville, NSW: Harcourt Brace and Co., pp. 1–25.

Johnson, L. (1993) *The Modern Girl. Girlhood and Growing Up*, Sydney: Allen and Unwin.

KENWAY, J. (1993) 'Learning from girls: What can girls teach feminist teachers?', in YATES, L. (ed.) *Feminism and Education: Melbourne Studies in Education 1993*, pp. 63–77.

MACINTYRE, S. and WEST, P. (1991) 'Social, developmental and health correlates of "attractiveness" in adolescence', *Sociology of Health and Illness*, **13**, 2, pp. 149–67.

MANGAN, J.A. (1981) *Athleticism in the Victorian and Edwardian Public School*, Cambridge: Cambridge University Press.

MORGAN, D.H.J. and SCOTT, S. (1993) 'Bodies in a social landscape', in SCOTT, S. and MORGAN, D. (eds) *Body Matters*, London: Falmer Press, pp. 1–21.

NATIONAL WOMEN'S HEALTH POLICY (1989) *Advancing Women's Health in Australia*, Canberra: AGPS.

NEWELL-WITHROW, C. (1986) 'Identifying health-seeking behavior: A study of adolescents', *Adolescence*, **21**, pp. 641–58.

OFFICE OF SCHOOLS ADMINISTRATION, MINISTRY OF EDUCATION, VICTORIA (1989) *The Personal Development Framework*, Melbourne, p. P-10.

OKELY, J. (1978) 'Privileged, schooled and finished: Boarding education for girls', in ARDENER, S. (ed.) *Defining Females*, London: Croom Helm, pp. 109–39.

OLDENHOVE, H. (1989) 'Girls, PE and sports', in GILAH, G., LEDER, N. and SAMPSON, S. (eds) *Educating Girls: Practice and Research*, Sydney: Allen and Unwin, pp. 39–48.

OTTAWA CHARTER FOR HEALTH PROMOTION (1986) World Health Organization/Health and Welfare Canada/ Canadian Public Health Association, Ottawa, Canada, November.

PALANK, C.L. (1991) 'Determinants of health-promotive behavior: A review of current research', *Nursing Clinics of North America*, **26**, 4, pp. 815–32.

PATIENCE, A. (1992) 'A cultural context for adolescent mental health', in KOSKY, R., ESHKEVARI, H.S. and KNEEBONE, G. (eds) *Breaking Out: Challenges in Adolescent Mental Health in Australia*, Canberra: AGPS, pp. 45–60.

POWLES, J. (1987) 'Naturalism and hygiene: Fascist affinities in Australian public health, 1910–40', Paper presented at the conference 'Attractions of Fascism', University of NSW, July (mimeo).

PROBYN, E. (1988) 'The anorexic body', in KROKER, A. and M. (eds) *Body Invaders: Sexuality and the Postmodern Condition*, London: Macmillan, pp. 201–11.

RICKWOOD, D. and D'ESPAIGNET, E.T. (1996) 'Psychological distress among adolescents and young adults', *Australian and New Zealand Journal of Public Health*, **20**, 1, pp. 83–6.

SCRATON, S. (1990) *Gender and Physical Education*, Geelong: Deakin University Press.

SHEEHAN, M. and BURNS, R. (1993) 'Evaluation of the role of individual teacher characteristics in the implementation of a multi-school health education project in Victorian primary schools', in CACOUAULT, M. and ORIVEL, F. (eds) *Evaluating Education and Training: Comparative Approaches*, Selected papers from the 15th conference of the Comparative Education Society in Europe, Dijon: IREDU-CNRS, Université de Bourgogne, pp. 361–83.

STEINER-ADAIR, C. (1991) 'When the body speaks: Girls, eating disorders and psychotherapy', *Women and Therapy*, **11**, 3, 4, pp. 253–66.

ST LEGER, L. (1991) 'The origins, growth and challenges of health education in Victorian schools', in WENT, S. (ed.) *A Healthy Start: Holistic Approaches to Health Promotion in School Communities*, Melbourne: Faculty of Education, Monash University, pp. 17–28.

Robin Burns

Sutton, H. (1933) 'The preschool child': Section of paediatrics and section of public health, preventive medicine and tropical hygiene, *Transactions of the Australasian Medical Congress*, British Medical Association.

The HIPS Project (1992) *Growing Girls*, Melbourne: Monash University and the Department of School Education.

Ussher, J.M. (1989) *The Psychology of the Female Body*, London: Routledge.

Victoria Advisory Committee Report, Health and Human Relations Unit (1980) Report of the Advisory Committee on Health and Human relations Education in Schools to the Honourable Norman Lacy, MP, Assistant Minister of Education, Melbourne, November.

Weiner, G. (1994) 'The gendered curriculum: Developing a post-structuralist feminist analysis', *Australian Educational Researcher*, **21**, 1, pp. 63–86.

Went, S. and Sheehan, M. (1991) 'The HIPS project', in Went, S. (ed.) *A Healthy Start: Holistic Approaches to Health Promotion in School Communities*, Melbourne: Faculty of Education, Monash University, pp. 3–16.

Wolf, N. (1990) *The Beauty Myth*, London: Vintage Books.

Yates, L. (1993) *The Education of Girls: Policy, Research and the Question of Gender*, Hawthorn, Victoria: Australian Council for Educational Research.

7 Education: A Site of Desire and Threat for Australian Girls

Victoria Foster

In a trend common to most western countries, Australia has in recent years experienced an *apparent* move towards sexual equality in schooling, offering the possibility of a significant change in girls' lived experiences of schooling (Foster, 1995; 1998; Weiner et al., 1997). This, potential, however, has not been realized because both Australian education policy and curriculum development have failed to address the public–private dialectic in social life and in schooling itself, and men's and women's different and asymmetrical relations with that dialectic. The term 'dialectic' is used here to emphasize the interconnected and shifting aspects of public and private life, which nevertheless remain fundamentally gendered in character.

This chapter develops the notion of the space-between: a heuristic device to analyse and explain girls' experiences of contemporary events in education. In particular, it explains the lack of change in post-school outcomes for girls, the insignificant degree of change in girls' participation in male-dominated curriculum areas, despite their successes in those areas, the endemic nature of sexual harassment and the inequitable use of school resources by girls.

Elsewhere (Foster, 1997), I explore the implications for the emerging field of citizenship education of this failure to address issues of public and private life in education.

The Space-between

This chapter presents the argument, elaborated in Foster (1994; 1996), that for women and girls, pursuing equal educational and citizenship rights entails entering a particular space — social, psychological and existential — between and beyond that which is prescribed for women, that is, women's 'place', and that which is proscribed to women. This is a space of lived experience, mediating between private and public spheres, where women and girls attempt to negotiate the conflicting, contradictory (at best), or violent and destructive (at worst) demands of a neo-liberal framework of equality, a framework which retains a masculinist subject at its centre (Leck, 1987; Martin, 1991). Both the individual learner-subject and the epistemological foundations of the curriculum are male-defined (Martin, 1981a, b; 1988). Girls are to be given equal opportunity to achieve parity in an education system which is normatively masculine.

The notion of a space is particularly applicable to a discussion of educational equality reforms. This space embraces both the actual, physical space of social relations, and a conceptual space which has cultural, ideological and experiential dimensions. 'Space' evokes meanings of sexual politics, of interconnection, and of positionality. It has a further sense of physical admission: allowing entry or access, and making room for, in an enclosed space. This is the sense inferred in equal opportunity provisions for women and girls, for example, in employment and education. There is a second more conceptual sense of space as representation and validation: to be admitted is to be fully recognized, acknowledged, and further, accepted as legitimately having a place. Feminist theorizing of difference, however, has shown that the first sense of admission in no way guarantees the second sense, of actually having a place.

Women's lived experience in the space-between revolves around two conflicting discourses: first, the neo-liberal discourse of equality with men — 'a woman's place is everywhere' and, second, the discourse of male supremacy which constructs women as transgressors on male territory — 'this is *not* your place'. The conflict of these two discourses makes the space-between a site of both desire and threat for women: the desire evoked by the promise of equal opportunities in a man's world, and the threat of punishment and violation which inevitably accompanies women's attempts to make that promise reality, to *live* the discourse of equality. Schoolgirls are aware of this contradiction when they make statements such as 'I believe that girls can do anything' and 'I believe in equality for women, but I wouldn't want to do it', speaking of careers in traditionally male-dominated fields (Foster, 1984). Of course, now many young women will easily say, 'sure women have equality', believing in 'presumptive equality' (Foster, 1995). However, that belief does not match up with the reality of most young women's lives.

The patriarchal power relations of schooling, and their connection with the public–private dialectic in society make the lived curriculum of schools a complex site of both desire and threat for girls. Equality-directed curriculum reforms require of girls that they attempt to transpose themselves from private realm status to a relatively different position as the equals of males in the public realm of the school. In this process, girls' status is defined and redefined as the 'other' in relation to males, in various ways which frequently define girls physically or sexually in terms of their bodies, and constitute reminders of difference. This central aspect of the space-between is a phenomenon distinct from, although clearly related to, the issue of girls' experience of a paradigmatically male-centred overt curriculum (Foster, 1992; Gilligan, 1990; Rich, 1977), and distinct also from the 'malestream' epistemological foundations of the curriculum (Martin, 1981a; O'Brien, 1984).

The Public–Private Dialectic: A Spectrum of Prohibition

A spectrum of prohibition constrains women's movement away from private realm status, or what is here referred to as 'women's place': the sphere of the personal, the domestic and intimate, so-called 'private life', of care and nurturance of others, characterized by unpaid and undervalued work.

The barriers women encounter when they attempt to move beyond their 'place', suggest clearly that such a move is in fact prohibited at profound psychic, structural and institutional levels of society (Cockburn, 1991). Prohibition occurs across a range of experiences, encompassing male employment bastions, to the area of sexuality, for example, the prohibition on women's refusing sexual exploitation, sexual harassment, and sexual violence. It is hardly surprising then, that Australian Bureau of Crime Statistics show that women's reporting of rape did not increase in the decade from 1983 to 1993, despite the efforts of the Bureau and many other organizations to encourage the reporting of rape. And women surveyed in the Australian study, 'The woman's view' (Office of Status of Women, 1992) believed strongly that violence, in particular domestic violence, was the price to be paid for changes in their status in society towards greater equality.

Both the idea and the concrete reality of public woman violates public–private norms, requiring women to give up the (dubious) protection of the private sphere, and expose themselves to the threat of violence in the public sphere. Similarly, for girls to take up the promises of reforms towards equality in education, in their present form, entails the threat of violence in one form or another. The space-between describes the relationship between women's attempts to gain equal entry to male terrain, and the prohibition exercised against these attempts. There is also an important epistemological dimension concerning the implications of women's and girls' experiences in the space-between for issues of knowledge and curriculum change. And finally, the space-between is an analytic construct developed to concretize and explore girls' experiences of schooling, and to give them a place. This construct has several themes or dimensions, which include both normative and behavioural aspects, and which are reinforced by ideological and symbolic structures of power, and relations of ruling which alienate women and their experience (Smith, 1990). These themes are elaborated in Foster (1996, 1997). This chapter takes up one theme in detail, the idea that girls' and women's place in education fundamentally centres on the expectation that they will be caretakers of males, and of masculinity, supporting the maintenance of male primacy and privilege in education.

Caretaking in the Classroom: What about the Boys!

Women's responsibility for unpaid domestic work and childcare is fundamental to the space-between. However, the critical aspect of the notion of a woman's place concerns *caretaking*. Although there has been a blurring of the public–private distinction, the contemporary imperative for women to take primary responsibility for caring work, which I refer to as 'caretaking' is the direct product of the public–private distinction.

The phenomenon of girls as caretakers of boys in the classroom, has not received any extended, formal discussion in Australian education policy, although Lewis (1990) discusses this dynamic in relation to the university classroom setting. It is, however, one of the most powerful, albeit subtle, determinants of girls' day-to-day schooling experience (see Ve, Berge, this volume). It is powerful because of its location in the public–private nexus, and specifically, as part of the unspoken sexual contract whereby the patriarchal meaning of femininity entails the provision of service, sexual and otherwise, to men (Pateman, 1988, p. 126). Within the sexual contract, the functions of caring, nurturance and emotional support are seen as women's functions. Women, as Benhabib (1987, p. 95) puts it, are the 'housekeepers of the emotions'. Men may carry out these functions but they are valued differentially according to whether they are done by men or women. Regrettably, curriculum reform in Australia has neglected an examination of the public–private dialectic in the curriculum, either in terms of curriculum content areas, or in the curriculum as it is lived by both female and male students.

The injunction placed upon girls to be caretakers of the learning environment, as well as persons in it, has a further *normative* sense which results in adverse consequences for girls and women when the norm is flouted. Furthermore, the equality discourse in girls' education produces what I will go on to describe as *desire* for equality which is tantamount to a flouting of the caretaking norm.

That male power and privilege are taken to be both subjective and objective reality explains why, despite a wealth of documented Australian evidence of girls' subordinate status to that of boys in education, the interests of males nevertheless continue to be of prior importance to those of females. This has been dramatically demonstrated in Australia over the past few years by a media-led campaign spearheaded by a handful of men, which incorrectly asserted that girls are now beating boys at maths and science. The possibility that girls might be outstripping boys on their own terrain was one which could not be tolerated and quickly led to a parliamentary inquiry (which had never been instigated to address the inequalities evident in girls' education), a widespread push for a 'Boys Education Strategy', and a plethora of programmes to address boys' 'educational disadvantage' and help them to regain their supremacy in the high-status curriculum areas. By contrast, boys' lesser skills in, for example, the care of children and domestic work, have never been identified as a problem for them, or for women.

These discussions of boys and their education are atheoretical (Foster, 1996), ignoring the social and educational context of gendered power relations. Instead, they rest on the shaky ground of presumptive equality (Foster, 1995). Internationally, policies and programmes have reverberated to the refrain, 'What about the boys!' effectively achieving a swift reassertion of male educational interests as prior, in the face of girls' perceived advances into male terrain. By contrast, male interests had earlier been strongly bolstered by a construction which emphasized girls as lacking, rather than viewing boys themselves as being advantaged (Eveline, 1994).

The curriculum and practices of schooling maintain a social reality which endorses the injunction that women should be the providers of care. The pervasiveness of this social reality means that a perceived conflict with the rights and interests of men is created in any educational setting, which seems to advocate in a major way, the needs and interests of women. This conflict is often keenly felt by women themselves, and it has been a significant aspect of the 'What about the boys!' campaign in Australia. This has resulted in a recasting of the issues concerning gender in education, primarily in terms of resources and benefits: too many are going to girls at the expense of boys, who are constructed as equally the victims of patriarchy as girls. This construction has succeeded despite the well-documented comparative positions of boys and girls in schools, including matters of differential resourcing, in terms of teacher time and attention, physical space, and equipment and facilities.

It is, however, the unexpressed subtext of the 'What about the boys!' refrain which is important, and relates directly to the expectation that women will be caretakers of men. In this subtext, notions of equality for girls entail taking something very crucial away from boys. What is seen to be taken from boys is their supremacy as learners, as well as the caretaking resources of women and girls, to which boys are assumed to be entitled.

So an unspoken question is, what would happen to boys if girls do become boys' equals and stop being their caretakers? Interestingly, during this backlash period in Australia, there has been no acknowledgment that girls' equal or better achievement in male-dominated subjects would actually be beneficial for boys in that it would give them an opportunity to see girls in a new, healthier light as peers and equals. This issue raises one of the most profound aspects of the space-between: that girls' and boys' schooling experiences are situated in what Alison Griffith and Dorothy Smith (1987) refer to as a 'mothering discourse'. This discourse, they suggest, operates according to a 'paradigm of the ideal mother', which can be traced back to Rousseau's prescriptions for Sophie's primary function as Emile's helpmate and nurturer in *Emile*.

For Australian schoolgirls, this paradigm is expressed in a constellation of required activities, for example, moderating the behaviour of boys, softening the classroom atmosphere, being 'good girls', and not exhibiting the kinds of undisciplined behaviours which are taken to be 'natural' for boys and which often gain sympathetic attention and resources for them. By contrast, there is no similar expectation for boys to be carers or nurturers. Indeed, it seems that boys and girls are involved in two quite different projects in education, in relation to issues of care and caretaking. For instance, it is current wisdom in Australia that a measure of girls' attainment of equality is their greater participation in leadership and positions of responsibility in schools. While boys see this kind of work as simply unnecessary as a qualification for what Teese

(1994) calls 'the male career trajectory', this extra work is not paying off for girls postschool.

The expectation placed upon women to take responsibility for males in the classroom can be seen on one level to be a transfer of the practices of the private, domestic sphere into the public setting of the school's learning situation, the classroom. Specifically, 'private' imperatives relating to women's perceived primary functions in the areas of sexuality, motherhood and caretaking are brought into the micro-public domain of the school. On another level, however, the injunction can also be seen to be a particular feature of educational settings. At this second level, there is a profound sense in which despite the discourse of educational equality, it is still widely believed that boys' interests and their learning are of prior importance to girls'.

There are many examples of the greater importance placed on boys' learning and associated problems, such as the greater amount of teacher time devoted to boys, the attention given to boys' learning difficulties and discipline problems, the greater amount of physical space and school sporting facilities used by boys, and boys' domination of technical and computer equipment. In New South Wales up to 90 per cent of specialist education resources currently go to boys. These barriers to girls' equal status in education have been repeatedly documented in Australia since the 1975 Report, *Girls, School and Society* (Schools Commission, 1975).

The persistence of these barriers is the outcome of deeply held and largely unexamined assumptions about the relationship of women to education, assumptions which are endemic in educational philosophy and schooling practices. They lead easily to the expectation that girls are responsible for making the learning environment a positive one for boys, rather than making that environment work for themselves. An especially clear example of this expectation in practice is that of the coeducation debate in Australia, where it has emerged clearly that it is expected by both boys and girls that girls should perform a function in the classroom quite distinct from that of learners. This has been variously described as 'socializing' boys and regulating their behaviour, providing a civilizing atmosphere and helping boys with learning difficulties. It is not surprising then that boys prefer coeducation and feel that their capacity to learn is enhanced by the presence of girls (Regan, 1993). On the other hand, many girls both prefer and perform better in single-sex classrooms, a finding which surprisingly has so far not been investigated in Australian research.

It is because of the priority placed on boys' learning that little serious attention has been given to the fact that the climate of the coeducational school is a negative and hostile one for many girls, characterized by endemic sexual harassment, and that girls' learning very likely suffers in coeducational classrooms (Australian Education Council, 1992), and conversely, is enhanced in girls-only learning situations (Regan, 1993; NSW Dept of School Education, 1994). Great importance has been placed on the 'social benefits' of coeducation, largely related to the school's perceived function of preparing students for the 'realities' of a coeducational, that is, gendered society, rather than how the educational interests of girls would best be served.

These 'social benefits' and 'realities' of the coeducational school setting are, however, conflated with the injunction on women to take care of and nurture the interests of others, in particular those of males, to the exclusion of important educational arguments. Furthermore, the caretaking injunction placed on girls becomes intensified and more threatening the more strongly sexually delineated the particular learning context. For example, girls in home economics classes are usually expected to help boys to pick up unfamiliar skills. No such expectation is made of boys in technical classes, where girls frequently report harassment which results in their discontinuing the subject.

Girls know that the ostensibly public space of the school is not equally shared by boys with girls. Girls accommodate boys' domination of the physical, especially teaching and learning, spaces of the school in various ways (Foley, 1993; Australian Education Council, 1992). A few girls act out, and as a consequence, are labelled as troublemakers and resisters, often in sexually explicit terms (Samuel, 1983, see also Berge, this volume). In relation to sex-based harassment, which many boys regard as natural and normal (Quality Assurance Review, 1994), the Australian Education Council (1992) states that in the cases of the majority of girls,

> Girls accommodate this harassment differently. Some react with hostility and anger, but it causes many to be passive and docile, restricts their access to space, equipment and attention of the teachers, and undermines their feelings of safety, self-confidence and worth.

Girls frequently accommodate their lack of space by withdrawing and creating their own cherished 'girls' spaces' (Australian Education Council, 1992, p. 8). Girls 'are not inclined to compete with outsiders for public social space. Instead they create space for themselves within their subjective group culture' (Foley, 1993). The Australian Education Council (1992, p. 8) reports on the ways in which girls, from an unequal position, negotiate for space in schools:

> It can be a particular piece of lawn or yard, or a commonroom, classroom or library where behaviour is regulated by school staff. In both primary and secondary schools it is surprisingly common to find that the girls' toilets are used as girls' meeting places, a place to call their own. 'It's the only place they can't get you', said one 13-year-old girl, echoing sentiments expressed time after time by many girls in many schools. When the levels of harassment in the school are high, the girls' toilets in many schools have become unsavoury sanctuaries, highly valued by some girls.

It is deplorable that for many girls, the toilets are the only 'public' space which they feel safe to occupy. In one school, the girls ate their lunch in the toilets, rather than the playground.

The space-between has the potential to challenge the norms just described. For girls to engage the curriculum equally with boys alters the dynamics of accommodation and negotiation, and makes the curriculum and the school setting itself, a site of both desire and threat for girls. The final section of this chapter examines the nexus of desire and threat in girls' schooling experiences.

Girls, Desire and Schooling/ Girls' Desire of Schooling: Philosophical Interpretations of Desire

The following discussion offers an interpretation of girls' experiences of the curriculum and the school setting, drawing on Grosz' (1989) discussion of philosophical approaches to the question of desire. Elsewhere (Foster, 1994), philosophical approaches are contrasted with two other theoretical interpretations of desire: the material-sexual interpretation, exemplified by Young (1993) and Spivak (1987), and the post-structuralist interpretation, exemplified by Davies (1990).

Grosz (1989, p. xv), describes desire as a pivotal concept having two quite different intellectual traditions. The first tradition, which encompasses Plato, Hegel and Lacan, conceives of desire as a 'fundamental lack in being, an incompletion or absence within the subject which the subject experiences as a disquieting loss, and which prompts it into the activity of seeking an appropriate object to fill the lack'. Grosz notes that for Lacan, 'desire is an ontological lack which ensures the separation of the subject from the immediacy of its natural and social environment, and the impulse of that subject to fill in this space through, in the first instance, the desire of the (m)other; and in the second, through its access to language and systems of meaning'.

In the second tradition which Grosz (1989), sees as encompassing Spinoza, Nietzsche, Foucault and Deleuze, desire is conceived not as a lack but as a positive force of production and self-actualization. In this second sense, at the level of the subject, desire functions insofar as the subject 'desires the expansion or maximisation of its power . . . it is not an unactualised or latent potential; it is always active and real'.

A crucial question is: What desire(s) do girls actually experience in and of schooling? There are very good reasons to believe that girls desire to learn, that they value their schooling and the learning environment. During the past decade in Australia, there is no doubt that this desire has been encouraged and nurtured by girls' education policies which in particular have stressed the need for girls' greater achievement in male-dominated subjects.

Policy discourse concerning the desirable educational achievements of girls has at different times philosophically encompassed both the senses of desire which Grosz has delineated. Earlier, girls were constructed as lacking the necessary masculine learner subjectivity as well as the necessary male-defined knowledge. The very meaning of 'girl' included a negativity or lack (Jones, 1993, p. 12). In this construction, the lack was to be removed by increasing girls' access to masculine knowledge areas, but not it transpired, by enhancing their achievement relative to boys in those areas. This first platonic sense of desire as lack resonates with the philosophical and social construction of femininity as 'other' to the masculine. Thus, it could be argued that for girls, the philosophical construction of desire in this first sense would have a logical consistency to which they could relate, given the normative climate of the school in relation to its curriculum, and its material-ideological practices.

The second sense of desire referred to by Grosz is, however, much more problematic for girls, because it invokes a more inherently masculine orientation to desire, that of actively seeking and pursuing achievement, and to an extent, power. To date, even more problematically for girls, that achievement has centered specifically on masculine curriculum areas and subject domains. Although the discourse of reform is couched philosophically in Grosz's first platonic sense, the implications for girls of following that discourse, as well as the outcomes, relate directly to Grosz's second sense of self-actualization. In concrete terms, this has resulted in the perception that girls are interlopers or 'space invaders' (Foster, 1996) in male educational terrain, depriving boys of their rights. The crucial point here then is that for girls to desire in this second sense places them not only in a contradictory position as 'educated women' (Martin, 1991), but also in a position of threat, which is both actual in school, and potential in relation to post-school life. It is significant that the 'What about the boys!' movement emerged at the precise moment (and not a moment earlier) that girls were perceived to be outstripping boys in the areas of male power and privilege. Prior to that, boys' education was only an issue for feminists and educationists concerned with improving gender relations. This point is obvious if one asks whether there would have been such concern about boys and their schooling if the contested areas had been different. What if the newspapers had reported, 'girls beating boys at childcare and home management!'?

The Nature of Threat: Its Relationship to Desire

The first construction of desire as lack, and girls as lacking masculine learner subjectivity, can be seen to pose no particular threat to hegemonic masculinity. In fact, it could be argued that the construction of girls as lacking in relation to hegemonic masculinity might have the effect of reinforcing that hegemony. It might further be argued that the earlier construction of girls as lacking essential knowledge in a paradigmatically masculine curriculum would have the effect of reinforcing that paradigm in the curriculum. Until mid-1993 in Australia, that was the case. The first sense of desire (as lack), in which girls are seen as disadvantaged, is relatively safe for girls, posing no threat to hegemonic masculinity and possibly reinforcing it. It is the second self-actualizing sense of desire in the educational setting which, by challenging male privilege, becomes threatening for girls and women. This is the sense which comes into play when women refuse to be constructed as lacking as in the first sense of desire and actively pursue their educational and occupational goals.

This discussion of desire and threat in girls' schooling raises several questions. For instance, what might happen if girls move outside the frame of their construction as lacking in relation to boys? How could girls be the caretakers of boys if they are equal (or better?) achievers? Such a prospect could be very threatening for girls and their education. For example, the current reaction to girls' perceived advances in maths and science may well make it very difficult for girls to pursue excellence in those subjects, if they are seen as depriving boys of their rights as the high achievers in those areas. In fact, girls' performance in those subjects actually declined from 1993 to 1994 (NSW Board of Studies, 1996), when the backlash period was beginning to gain momentum. The interesting question is also raised of whether, and to what extent, girls and women use caretaking as a means of controlling the threat against them which is posed by greater equality? Finally, given that the value-added dimensions (to use an economic rationalist concept) of care and caretaking are vastly different according to whether they are done by men or women, where does this leave care as a curriculum issue? This question is very pertinent in Australia where care-related matters have been relegated to the bottom of the curriculum hierarchy.

The mere existence of policies on girls' education has begun to provoke indignation about the harm they may do to boys' interests. These policies together with their success in terms of girls' improved participation and performance in specifically male-defined areas, have produced a subtle shift from the perspective of girls as lacking, into Grosz's second sense of desire, in which girls can be seen to be actively seeking educational success. It might be predicted, then, that this shift could prove in the near future to be a threatening one for girls. The rush to develop compensatory programmes for boys is the beginning of a threatening response to girls and to policies concerning their education.

Desire and Threat As Dialectical Experiences in Girls' Schooling

Education for women is both contradictory (Martin, 1991) and inasmuch as it entails movement into male terrain, potentially threatening and dangerous. Noting that it is not uncommon for women to experience male violence in connection with educational participation, Rockhill (1987, page 316) observes that 'we know little about how it is lived in women's lives'. Specifically discussing literacy, Rockhill (1987, page 315) notes that for many women, education is a means of becoming 'somebody', and that it has functioned as a primary site of both 'regulation and of rebellion'. In the Australian context, some recent research reinforces these themes. Narelle Glass (1993), in a study of nurses who gained tertiary qualifications, found that these nurses believed they had a lot to risk if they continued to further their careers. The experience of hostility from their male partners, and the feeling that they risked losing their family relationships made them reluctant to pursue career advancement. Cheryl Hercus (1993) conducted a follow-up study of 45 women who attended a weekend workshop on feminism. She found that 'many of the women experienced subtle and not so subtle attempts to not only circumscribe their involvement in terms of active participation, but to prevent them from speaking of their experiences in feminist language'.

This chapter has raised questions about the ways in which girls may experience and resolve for themselves the simultaneous desire to be 'somebody' which education offers, and the potential threat to them from those who in turn feel threatened by girls' living out of this desire. This last statement contains two important points: the mutuality of threat in the space-between, and the fact that this threat is itself the product of girls' desire for learning. This is not at all to suggest that girls themselves cause this threat or bring it upon themselves. Rather, both desire and threat are in turn produced by the neo-liberal equality framework, and that they form a dialectical relationship, in that framework. That relationship is described as dialectical because of the apparent opposing connotations of the notions of desire and threat, and because of the dynamic interplay of them in girls' schooling lives. Far from being unaware of the conflicting nature of these forces, girls are keenly aware of both, and of their dialectical influence on their schooling and its outcomes. And it is this awareness that leads to girls' self-regulatory behaviour, for example, in relation to male-dominated occupations.

The elaboration of the space-between, however, reveals a potentially better space of experience for girls. It is a space in which it now becomes possible for them to investigate and take greater command of their relationships with public and private life, and through the curriculum, to build positively and creatively on female difference.

References

AMERICAN ASSOCIATION OF UNIVERSITY WOMEN (1994, May) 'The effect of school climates on girls: A view from inside middle schools', a request for proposals for the Eleanor Roosevelt Fund for Women and Girls: Intergenerational Partnerships, Washington DC.

AUSTRALIAN BUREAU OF STATISTICS (1993) *Women in Australia* (Cat.No.4113.0), Canberra: Australian Bureau of Statistics.

AUSTRALIAN EDUCATION COUNCIL (1992) *Listening to Girls*, Melbourne: Australian Education Council.

BENHABIB, S. (1987) 'The generalized and the concrete other: The Kohlberg-Gilligan controversy and feminist theory', in BENHABIB, S. and CORNELL, D. (eds) *Feminism as Critique: Essays on the Politics of Gender in Late-capitalist Societies*, Cambridge, UK: Polity Press.

COCKBURN, C. (1991) *In the Way of Women: Men's Resistance to Sex Equality in Organizations*, Basingstoke: Macmillan.

DAVIES, B. (1990) 'The problem of desire', *Social Problems*, **37**, 4, pp. 501–16.

EVELINE, J. (1994) 'The politics of advantage', *Australian Feminist Studies*, **19** pp. 129–54.

FOLEY, C. (1993, December) 'Creating space: An exploration of a girls' subculture', Paper presented at The Australian Sociological Association 1993 Conference, Macquarie University, Sydney.

FOSTER, V. (1984) *Changing Choices: Girls, School and Work*, Sydney: Hale and Iremonger.

FOSTER, V. (1992) 'Different but equal? Dilemmas in the reform of girls' education', *Australian Journal of Education*, **36**, 1, pp. 53–67.

FOSTER, V. (1994) 'Making women the subject of educational change: An interdisciplinary and comparative study', Unpublished doctoral dissertation, Macquarie University.

FOSTER, V. (1995) '*What about the boys!*', Presumptive equality in the education of girls and boys, Published proceedings of the National Social Policy Conference 'Social Policy and the Challenges of Social Change' vol. 1: University of New South Wales, pp. 81–97.

FOSTER, V. (1996) 'Space invaders: Desire and threat in the schooling of girls', in *Discourse: Studies in the Cultural Politics of Education*, **17**, 1, pp. 43–63.

FOSTER, V. (1997) 'Feminist theory and the construction of citizenship education in the modern state', in KENNEDY, K. (ed.), *Citizenship Education and the Modern State*, London: Falmer Press.

FOSTER, V. (1998) 'Gender, schooling achievement and post-school pathways: Beyond statistics and populist discourse', in DINHAM, S. and SCOTT, C. (eds) *Teaching in Context*, Australian Council for Educational Research.

GILLIGAN, C. (1990) 'Teaching Shakespeare's sister: Notes from the underground of female adolescence', in GILLIGAN, C., LYONS, N.P., HAMMER, T.J. (eds), *Making Connections — The Relational Words of Adolescent Girls at Emma Willard School*, Cambridge, MA: Harvard University Press.

GLASS, N. (1993) 'Rocking the boat: Women nurses speak out', Paper presented at The Australian Sociological Association Conference, Macquarie University, December, Sydney.

GRIFFITH, A.I. and SMITH, D.E. (1987) 'Constructing cultural knowledge: Mothering as discourse', in GASKELL, J.S. and MCLAREN, A.T. (eds) *Women and Education: A Canadian Perspective*, Calgary: Detselig Enterprises Limited.

GROSZ, E. (1989) *Sexual Subversions: Three French Feminists*, Sydney: Allen and Unwin.

HERCUS, C. (1993) 'Stepping out of line: Social control and women's involvement in feminism,' Paper presented at The Australian Sociological Association 1993 Conference, Macquarie University, Sydney.

JONES, A. (1993) 'Discourses of disadvantage: The construction of girls at school', Keynote address for National Transition Conference, Christchurch, 23 August.

LECK, G.M. (1987) 'Feminist pedagogy, liberation theory and the traditional schooling paradigm', *Educational Theory*, **37**, 3, pp. 343–54.

LEWIS, M. (1990) 'Interrupting patriarchy: Politics, resistance and transformation in the feminist classroom', *Harvard Educational Review*, **60**, 4, pp. 467–88.

MARTIN, J.R. (1981a) 'The ideal of the educated person', *Educational Theory*, **31**, 2, pp. 97–109.

MARTIN, J.R. (1981b) 'Needed: A paradigm for liberal education', Offprint from the *Eightieth Yearbook of the National Society for the Study of Education: Philosophy and Education*, Chicago: The National Society for the Study of Education, pp. 37–59.

MARTIN, J.R. (1988) 'Science in a different style', *American Philosophical Quarterly*, **25**, 2, pp. 129–40.

MARTIN, J.R. (1991) 'The contradiction and the challenge of the educated woman', *Women's Studies Quarterly*, **1**, 2, pp. 6–27.

NATIONAL WOMEN'S CONSULTATIVE COUNCIL, OFFICE OF THE STATUS OF WOMEN, DEPARTMENT OF THE PRIME MINISTER AND CABINET (1992) 'The women's view', Market research study on women's perceptions of themselves and government programs and policies.

NSW BOARD OF STUDIES (1996) *The Report of the Gender Project Steering Committee*, Sydney: NSW Board of Education.

NSW DEPARTMENT OF SCHOOL EDUCATION (1994) *Evaluation of Educational Outcomes for Girls in NSW Government Secondary Schools*, Sydney: NSW Department of School Education.

NSW GOVERNMENT ADVISORY COMMITTEE ON EDUCATION, TRAINING AND TOURISM (1994) Draft report on the inquiry into boys' education.

O'BRIEN, M. (1984) 'The commatization of women: Patriarchal fetishism in the sociology of education', *Interchange*, **15**, 2, pp. 43–60.

PATEMAN, C. (1988) *The Sexual Contract*, Cambridge, UK: Policy Press.

REGAN, L. (1993) 'The results of a survey of the attitudes of Year 9 students and their teachers towards single-sex and mixed-sex classes in science or mathematics at three North Coast high schools', Project funded by the NSW Department of School Education (North Coast Region).

RICH, A. (1977) *Of Woman Born: Motherhood as Experience and Institution*, New York: Bantam.

ROCKHILL, K. (1987) 'Literacy as threat/desire: Longing to be somebody', in GASKELL, J.S. and McLAREN, A.T. (eds) *Women and Education: A Canadian Perspective*, Calgary: Detselig Enterprises Limited.

ROMAN, L.G. (1993) 'Double exposure: The politics of feminist materialist ethnography', *Educational Theory*, **43**, 3, pp. 279–308.

SAMUEL, L. (1983) 'The making of a school-resister: A case study of Australian working-class secondary schoolgirls', in BROWNE, R.K. and FOSTER, L.E. (eds) *Sociology of Education* (3rd edition), Melbourne: Macmillan.

SCHOOLS COMMISSION (1975) *Girls, School and Society: Report of a Study Group to the Schools Commission*, Canberra: Schools Commission.

SMITH, D.E. (1990) *The Conceptual Practices of Power: A Feminist Sociology of Knowledge*, Boston: North-eastern University Press.

SPIVAK, G. (1987) 'French feminism in an international frame', in SPIVAK, G. (ed.) *In Other Worlds*, New York: Methuen.

TEESE, R. (March, 1994) 'Evaluating school systems: Provider versus client perspectives on performance', Paper for the Centre for Economic Policy Research, Research School of Social Sciences, Australian National University and the Schools Council, *Public Investment in School Education: Costs and Outcomes Conference*, Canberra: Australian National University.

WEINER, G., ARNOT, M. and DAVID, M. (1997) 'Is the future female? Female success, male disadvantage and changing gender patterns in education', in HALSEY, A.H., BROWN, P. and LAUDER, H. (eds) *Education, Economy, Culture and Society*, Oxford: Oxford University Press.

YOUNG, I.M. (1993) 'Gender as seriality: Thinking about women as a social collective', Paper presented at the Australian Women and Philosophy Conference, Adelaide, (forthcoming in *Signs: A Journal of Women in Culture and Society*).

8   Who Benefits from Schooling? Equality Issues in Britain

Gaby Weiner with Madeleine Arnot and Miriam David

If we are to believe recent media claims in the UK and elsewhere, we have witnessed in the 1980s and 1990s for the first time, a change in performance and aspiration patterns of girls and boys, with boys showing signs of significant underachievement in contrast to girls' increasing success and confidence. Are we, then, at a point of transition in gender relations? If so, what is the evidence for such claims? In the UK for example, there may be shifts in the relative experience of, and aspirations related to, schooling, but the translation of such shifts into the transformation of labour-market and family patterns, and in women's increased power in the private and public spheres, is not at all clear cut. This chapter seeks to untangle some of the issues contained in the above questions by drawing on debates about gender and schooling in the UK, and, in particular on recent research project findings. The chapter is divided into five sections. It first outlines briefly past developments in gender and schooling in the UK, bringing the story up to date in the second section with a brief overview of recent reforms in British education. The third section describes the Educational Reform and Gender Equality in Schools Project (1994–5) which sought to examine the state of gender relations in English and Welsh schools and, in particular, the impact of the reforms. The fourth section reports on the findings while the final section discusses possible explanations for any changes that have been identified.

UK Debates on Gender and Education

At various stages in the twentieth century, equality has been a target of British government policy-making, though it has rarely been perceived as high priority. From the 1944 Education Act onwards, 'equality of opportunity' was included in the rhetoric of schooling though gender was not a specific consideration until the 1970s.

In the decades before the Thatcher administration began in 1979, policies under both Labour and Conservative governments were orientated towards the twin goals of greater equality and increased economic growth — with the former seen as contributing to the latter. Nineteenth-century assumptions about the natural characteristics of males and females, continued to be used as foundations upon which to frame and build the post-War British welfare state. Coppeck, Haydn and Richter (1995, p. 12) suggest that women were sacrificed to the perceived needs of the welfare state and post-war reconstruction:

> For the sake of rebuilding the war-stricken nation, women's primary role was defined in British social policy as that of homemaker and childrearer. The Beveridge Report (1942) relied on the reassertion of traditional sex roles.

Thus the structure of the British welfare state and indeed, the school day assumed that women would work primarily in the home and would be dependant economically on their husbands' wage. What this meant in terms of education was that in the 1960s and 1970s, equality issues were viewed wholly in terms of social class inequality. Implicitly, ideas about the naturalness of gender differences were maintained and reproduced through schooling, disseminated, for example, by the incorporation within teacher training of Bowlby's theories of maternal deprivation and Parson's functionalist perspectives on distinctive sex roles (Bowlby, 1953; Parsons, 1952).

The main legislation associated with gender and equal opportunities during this period were the Equal Pay Act (1970, coming into force in 1975) the Sex Discrimination Act (1975) and with respect to 'race' issues, the Race Relations Act (1976). This set of legislation led to a range of policy strategies instituted by individual teachers (many of whom were feminists), schools and local authorities, anxious to see enacted the spirit as well as the letter of the legislation. However, by the end of the 1970s, partly as a consequence of the ending of the post-war boom period and an increasing concern for value-for-money in education, a debate began to develop about the extent to which policies aimed at increased equality might be at odds with those aimed at economic growth and individual aspiration.

At the same time, a number of consistent research findings began to emerge pointing to inadequacies in schooling for girls. In terms of the formal curriculum, syllabuses and content were found to exclude the experiences of girls and women (Northam, 1982; Stanworth, 1981; Chisholm and Holland, 1987) and where choice was available, usually at secondary level, girls tended to prefer the humanities, languages and social science, and boys, science, mathematics and technological subjects (Pratt et al., 1984). Also, students tended to be directed into conventionally male and female subjects and careers, and in the main, girls' careers were believed to be less important than boys' (Arnot and Weiner, 1987).

In terms of performance, girls were generally found to be achieving well at primary level although they tended to slip back at secondary level, particularly in mathematics and science (Kelly, 1985; Burton, 1986). Boys' poor performance in English and languages throughout schooling was seen to be offset by their progressively better performance in examinations as they reached school-leaving age (Spender, 1980). In general, young men had an advantage in the labour market because of employer bias, and also because many young women had low occupational aspirations, tending to opt for low status and low paid 'feminine' jobs to bridge the gap between leaving school and marriage.

The hidden or unwritten curriculum of schooling was also found to exert pressure on students (and staff) to conform in sex-specific ways; for example, there were different rules on uniform and discipline for girls and boys, and sexual and racial harassment, and verbal abuse were identified as regular features of school life (Lees, 1987; Wright, 1987; Troyna and Carrington, 1990).

As a consequence, by the early 1980s, a range of local authority and school-based strategies were developed to counter these inequalities, though gender in/equality was rarely a high priority of government and never awarded extensive resources for research and evaluation. Nevertheless, because of the relative decentralization of British education at the time, local projects were able to flourish aided by feminist work in universities and colleges. Most notably, strategies were developed which acknowledged that individual children had multiple identities relating to their sex, social class, ethnicity, family culture etc., all of which needed to be addressed if social inequality was to be reduced or eliminated (ILEA, 1986a, b).

Towards the mid 1980s, a number of labour-controlled Local Education Authorities (LEAs) adopted increased support for equality projects and initiatives, as part of their challenge to the Thatcher government's New Right policies. The upshot of the power struggle that ensued was that the powers of the local authorities were sharply curtailed by the 1988 Education Reform Act and subsequent legislation (David, 1993), and funding and resources were gradually withdrawn from initiatives on gender and other work orientated towards increasing social justice in education.

Simultaneously, feminist and equality activists were confronted by what seemed to be a fragmentation of political effort with the emergence of identity politics around different forms of feminist, masculine, black and minority ethnic voices (Weiner, 1994). Also, the Conservative government retained its own particular interpretation of concepts of equality of opportunity and social justice; which were recast as 'entitlement' and promoted rhetorically through support for individualism and entrepreneurism. Thus, the capacity to survive and succeed in the turbulence of the market and the aspirations of the individual were superimposed over post-war welfarism and equality initiatives systematically targeted at identifiable social groups and communities.

The period from the mid 1970s until the mid 1980s in Britain, thus, might be viewed as one where equality issues were hotly contested and voluntary, of interest mainly to committed politicians, teachers and local authorities, and having different meanings for different groups. Initiatives were often short-term, small-scale, temporary and local, and the national picture was difficult to ascertain. Also, there was little opportunity to evaluate the long-term effects of any policies and practices, though short-term evaluations suggested that the perceptions of some teachers and pupils were changing (Whyte et al., 1984; ILEA, 1986a, b).

By the late 1980s, as government increasingly focused on achievement, standards and data collection, interest in gender shifted from policy and practice *inputs* to examination and assessment *outcomes*, in particular as they related to girls and boys of different social groups (Gipps and Murphy, 1994). This coincided with, and was the consequence of, the educational reforms: thus much debate and analysis focused on the significance and effects (anticipated and actual) of the Educational Reform Act and, particularly, of the new national curriculum (see, for example, Arnot, 1989; Burton and Weiner, 1990; Miles and Middleton, 1990; Shah, 1990).

British Educational Reforms (1983–94)

The reforms introduced in the UK between 1988 and 1994 were sweeping and extensive, aimed at destabilizing and breaking up the post-war professional culture of schooling which was perceived by some on the New Right as mediocre, collectivist and self-serving, and by equality activists including feminists, as excluding, discriminatory and elitist. Briefly, the key curriculum reforms affecting issues outlined in this chapter are:

- The Technical, Educational and Vocational Initiative (TVEI), initially a pilot experiment in 14 LEAs in 1983, which aimed at stimulating curriculum development in technical and vocational subjects for the 14–18 olds. It was later extended nationwide.
- Changes in examinations for 16-year-olds at the end of secondary school, particularly the introduction of the General Certificate of Secondary Education (first examined in 1988), which replaced both the General Certificate of Education (GCE O-level) and the Certificate of Secondary Education (CSE). These changes included new criteria for examination and assessment, and increased emphasis on coursework.
- Creation in 1986 of a new set of vocational qualifications *viz.* National Vocational Qualifications (NVQ) and General National Vocational Qualifications (GNVQs) which aimed to enhance the status of vocational subjects and also to standardize and simplify the vocational award structure.
- The Educational Reform Act of 1988 and particularly:
  — compulsory national curriculum, with three core subjects and seven foundation subjects;
  — national forms of assessment for the national curriculum including Standardized Assessment Tasks (SATs);
  — local management of schools (LMS) giving stronger powers to governing bodies and devolving school budgets;
  — open enrolment for schools, requiring schools to accept pupils up to capacity;
  — provision for schools to opt out of LEA control and become Grant Maintained.

- Education Act of 1992 and 1993, and particularly:
  - — abolition of Her Majesty's Inspectorate (HMI) and the creation of the Office for Standards in Education (OFSTED);
  - — new system of regular, statutory inspections for schools, conducted by OFSTED inspectors;
  - — increased emphasis on the role of parents;
  - — statutory performance tables of school examinations, particularly at the end of compulsory schooling (16 plus) and for A-levels.
- Dearing Report (1994) which led to a more streamlined National Curriculum with the introduction of limited curriculum choice at 13 plus.

The reform agenda has continued apace since 1994, and has included plans for primary school league tables which rank schools on performance, formal identification and dismissal of 'failing' teachers, a nursery voucher scheme, more targeted inspection of schools, and so on. As might be expected, much has been written about both the intentions and the impact of the reforms. Initially, there was considerable concern about the lack of equality discourses available in the reform rhetoric; however it quickly became evident that government policy-making does not necessarily translate directly into changed practice, and that resistances and alternative readings of the reform agenda are both possible and likely.

Further complications have also resulted from divisions within the British Conservative Party itself, arising from its composition of two main ideological groups: the market-liberals and neo-conservatives (Hickox, 1993). To counter the 'production capture' of the large state bureaucracies and institutions such as education, according to Hickox, market-liberals identify as strategies, increased consumer choice and greater efficiency within a highly competitive market framework. In contrast, neo-conservatives emphasize the pivotal role of education in consolidating and transmitting a national, firmly British, culture. The reforms reflect this ideological split with the heavily centralized and prescriptive curriculum and assessment changes representing the views of the neo-conservatives, and the atomized, deregulation of the organizational changes, representing those of the market-liberals.

The Research

The publication of an invitation to bid for a research project in 1993, and subsequent discussions with the funding body, the Equal Opportunities Commission (EOC), when we were awarded the project, suggested a period of renewed interest in gender and education in the early 1990s. The education department at the EOC had been deliberately run down at the end of the 1980s because it was felt that subsequent to the passage of the Sex Discrimination Act (1975) and the follow-up work done by the EOC concerning clarification of the legislation and guidelines to schools on policy and practice, there was little more work to do. Gender equality in education in its formal sense, it was believed, had been achieved. However, the education reforms of the late 1980s and early 1990s were viewed by the EOC as potentially destabilizing: therefore it commissioned a thorough survey of gender relations in schools in order to evaluate the impact of the legislation. As researchers, we were equally intrigued about the dual consequences of Thatcher/Majorism and the education reforms, if fairly pessimistic given the stated anti-egalitarianism of the government and its appointees.

In the project entitled *Educational Reforms and Gender Equality in Schools*, the research team employed three different approaches to data collection and analysis in order to elucidate and explain the various patterns and trends in gender equality in schools over the last decade, as follows:

- *Analysis* of published examination and performance data for the period 1984–94.
- *Questionnaire* surveys of:
  — national sample of primary and secondary maintained schools in England and Wales;
  — all LEAs in England and Wales.
- *Case studies* of equal opportunities policy and practice in seven selected LEAs in England and Wales.

Outcome of the Research

The findings of the project were notable if less dramatic than the media would have us believe. While researching one of the case-studies, I remember the exhilaration of seeing how different the girls and young women I had talked to for the project seemed, compared to those growing up in previous decades, including myself. In particular, today's schoolgirls seemed more ambitious and practical, less romantic and innocent than in the past. One striking factor was their apparent rejection of dependence on men. According to a group of inner-city 10-year-old girls interviewed for the project, for example, the main cause of this was men's unreliability. They asserted that men could be on drugs and couldn't be trusted to be supportive in the home. Therefore they did not see their future lives principally in domestic terms. In fact they had 'all sorts of ideas . . . about how to look after children when working'. 'Overall', one researcher noted, 'the girls seemed very practical and focused. Very independent and unromantic/unsentimental' (Arnot et al., 1996, p. 138).

At other points in the research, the research team were less convinced about the extent of change. This was particularly notable in the case of the conspicuous dominance of white male cultures in schools and LEA hierarchies. A quote from a male headteacher usefully illustrates the perceptions of LEA management held by some, as: 'grey suited men running the authority in a paternalistic rather than partnership sort of way' with 'blunt autocratic reputations' and with 'uncomfortable, defensive, dismissive, sceptical, [and] hostile' responses to gender issues (Arnot et al., 1996, p. 133). The project findings are divided into three sections: patterns of qualifications over a 10-year period; impact of the reforms; and changing student and school cultures.

Patterns of Qualifications

Overall, the new national curriculum extended the previous set of core subjects to science, and required that students in the state sector take all core and foundation subjects (notably, the independent sector was not compelled to observe the new curriculum). Assessment and testing became more regular and systematic, and there were fewer possibilities for choice of subject at secondary level. As a consequence of the Dearing Report (1994) and because of complaints of curriculum overload, the number of compulsory subjects in the initial national curriculum was reduced and limited choice re-introduced.

More specifically as a consequence of the reforms, primary assessment focused more heavily on the core subjects (English, mathematics and science) with girls registering higher level achievements overall, especially in English. Up to 16, the main change from previous decades was the introduction of one examination, GCSE (first examinations in 1988) to replace and streamline the previous two-tier examination track — O-level and CSE. This change, more than any other, we suggest, has caused the shifts picked up by the press and others (i.e. the improved examination entry and performance patterns of girls) as it encouraged more students to be entered for examinations, and in a broader range of subjects. Largely because of this, girls have caught up with boys in mathematics and science at GCSE and there has been an increased entry and a closing gender performance gap in most subjects apart from chemistry and economics which are still largely taken by boys, and social sciences, largely taken by girls. Male students continue to achieve relatively less well in English and the arts, humanities, modern foreign languages and technology. Also, single sex girls' schools continue to be particularly successful in examination performance.

At the age of 18, conventional stereotypes re-emerge. There is higher male entry into A-level sciences (physics, technology, computer studies, geography, chemistry, mathematics) and an increasing male entry into English and modern foreign languages. There is a higher female entry for the arts and humanities, though overall, males gain higher A-level grades in nearly all subjects, especially mathematics, chemistry, technology, history, English and modern foreign languages. However, this male grade superiority is gradually being eroded with a marked improvement in female performance at A-level, particularly in biology, social sciences, art and design. Interestingly, male students tend to score at the extremes, constituting the majority of both the weakest and the strongest students.

Conventional stereotyped entry and performance patterns also re-emerge post-16 for those students seeking vocational rather than academic qualifications. Here we found that young men have a slight (7 per cent) advantage over young women in numbers gaining vocational qualifications and are also more likely to gain higher awards. Young women and men also choose different subjects, courses, and levels of award, related to the labour market sector to which they aspire, many of which are conventionally confined to one or other sex.

Impact of the Reforms

Project findings suggest that despite the immense public controversy and debate engendered by the reforms, many are now viewed positively in terms of increased gender equality, although there are still widespread concerns.

Changes to curriculum and examinations (e.g. TVEI, GCSE, national curriculum) were viewed by project respondents as having had largely *positive* effects on promoting gender equality, in particular for secondary schools. TVEI was reported to have had a positive (or even very positive) effect on gender equality by 87 per cent of secondary schools; similarly, 72 per cent saw positive effects of GCSE.

Reforms and administrative and financial changes in the direction of market forces, choice and freedom of parental choice were viewed as having had largely *negative* effects on gender equality. These include the introduction of Local Management of Schools, the creation of league tables, competition between schools and loss of power of the LEAs.

The overall perception was that gender as an issue had shifted *downwards* in the policy agenda particularly in LEAs with a greater commitment to equal opportunities. Small shifts *upwards*, however, were discerned in other schools and LEAs which for the first time, post-1988 were required to address gender issues in their reporting and evaluation procedures.

Table 8.1 provides an overview of the perceived impact of various educational reforms on gender equality. It shows that reforms influenced by the neo-conservatives concerning curriculum and assessment have been more popularly

Table 8.1   Pattern of findings: Reforms and their positive or negative impact on equality issues

Reform Cluster	Specific Reform	+ or −
Curriculum and Assessment	GCSE	+
	TVEI	+
(neo-conservative influence)	National Curriculum	+
	Data Collection	+
	Focus on Performance	+
	SATs	+
	OFSTED Inspections	+
Changes in Organization	National Targets	+
	League Tables	−
(market liberal influence)	LMS	−
	Opting out and GMS	−
	Loss of LEA powers	−

received than those concerning school and organizational issues, originating from the market-liberals.

Changing Student and School Cultures

This aspect of the research was mostly encouraging. Gender issues in British schools were seen as having been altered and reshaped to accommodate the new language of schooling of the post-reform era. Some schools had brought gender issues into line with concerns about performance, standards, school improvement and value-added policies; others had focused on broader based and more inclusive concepts of entitlement and effective citizenship. Thus the language of equal opportunities policy-making had, to some extent, adapted to, and become part of the new mainstream culture of schools.

Additionally, students' perceptions of gender issues, across a range of ages and social groups and localities were viewed as more open and more sensitive to changing cultural expectations and/or changes in the labour market than previously. Thus, girls and young women appeared more confident and positive about their future working lives and opportunities and boys and young men also seemed aware of gender debates about women's working lives. Nevertheless occupational choices for both sexes remained generally conventional and stereotyped.

Despite the anti-egalitarian government rhetoric of recent years, new gender projects and initiatives have continued to be developed in some LEAs and schools, although they have tended to remain local, with little attempt at wider publicity or dissemination. Such initiatives have tended to address specific local concerns within the post-reform context (e.g. OFSTED inspections, value-added policies, monitoring of performance, governor training, women in management), fusing prior considerations premised on social justice with more recent concerns about performance standards.

More negatively, there was still a clear bias in favour of men, in the management of LEAs and schools. Evidence from both the case-studies and surveys suggests that few women have been able to enter the higher levels of educational management and moreover, that many female LEA officers and teachers have been intensely aware of such gender biases in management and policy. Female teachers' concerns and levels of gender awareness more generally have also tended to be constrained by the lack of interest (and sometimes hostility) of senior male colleagues and LEA managers.

Discussion

How may we interpret the issues raised by this chapter and the research on which it draws? Can we say that there have been any substantial changes in gender relations in British schools? If so, what explanations or theoretical frameworks are available, and what outcomes are likely?

The project report was reasonably well covered in the press, generating both favourable and hostile comments. As MacKinnon (1987, p. 8) suggests, gender is fundamentally about power rather than difference: 'Gender is an inequality of power, a social status based on who is permitted to do what to whom'. Thus, merely to speak of gender creates a tension, a challenge to the dominant male order.

This is neatly illustrated in a highly charged response to the project report, written a couple of months after its publication, entitled 'Perils of ignoring our lost boys' (Evans, 1996). While acknowledging and admitting to 'delight' about the evidence of girls' successes, Evans argues that 'the chronic underachievement of boys' must now be 'a cause of profound concern'. He castigates the project report for 'complacency' over its assertion of the disappearance of male underachievement at 16 when many young men reassert their advantage over young women at A-level and in the labour market, suggesting that this refers to but a small relatively privileged group.

> This [group of boys] is a relatively small selective group whose achievement does not reverse the disturbing fact that at the age of 16, up to 40 per cent of boys are 'lost' to education.

The spectre of a bleak millennium of male unemployment and crime is evoked in Evans' plea for attention now to be diverted towards the 'lost boys' (a reference, one supposes, to the orphaned boys in J M Barrie's *Peter Pan*) and one assumes, away from any 'lost girls'.

> Unless major priority is given to combating the underachievement of boys, the new millennium will herald a bleak future for hundreds of thousands of young men because they are unable to secure employment, because they lack qualifications and equally serious, because they lack confidence and application to take advantage of post-school training and educational opportunities.
>
> The prospect of up to half the young men between the ages of 18 and 30, who live in urban areas in Britain, being unemployed, on probation or in jail is one which no civilized society should contemplate. (Evans, 1995, p. 20)

A key issue for discussion must be, to what extent this panic over boys has been allowed to push other gender areas to the periphery, and why male underachievement has been given such wide publicity in the media and by policy makers, nationally and internationally (Foster, 1995; Kenway, 1995; Haywood and Mac An Ghaill, 1996). We have suggested elsewhere that this moral panic may owe its origins to a number of white, middle-class male fears – of male youth violence, loss of middle-class male job security, unbiddable female lone parents, unstoppable influence of feminism and so on (Weiner et al., 1997). There is a crisis in middle-class masculinity, we suggest, because of a perception of a leaking away of patriarchal power, for which women (particularly those who raise gender issues) are to be blamed.

That some boys are underachieving is certainly true, and it is also factually correct that they constitute a slightly larger group of under-achievers than their female peers. However the spectre raised by Evans — of male unemployment, male crime, and male alienation — should not be laid at the school gate. The forms of masculinity adopted by boys and young men which, in many cases, are proving so resistant to schooling, have been framed not by schools but largely by the economic restructuring of the 1980s and 1990s. As Haywood and Mac An Ghaill (1996, p. 23) point out:

> The political-economic legacy of the 1980s for large sectors of working class students, is that of a post-school anticipation of a condition of dependency, on low skilled central government training schemes, as surplus labour in late industrial capitalism.

Part of the problem for boys and young men, it seems, is that not only are traditional forms of male work no longer open to them, but because the 'masculine' manufacturing base is being displaced by the 'feminine' service sector, they are having to develop new anti-masculine masculinities to cope with the changed conditions. Haywood and Mac An Ghaill suggest that these issues must necessarily be seen as part of the British 1990s political context, relating to class rather than to any errors in previous policies concerning gender and 'race'.

We suggest that far from the gloomy predictions of some regarding gender relations in British schools and LEAs in the mid 1990s, what we have seen is a mixed picture of beneficial procedures and policies arising from some of the reforms, pockets of thoughtful and knowledgeable practice from committed individuals and groups. Cultural, demographic and labour market changes have quite clearly influenced the way male and female students and teachers think about schooling such that few now openly assert female education to be less important. In fact high-scoring female students are proving attractive to schools in the competitive climate of the 1990s, and it is poorly behaved and low achieving boys who are the objects of greatest concern.

What is needed, however, is not a reversal of past successful policies aimed at girls, but a greater understanding of why certain groups do not, perhaps cannot, benefit from schooling. We need to examine with some sensitivity which causes of educational underachievement, whether of boys or girls, can be attributed to the quality of schooling, and which are due to the instabilities of late capitalism. A recent review of international comparisons of educational achievement shows that when compared to other countries, England has a greater proportion of low achieving pupils and a wider distribution of achievement (Reynolds and Farrell, 1996). Our research shows that more of the low achievers are likely to be boys but also that males, even if from a relatively small and privileged group, continue to dominate education and other public domains. Given this complexity, we might expect that both ends of the male equation — the low achieving boys and the high achieving men

— deserve some attention but within a framework of equity and opportunities to benefit from schooling. If this happens, we might see a genuine shift for hitherto disenfranchised groups, though to mount such a twin challenge (on the basis of both gender and class), we suspect, might be viewed as one challenge too far!

References

ARNOT, M., DAVID, M. and WEINER, G. (1996) *Educational Reform and Gender Equality in Schools*, Manchester: EOC.

ARNOT, M. and WEINER, G. (1987) *Gender and the Politics of Schooling*, London: Hutchinson.

BOWLBY, J. (1953) *Childcare and the Growth of Love*, Harmondsworth: Penguin Books.

BURTON, L. (1986) *Girls into Maths Can Go*, East Sussex: Holt, Rinehart and Winston.

BURTON, L. and WEINER, G. (1990) 'Social justice and the National Curriculum', *Research Papers in Education*, **5**, 3, pp. 203–28.

CHISHOLM, L. and HOLLAND, J. (1987) 'Anti-sexist action research in schools: The girls and occupational choice project', in WEINER, G. and ARNOT, M. (eds) *Gender under Scrutiny*, London: Hutchinson.

DAVID, M. (1993) *Parents, Gender and Education Reform*, London: Polity Press.

EVANS, A. (1996) 'Perils of ignoring our lost boys', *Times Educational Supplement*, 28 June, p. 20.

FOSTER, V. (1995) 'What about the boys! Presumptive equality in the education of girls and boys', *Social Policy and the Challenges of Social Change*, **1**, University of New South Wales.

GIPPS, C. and MURPHY, P. (1994) *A Fair Test? Assessment, Achievement and Equity*, Buckingham: Open University Press.

HAYWOOD, C. and MAC AN GHAILL, M. (1996) 'What about the boys? Regendered local labour markets and the recomposition of working class masculinities', *British Journal of Education and Work*, **9**, 1, pp. 19–30.

HICKOX, M. (1993) 'The Crisis of Education', *Questions of Ideology*, Occasional Papers, **1**, London: South Bank University.

INNER LONDON EDUCATION AUTHORITY (1986a) *Primary Matters*, London: ILEA.

INNER LONDON EDUCATION AUTHORITY (1986b) *Secondary Issues*, London, ILEA.

KELLY, A. (1985) 'Changing schools and changing society: Some reflections on the girls into science and technology project', in ARNOT, M. (ed.) *Race and Gender: Equal Opportunities Policies in Education*, Oxford: Pergamon.

KENWAY, J. (1995) 'Masculinities in Schools: Under siege, on the defensive and under reconstruction?', *Discourse: Studies in the Cultural Politics of Eduction*, **16**, 1, pp. 59–79.

LEES, S. (1987) 'The structure of sexual relations in school', in ARNOT, M., WEINER, M. and G. (eds) *Gender and the Politics of Schooling*, London: Hutchinson, pp. 175–88.

MACKINNON, C.A. (1987) *Feminism Unmodified: Discourses on Life and Law*, Cambridge: Harvard University Press.

MILES, S. and MIDDLETON, C. (1990) 'Girls' education in the balance: The ERA and inequality', in FLUDE, M. and HAMMER, M. (eds) *The Education Reform Act 1988: Its Origins and Implications*, Basingstoke: Falmer Press, pp. 187–206.

NORTHAM, J. (1982) 'Girls and boys in primary maths books', *Education*, **10**, 1, Spring, pp. 11–14.

PARSONS, T. (1952) *The Social System*, London: Tavistock.

PRATT, J., BLOOMFIELD, J. and SEALE, C. (1984) *Option Choice: A Question of Equal Opportunity*, Slough: NFER-Nelson.

REYNOLDS, D. and FARRELL, S. (1996) *Worlds Apart: A Review of International Surveys of Education and Achievement Involving England*, London: OFSTED.

SHAH, S. (1990) 'Equal opportunity issues in the context of the National Curriculum: A black perspective', *Gender and Education*, **2**, 3, pp. 309–18.

SPENDER, D. (1980) *Man Made Language*, London: Routledge and Kegan Paul.

STANWORTH, M. (1981) *Gender and Schooling: A Study of Sexual Division in the Classroom*, London: Hutchinson.

TROYNA, B. and CARRINGTON, B. (1990) *Education, Racism and Reform*, London: Routledge.

WEINER, G. (1994) *Feminisms in Education: An Introduction*, Buckingham: Open University Press.

WEINER, G., ARNOT, M. and DAVID, M. (1997) 'Is the future female?: Female success, male disadvantage and changing gender patterns in education', in HALSEY, A.H., BROWN, P. and LAUDER, P. and H. (eds) *Education, Economy, Culture and Society*, Oxford: Oxford University Press.

WHYTE, J., DEEM, R., KANT, L. and CRUICKSHANK, M. (1984) *Girl Friendly Schooling*, London: Methuen, pp. 7–23.

WRIGHT, C. (1987) 'The Relations Between Teachers and Afro-Caribbean Pupils', in WEINER, G. and ARNOT, M. (eds) *Gender Under Scrutiny*, London: Hutchinson.

9 'Us Guys in Suits Are Back': Women, Educational Work and the Market Economy in Canada

Rebecca Priegert Coulter

History is better made than predicted but even the most cursory reading of contemporary events and current trends in Canada suggests that for women in education, the 21st century will provide dangerous terrain indeed. The cumulative effects of the government-supported, corporate effort to implement the neo-liberal economic agenda in Canada (Bakker, 1996b; Brodie, 1996b) and the ongoing destruction of public services and the commercialization of education will have specific consequences for women as educational workers.

The pernicious effects of economic restructuring on social services and health care have already been documented and several recent studies have examined the specific impact on women (Armstrong, 1996b; Dacks, Green and Trimble, 1995; Evans, 1996). Some consideration also has been given to the way in which the Canada–US Free Trade Agreement (FTA) and the North American Free Trade Agreement (NAFTA) are reshaping public education (Calvert and Kuehn, 1993; Kuehn, 1996) and how the mania for deficit reduction (McQuaig, 1995) is threatening the viability of provincial school systems (Robertson and Barlow, 1995; Robertson, Soucek, Pannu and Schugurensky, 1995; Soucek and Pannu, 1996). However, with only a few exceptions (Coulter, 1996c; Reynolds and Smaller, 1996), virtually no attention has been given to the specific consequences for women of educational restructuring and the empirical and theoretical work necessary to reach firm conclusions is missing. Nonetheless, by probing the specific case of Ontario, the country's largest and most populated province, it becomes possible to speculate about some of the gender dimensions of educational down-sizing and government initiatives to deskill and discipline the teaching force. As the 21st century approaches, it appears that the dangers to Canadian women in education are to be found largely in deficit reduction and down-sizing, deregulation of the economy, harmonization with the United States and Mexico, and efforts to destroy the discourses of equality and social justice.

The Wider Context

The relationship between women and the Canadian state has always been troubled but, as Cohen (1996) observes, 'through the market-controlling institutions of the state, women and minority groups have been able to pursue equality and redistributive goals' with some success (p. 189). However, the neo-liberal economic agenda of transnational corporations reflected in international trade agreements such as NAFTA threatens the ability of equality seeking groups to influence social policy. The demands of global capital for reductions in public spending and government regulation coupled with an emphasis on an ethic of self-reliance, self-interest and competition undermine the earlier social consensus based on a caring welfare state, empowered to restrain the worst excesses of the market (Bakker, 1996a; Brodie, 1996a). The FTA and NAFTA do far more than provide a framework for international trade and are dangerous to women and other disadvantaged groups because 'they codify social, economic, and political behaviour in ways that used to be left to the nation-states' (Cohen, 1996, p. 188) and impose a minimalist role for government regulation while giving free rein to an unfettered market. It will become increasingly difficult for women and other popular sector groups to ameliorate disadvantage through state mechanisms or to seek redress through programmes of positive action.

The free trade agreements are of particular significance to education because they require the harmonization of the Canadian, American and Mexican economies in all areas including services, one of which is education. Given that Canada has had a relatively strong welfare state orientation and the public sector has played a key role in controlling the market and supporting national social and cultural programmes, harmonization for Canadians means harmonization down. As Calvert and Kuehn (1993) observe:

> Harmonization will have a downward impact on public education in Canada in at least four areas: pressure to decrease the level of funding to education; reduction in social programs that improve the quality of the lives of children; demands to limit the collective bargaining rights of teachers; and pressure to open delivery of education services to privatization and 'market solutions'. (p. 90)

Although Calvert and Kuehn do not say so, the impact of harmonization in these contexts is also gendered because most educational workers are women and because it is women whose lives are most intimately connected to those of children.

Decreased Funding: Tightening the Screws

In concrete terms, educational restructuring is having and will continue to have profound effects on educational work, most of which is done by women. The longer history of re-tooling the Ontario school system cannot be told here but it is important to note that all three major political parties in the province have shared the same general direction. The social democratic party, the New

Democratic Party (NDP) under Bob Rae, forced spending reductions in education in 1993 through the so-called Social Contract. The Social Contract ignored existing collective agreements between teachers and school boards and imposed province-wide wage cuts for teachers and other educational workers (Martell, 1995). The assault on free collective bargaining profoundly disturbed the NDP's usual constituency and led directly to the election of the Conservative government of Mike Harris in 1995. Like the Klein government in Alberta, the Harris government is deeply committed to the free market and to deregulation. Its agenda will dominate the provincial scene until the dawning of the 21st century, although it should be noted that public protest and organizing against the new right agenda is mushrooming. The next round of reductions in public spending in Ontario was implemented almost immediately by the Conservatives after their election win. Ostensibly designed to reduce the provincial deficit, the cuts meant that over two years and by the end of 1997, one billion dollars less would be available from the province for education. The local school boards initially responded in predictable ways to these cutbacks in provincial support. Information collected by the Ontario Secondary School Teachers' Federation (OSSTF) indicated that by May, 1996 at least 4,200 teachers had received lay-off notices (personal communication, 13 May 1996). Since the vast majority of teachers are women, lay-offs reflected that gendered pattern. In the case of the lay-off of approximately 1,000 educational assistants and clerical workers, job categories where 95 per cent of the employees are female, there can be no doubt that women's jobs were targeted (personal communication, OSSTF, 13 May 1996).

Women's employment in education was challenged in some other ways, as well. Despite very strong recommendations from Ontario's Royal Commission on Learning (1994) in support of an expanded, publicly funded early childhood programme in the schools, the Conservative government rescinded the legal requirement for school boards to offer junior kindergarten programmes for 3- and 4-year-olds. Since virtually all kindergarten teachers are female, this decision marks another diminution of reasonably paid work opportunities for women. This move was coupled with musings from the Minister of Education which suggested that the province was considering allowing personnel without teaching certificates to teach in the remaining early childhood programmes. Replacing women with women but at half the cost is a trend also observed in health care and social services (Connelly and MacDonald, 1996) and has especially pernicious ramifications because it potentially pits women against women while at the same time reflecting a literal and ideological effort to devalue women's work. Caring work, whether in the teaching of the very young or the care of the ill and aged, is constructed as 'natural' for women, as not needing substantive education, and certainly as not requiring a decent wage.

Although the school boards initially reacted quickly in response to government funding cutbacks, sober second thought encouraged by intense lobbying from parent and teacher groups, produced a somewhat different picture. Many Ontario boards responded to government cutbacks by raising more money locally through increased property taxes, thus defeating the Conservative's agenda of down-sizing the system and restricting teacher numbers and wages. In the end, through early retirement schemes and other devices, boards were able to rescind the majority of lay-off notices.

In January, 1997, the government struck back. Justifying the move by arguing that school boards had raised taxes on average by 5 per cent for each of the preceding 10 years, had refused to cut expenditures in the previous year despite reductions in government grants, were top-heavy with administration and wasteful with their spending, the Minister of Education and Training announced plans for a major restructuring of the funding and governance of education and the *Fewer School Boards Act* was introduced (Ontario Ministry of Education and Training [MOET], 1997). The province will assume full responsibility for education costs, thus acquiring the most powerful tool for shaping the direction of public education. By implication, teachers will move from a local to a provincial collective bargaining system.

Attacking Collective Bargaining and Teacher Federations

There is little doubt that schools and teachers will have to make do with less. The government is bent on reducing public expenditures in order to pay for the 30 per cent reduction in income tax that was promised during the election campaign. Since salaries are the largest cost in education, teachers and other educational workers can expect another round of lay-offs and attacks on their salaries and collective agreements. Indeed, in the fall of 1996, the Minister of Education appointed lawyer Leon Paroian to examine the teacher–school board collective bargaining process. Paroian (1996) advised the Minister to remove the teachers' right to strike and to make major changes in a bargaining process that has been working so well that 98.2 per cent of all contract talks have concluded without a strike (OSSTF, 1996). Paroian also suggested changes be made to the *Education Act* to redefine the duties of teachers so that preparation time could be eliminated and teachers could be forced to supervise extra-curricular activities. He implied that a teaching day should be defined as those hours between 8am and 5pm, a time frame which would give sufficient scope to include at least five hours of instruction for students, time for preparation and time for the supervision of extra-curricular activities. Paroian also envisioned restricting the scope of bargaining and returning items such as class size to the realm of management rights. In other words, the major emphasis of the Paroian Report was on the proletarianization of teaching work.

It is unionization and collective bargaining which have made teachers the female aristocracy of labour. Collective action has been the key to attaining and retaining decent salaries, some control over working conditions and programmes of maternity and family leaves, sexual harassment procedures and other policies of particular import to women. An attack on the bargaining rights of teachers is a direct challenge to women in the profession. Of course, efforts to break the power of the teacher federations are an open objective of the Conservative government. Speaking to investors on Wall Street, Premier Mike Harris was explicit on this point. The Ontario Teachers' Federation, he said, was the most powerful union in the world and concessions must be wrung from teachers (Milner, 1996). What he did not acknowledge was that most of those teachers are women. Harris' position, however, fits nicely with the view of the World Bank that 'teachers are essentially not as productive as they could be and [are] overly reimbursed for the work they perform' (Meaghan, 1996).

As part of a strategy to control teachers and decrease the power of their federations, the province also has introduced a College of Teachers. Although the promise was that the College would make teachers autonomous professionals, there is no evidence that teachers themselves wanted a college. Indeed, workplace votes conducted by the OSSTF and the Ontario Public School Teachers' Federation (OPSTF) revealed overwhelming opposition to the idea. In reality, the College of Teachers is another tool for controlling teachers' work (Coulter, 1996b; Smaller, 1995). For example, the College is currently developing competency based criteria with which to judge teacher education programmes and appraise individual teachers over the course of their careers and it has taken on many of the responsibilities for professional governance and relations that were once within the purview of the federations. Given the similarities between these strategies and the ones used by the Conservatives in Britain (Hatcher, 1994), it is not too difficult to imagine that the government's next step might be an attempt to remove the compulsory membership clause from the *Teaching Profession Act*, hence eliminating the closed shop in public school teaching. This move would open the door to the possibility of legislation eliminating collective bargaining for teachers altogether and introducing a system built on individually negotiated contracts of employment. However, teachers are highly organized and their unions are well-funded and strong. They have been actively making alliances with the wider community, including organized labour, and with parents, and the support of Canadians for public education remains strong (Barlow and Robertson, 1994). It remains to be seen whether the government will decide to do battle over collective agreements and the closed shop.

Eliminating Employment Equity

It should not escape our notice that these threats to teachers come at a time when women are making some inroads at the senior administrative level in school systems. Historically, schools have been institutions where a predominantly female work force has been managed and controlled by a select group of men who served as agents of the state and exercised authority through their positions as principals, superintendents, inspectors and directors (Abbott, 1986; Curtis, 1992). For the last two decades the significant under-representation of women in positions of educational leadership has occupied women teachers, especially those organized through the Federation of Women Teachers' Associations of Ontario (FWTAO). Until 1989, the Ministry of Education, while occasionally expressing a shared concern with the FWTAO, did little.

Finally, in 1989, a small but important amendment was made to the *Education Act* to allow the Minister of Education to require school boards to establish and maintain an affirmative action policy with respect to the employment and promotion of women. Between 1989 and 1995, Ministers of Education exercised this power by ordering school boards to seek to achieve a goal of 50 per cent representation by women in supervisory officer, principal and vice-principal positions by the year 2000. Although progress toward the goal was very slow, the symbolic significance of the amendment was great. In 1992, the NDP government expanded the ambit of the legislation to include members of other designated groups, namely visible minorities, aboriginal peoples and the disabled.

When the Conservative government assumed office in 1995, it immediately repealed all employment equity legislation in Ontario, including the small amendment to the *Education Act.* While some boards have maintained an equity approach, many others have used financial stringency and the absence of any legislation to rid themselves of their mostly female equity officers and to close down their employment equity programmes.

For many women, the removal of employment equity legislation and the special glee with which it was done (Martin, 1995) highlight some new dangers. The discourse of equity and the understanding of discrimination as systemic are rapidly being displaced by the more limited view of individual rights and equality of opportunity and by an uncritical call to a merit principle and standards of excellence as though these were objective criteria. In fact, the truth is more likely revealed in the comment from one old-time Conservative who is reported to have explained simply, 'Us guys in suits are back' (Landsberg, 1996).

Gender Work in Classrooms

Important progress has been made in Canada with respect to understanding gender and education and implementing anti-sexist and anti-racist teaching practices (Coulter, 1996a). In Ontario, the elementary and secondary programmes of study recognize the importance of equity in the school context. However, here again the discourse of equity is disappearing, only to be replaced by a pale version of equality of opportunity. Where the current programme of studies for secondary schools calls for the philosophy of sex equity to 'permeate all aspects of the school's curriculum, policies, teaching methods and materials, and assessment procedures, as well as the attitudes and expectations of its staff' (Ontario MOET, 1989, page 11), the new programme to take effect in 1998 contains an anti-discrimination clause that makes no mention of gender at all (Ontario MOET, 1996, p. 41). Instead, vague wording about equal access and full participation for all individuals is the order of the day. Girls and women are about to drop off the educational map though a concern for gender, race and sexual orientation lingers in *The Common Curriculum*, the programme of studies for grades 1 to 9 (ages 6–14).

Gender work with students is further threatened by the loss of school board employment equity officers since they often were responsible for educational equity work, as well. Indeed, a few key local school boards have been instrumental in providing leadership in the province with respect to the development of programmes and materials and this work may be stymied as these boards lose their identities inside much larger district boards. Teacher federations, the other organizational entity responsible for a considerable amount of programme and resource development in the area of gender equity, are so harried by the fast and furious pace of change and by attacks on their very being that there is little time to devote to equity initiatives. Many feminist teachers have opted to become more active in their unions in order to protect the interests of public education more generally but this has meant less time for gender work (Coulter, 1996c).

There is also a sense in which teacher unions choose to ignore the gender implications of attacks on public education in the interests of presenting a united front as an undifferentiated group — teachers. In fact, the long-standing dispute between the female elementary teachers represented by the FWTAO and the male elementary teachers represented by the OPSTF is over. The dispute centred on a disagreement over the Ontario Teachers' Federation by-laws which used sex as the determining factor for membership in one federation or the other. The OPSTF claimed that assigning membership on the basis of sex was discriminatory because individual women could not choose to be members of the OPSTF. The FWTAO argued that the membership by-laws promoted sex equality by recognizing women's inequality and providing a mechanism, an all-women organization, to promote women's equality. After 11 years of litigation, the two federations decided in the summer of 1996 to join together to form one new federation to face the common enemy, the Conservative government. The decision to retire what is thought to be the last remaining women teachers' union in the world is itself a move into dangerous territory for women in Canada for the FWTAO has a long history of working with and financially supporting the Canadian women's movement as well as supporting a wide range of educational initiatives in the elementary schools of the province.

An additional challenge to gender work in the classrooms can be found in demands for system accountability. Standardized testing at the provincial, national and international levels has been imposed on teachers. In Ontario, an Education Quality and Accountability Office (EQAO) has been established to oversee the testing of student achievement in the province. The precise impact this will have on girls' schooling is unclear. There is an occasional instance where girls have not performed as well as boys such as on the grade

12 (ages 17–18) social studies examinations in Alberta (Walter and Young, 1997). However, on the Third International Mathematics and Science Study, there were no significant differences between young men and women in mathematics and only slight differences in science (EQAO, 1996). The School Achievement Indicators Program which tested 13- and 16-year-olds across Canada in reading and writing found that girls significantly outperformed boys (Canadian Education Association, 1995). In fact, with respect to achievement, a growing concern with boys' inadequate school performance is discernible.

At this point, the 'boy problem' is being attributed to single mothers/ absent fathers and to the decline in the numbers of men teaching in elementary schools. The overriding explanation for poor performance in schools, then, is the failure of school to provide strong male role models. This explanation receives support from many male elementary teachers, and in Ontario, from their union. The OPSTF also has made concerted efforts to influence Faculties of Education to take a more aggressive stance towards recruiting males into elementary teaching (Coulter and McNay, 1993) but this has met with little success.

Part of the danger for girls lies with the possibility that standardized tests will become the only measure of school success and accountability. 'Teaching to the test' will override concerns for an inclusive curriculum and it will be argued that schools do not discriminate against girls since their achievement is comparable to, or even better than, that of boys. More resources may be earmarked for boys although they are already in the majority in special education programmes and hence are receiving considerable additional support. Men's rights groups and the media will intermittently mount attacks on what they call the 'feminized school' as they have done in the past, but there is little evidence to suggest that much will come of this.

The more significant danger arises not from immediate concerns about boys' achievement in school but from changes to men's work and how this might affect schools. The loss of traditional men's work in the Canadian economy as a result of globalization and the free trade agreements is significant and young men experience higher rates of unemployment than do young women. Overall, the labour market has been 'feminized', not just because more women are working, but because the position of men has deteriorated. As Armstrong (1996a) puts it, 'many of the good jobs dominated by men are not so good any more' (p. 42). Men and women will increasingly compete for bad jobs in the service sector, jobs which are often part-time, pay the minimum wage and offer little security or hope for advancement.

Weis (1990) has argued that the loss of relative privilege among young, white, working class males that comes with the disappearance of industrial work creates a crisis of gender identity and triggers a more direct form of domination over women, a process which can be seen in operation in classrooms. Young men who have nothing to look forward to but employment in the low wage service sector express anger in virulent forms of sexism and racism and become open to the New Right which seeks to reassert narrow pro-family values and dismantle the gains made by women, racial minorities and homo-sexuals. Certainly, in Canada, there is an active anti-feminist and coded racist agenda evident in much of the opposition to employment equity, pay equity and public spending on social services for single mothers, women's shelters and sexual assault centres. This hostility may well manifest itself in schools.

Conclusion

It is no accident that there is a significant gender gap in support for neo-liberal economic policies in Canada (Kenny, 1996; Toughill, 1996). The dangers con-fronting women workers in education in Ontario are but one example of the pernicious effects of global restructuring and international harmonization as they unfold in a localized context. The dangers are real and immediate and they challenge the gains that have been made over the last 30 years. However, 'women's transformed view of themselves' (McCorduck and Ramsey, 1996) as deserving of equality and as agents of change allows an optimistic reading of the eventual outcome of contemporary struggles. Women working for equality and social justice have always met resistance, they have faced setbacks, but ultimately they have 'managed to change the way our society operates and the way in which people think about women' (Cohen, 1995, p. vi). The road ahead for women in education runs through dangerous terrain but the destina-tion will be reached.

References

Abbott, J. (1986) 'Accomplishing "a man's task": Rural women teachers, male culture, and the school inspectorate in turn-of-the-century Ontario', *Ontario History*, **78**, 4, pp. 313–30.

Armstrong, P. (1996a) 'The feminization of the labour force: Harmonization down in a global economy', in Bakker, I. (ed.) *Rethinking Restructuring: Gender and Change in Canada*, Toronto: University of Toronto Press, pp. 29–54.

Armstrong, P. (1996b) 'Unravelling the safety net: Transformations in health care and their impact on women', in Brodie, J. (ed.) *Women and Canadian Public Policy*, Toronto: Harcourt Brace, pp. 129–49.

Bakker, I. (1996a). 'Introduction: The gendered foundations of restructuring in Canada', in Bakker, I. (ed.) *Rethinking Restructuring: Gender and Change in Canada*, Toronto: University of Toronto Press, pp. 3–25.

Bakker, I. (1996b) *Rethinking Restructuring: Gender and Change in Canada*, Toronto: University of Toronto Press.

Barlow, M. and Robertson, H-j. (1994) *Class Warfare: The Assault on Canada's Schools*, Toronto: Key Porter.

Brodie, J. (1996a) 'Canadian women, changing state forms, and public policy', in Brodie, J. (ed.) *Women and Canadian Public Policy*, Toronto: Harcourt Brace, pp. 1–28.

Brodie, J. (1996b) *Women and Canadian Public Policy,* Toronto: Harcourt Brace.

Calvert, J. and Kuehn, L. (1993) *Pandora's Box: Corporate Power, Free Trade and Canadian Education,* Toronto: Our Schools/Our Selves Education Foundation.

Canadian Education Association (1995) 'CMEC releases SAIP results on language', *Newsletter,* January, p. 3.

Cohen, M.G. (1995) 'Preface', in Pierson, R.R. and Cohen, M.G. (eds) *Canadian Women's Issues, Volume II: Bold Visions,* Toronto: James Lorimer, pp. v–vi.

Cohen, M.G. (1996) 'New international trade agreements: Their reactionary role in creating markets and retarding social welfare', in Bakker, I. (ed.) *Rethinking Restructuring: Gender and Change in Canada,* Toronto: University of Toronto Press, pp. 187–202.

Connelly, M.P. and MacDonald, M. (1996) 'The labour market, the state, and the reorganizing of work: Policy impacts', in Bakker, I. (ed.) *Rethinking Restructuring: Gender and Change in Canada,* Toronto: University of Toronto Press, pp. 82–91.

Coulter, R.P. (1996a) 'Gender equity and schooling: Linking research and policy', *Canadian Journal of Education/Revue canadienne de l'éducation,* **21**, 4, pp. 433–52.

Coulter, R.P. (1996b) 'Re-certification: Inspection by another name?', in Milburn, G. (ed.) *Ring Some Alarm Bells in Ontario: Reactions to the Report of the Royal Commission on Learning,* London, Ontario: Althouse Press, pp. 119–26.

Coulter, R.P. (1996c) 'School restructuring Ontario style: A gendered agenda', in Robertson, S. and Smaller, H. (eds) *Teacher Activism in the 1990s,* Toronto: James Lorimer, pp. 89–102.

Coulter, R.P. and McNay, M. (1993) 'Exploring men's experiences as elementary school teachers', *Canadian Journal of Education/Revue canadienne de l'éducation,* **18**, 4, pp. 398–413.

Curtis, B. (1992) *True Government by Choice Men? Inspection, Education, and State Formation in Canada West,* Toronto: University of Toronto Press.

Dacks, G., Green, J. and Trimble, L. (1995) 'Road kill: Women in Alberta's drive toward deficit elimination', in Harrison, T. and Laxer, G. (eds) *The Trojan Horse: Alberta and the Future of Canada,* Montreal: Black Rose Books, pp. 270–85.

Education Quality and Accountability Office (1996) *The Third International Mathematics and Science Study (TIMSS): Ontario Release,* Toronto: EQAO.

Evans, P. (1996) 'Single mothers and Ontario's welfare policy: Restructuring the debate', in Brodie, J. (ed.) *Women and Canadian Public Policy,* Toronto, Harcourt Brace, pp. 151–71.

Hatcher, R. (1994) 'Market relationships and the management of teachers', *British Journal of Sociology of Education,* **15**, 1, pp. 41–61.

Kenny, E. (1996) 'Battle of sexes looms in Alberta', *London Free Press,* 18 November, p. A4.

Kuehn, L. (1996) 'Teachers, NAFTA and public education in Canada: Issues for political action', in Robertson, S. and Smaller, H. (eds) *Teacher Activism in the 1990s,* Toronto: James Lorimer, pp. 27–34.

Landsberg, M. (1996) 'The ABCs on how women lose out in Tory power game', *The Toronto Star,* 10 November, p. A2.

Martell, G. (1995) *A New Education Politics: Bob Rae's Legacy and the Response of the Ontario Secondary School Teachers' Federation,* Toronto: James Lorimer.

Martin, S. (1995) 'The inevitable backlash', *The Toronto Star,* 19 November, pp. F1, F4, F5.

McCorduck, P. and Ramsey, N. (1996) *The Futures of Women: Scenarios for the 21st Century*, Reading, MA: Addison-Wesley.

McQuaig, L. (1995) *Shooting the Hippo: Death by Deficit and Other Canadian Myths*, Toronto: Penguin Books.

Meaghan, D. (1996) 'Transformational trends in higher education: Restructuring the academic labour process through the introduction of a corporate agenda', *Socialist Studies Bulletin*, **45**, pp. 23–42.

Milner, B. (1996) 'Province's school boards score low marks on Harris Test', *The Globe and Mail*, 7 June, p. A8.

Ontario Ministry of Education and Training (1989) *Ontario Schools: Intermediate and Senior Divisions*, Toronto: Queen's Printer.

Ontario Ministry of Education and Training (1996) *Ontario Secondary Schools (1998): Detailed Discussion Document*, Toronto: Queen's Printer.

Ontario Ministry of Education and Training (1997) *News Release, Speaking Notes and Backgrounder*, 13 January, Toronto.

Ontario Royal Commission on Learning (1994) *For the Love of Learning: Report of the Royal Commission on Learning*, Toronto: Queen's Printer.

Ontario Secondary School Teachers' Federation (1996) 'If it ain't broke, break it', *Update*, **24**, 6, p. 3.

Paroian, L. (1996) 'Review of the school boards'/teachers' collective negotiations process in Ontario', Toronto: Ministry of Education and Training.

Reynolds, C. and Smaller, H. (1996) 'Economic downturns affect women and men differently', *FWTAO/FAEO Newsletter*, **14**, 3, pp. 50–7.

Robertson, H-j. and Barlow, M. (1995) 'Restructuring from the right: School reform in Alberta', in Harrison, T. and Laxer, G. (eds) *The Trojan Horse: Alberta and the Future of Canada*, Montreal: Black Rose Books, pp. 194–208.

Robertson, S. and Smaller, H. (1996) *Teacher Activism in the 1990s*, Toronto: James Lorimer.

Robertson, S., Soucek, V., Pannu, R. and Schugurensky, D. (1995) 'Chartering new waters': The Klein revolution and the privatization of education in Alberta, *Our Schools/Our Selves*, **7**, 2, pp. 80–106.

Smaller, H. (1995) 'The Ontario College of Teachers: Whose interests would it serve?', *Our Schools/Our Selves*, **7**, 1, pp. 121–33.

Soucek, V. and Pannu, R. (1996) 'Globalizing education in Alberta: Teachers' work and the options to fight back', in Robertson, S. and Smaller, H. (eds) *Teacher Activism in the 1990s*, Toronto: James Lorimer, pp. 35–69.

Toughill, K. (1996) 'Tories' gender gap suggests new supporters decamping', *The Toronto Star*, 4 May, p. C4.

Walter, C. and Young, B. (1997) 'Gender bias in Alberta social studies 30 examinations: cause and effect', *Canadian Social Studies: The History and Social Science Teacher*, **31**, 2, pp. 83–6, 89.

Weis, L. (1990) *Working Class without Work: High School Students in a Deindustrializing Economy*, NY: Routledge.

10 Is It Really Worthwhile? Women Chemists and Physicists in Sweden

Sylvia Benckert and Else-Marie Staberg

> I think many women do not want to go to the top where you always have to fight and struggle and the workload is enormous.

These are words from a woman chemist who, like many others, questions the competitive atmosphere and the all engulfing work in the top positions of a university science department. She is one of about 25 chemists and physicists interviewed by us in a follow up study of a mapping of women chemists and physicists in Sweden 1900–89 (Benckert and Staberg, 1994). We selected women to interview from different universities, different areas of chemistry and physics and of varying ages in order to explore the conditions of women chemists and physicists in the academy. The roots to our study lie in our own background. We both have an interest and an education in science, one with a preference for physics the other for chemistry; one of us did post-graduate studies and made a career in physics, the other left the university immediately after her graduation and came back much later, and is now in education. Together and also individually we have pursued our interest in questions of gender and science and the feminist critique of science.

In an earlier study we looked at the careers of six very successful women scientists, born 1867–1920 (Benckert and Staberg, 1992). Four of the scientists in this study were Nobel prize winners and the two others were as eminent in the field; the oldest was Marie Curie and the youngest Rosalind Franklin. Findings worth mentioning in this context were the formal and informal resistance all these women met and the problems associated with being a woman and a scientist. For the older ones there was formal resistance concerning, for example, access to school or university positions, and all the women met different kinds of informal resistance during their careers. In this study, we stressed the importance of having the right husband – or none – and also the necessity of supportive colleagues. We also noted that the married women took a far greater part of the unpaid work for maintaining home and children than their husbands, a fact that influenced their careers.

Today half the undergraduate students in chemistry at Swedish universities are women but at research levels women chemists are relatively rare. In physics there are few women even at undergraduate level and very few women in research positions. Swedish equity policy for women and men is well known and there has been a debate in Sweden for some years about the need for more women scientists. Why does the equity policy not result in more women chemists and physicists at research level? Is it the problem of combining family and science that prevents women from participating in science or is there a resistance from the male science community or perhaps a combination of these and other factors? Does resistance, family and children and other factors (for example women's views of a good life or a meaningful job) result in a typical career for women differing from men's careers?

In this article we briefly discuss the difference in women's participation in the disciplines of chemistry and physics. We look at the career paths of the women and the connections between the character of these paths with the struggle of the women to combine family and science and the informal, conscious or unconscious, resistance from the science community.

Women in Chemistry and Physics

How many women chemists and physicists with a PhD are there in Sweden today and how have these numbers varied during the last century? The answer to this question is given in Figures 10.1 and 10.2.

Figure 10.1   Number and proportion of women awarded a PhD in chemistry

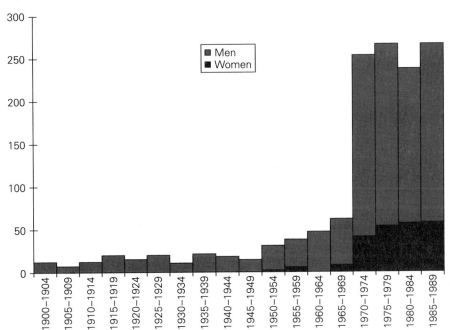

Source: Benckert and Staberg, 1994

Figure 10.2   Number and proportion of women awarded a PhD in physics

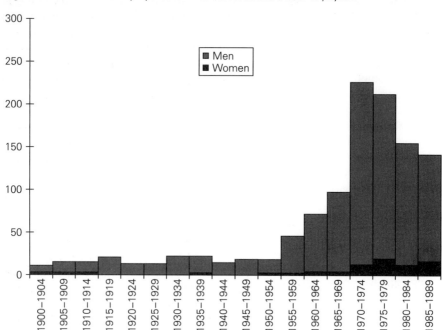

Source: Benckert and Staberg, 1994

From the figures we see that the number of persons with a PhD in chemistry or physics increases very rapidly at the beginning of the 1970s. There are several factors behind this increase. The large generation born in the 1940s reached the universities at that time and a greater part of the population in Sweden attended higher education. The introduction of a new doctorate is another factor. The number and the proportion of women with a PhD in chemistry or physics also increased in the 1970s. From the figures we can also see that at the beginning of the century there were women doctorates in physics but not in chemistry. Our informants among the women physicists tell us that physics is seen as difficult and elitist and theoretical physics even more elitist than experimental physics. They also agree that the status of the field/subfield probably is of more importance for men than for women. This could partly explain the higher proportion of women in chemistry compared to physics. According to women physicists, particle physics seems to be the subfield of physics with the highest status but more applied physics, like material physics, also has a high status at the technical universities. One woman physicist says: 'I think there is a lot of snobbery among physicists and not least among theoretical physicists'. Another physicist tells that: 'Some people certainly assert that elementary particle physics is the most. . . . But I am not so sure. Subjects dealing with materials and applications are economically big and important areas, so these subjects have another kind of status'. The chemists are less inclined to talk about the status of disciplines or subdisciplines, but on the other hand they sometimes show respect towards physicists.

Sharon Traweek, author of the book *Beamtimes and Lifetimes: The World of High Energy Physicists* (1988) found that the particle physicists at the SLAC-lab in California shared the assumption that particle physics is 'the spearhead of our penetration into the unknown'. The particle physicists also think that this spearhead has a shaft extending behind it; after chemistry and engineering comes biology, followed perhaps by the social sciences and humanities. The theoretical physicists in her study occupy the top floor in the physical building at this lab and they also occupy the top floor symbolically. These ideas, so expressively described by Traweek, also seem to exist in less pronounced form among the Swedish physicists.

What do our informants say about studies in chemistry contra physics? Many of the physicists do like mathematics but say that they do not like chemistry because in chemistry you cannot work out the result logically and you just have to swot. One of the chemists has an opposite point of view. She thought physics at school was very mechanical. Not so few of the physicists have nevertheless studied chemistry with the argument that it is easier to get a job with a background in chemistry. Chemistry is also seen as more appropriate for women. One of the physicists wanted to study physics but for many years was persuaded by her father and her boyfriend to study chemistry instead of physics. Differences in status, work prospects and traditions are some factors that can explain the difference in the participation of women in the two sciences.

A Typical Career for Women

I have never made an academic career. Rather, I have made a typical women's career, as I had children before I got my PhD. My son was one year when I was awarded my PhD. OK my husband stayed at home a lot when I was writing up the thesis. He had his PhD. Then we went to the US for a year and both of us were postdocs. I was lucky with the place I came to. I was the one who worked part time in the US. When we came back and they needed teachers here . . . My husband had a research position. So I came back and taught and managed to get along somehow. And since then I have managed to get along. I do research, but I have no research money of my own and no tenure.

Does this quotation describe a typical career for women and is there another ideal career? A common opinion is that in the ideal type career you must have your PhD before 30 and then go abroad for some years. When you come back you should seek a research position financed by the research council, based on the work you did as a postdoctoral student. During this period you are supposed to form your own group and then you should apply for more money for yourself and your group and after another few years you start applying for a professorship and eventually you become a full professor. In Sweden a full professor is often the leader of the department. Research positions with a lower rank are not titled 'professor'. None of the women interviewed fit the proper pattern. Some fit the beginning of this pattern but have not yet become full professors. They have, however, a good chance of succeeding.

A career similar to the 'typical career for women' described in the quotation above is not unusual. Often, the women never decided to make a career in academia. Many of the physicists for example planned to be teachers and some of them also worked as teachers for a couple of years before they started their doctoral studies. One of them tells us: 'As you see, it is no straight career so that you decide during high school that I am going to do research in the fundamental problems in physics. It is a winding track for most women, much more for women, I think'. She is using the same words 'straight roads' and 'winding tracks' as Inga Elgqvist-Saltzman (1992) in her analyses of women's careers.

Children and husband have influenced the typical career of women in important ways. To leave the country for a postdoc period abroad can (for example) be very difficult if you have the responsibility for a family and children. According to one of our informants you can move children but a husband is much more difficult to move. In every stage of the career family and children can cause the orientation towards a more typical career for women. One successful woman says:

> I have never applied for a professorship and I don't want to make such an investment, as I think it would be, if I should manage to be a leader for a whole department. I want to have time for my children and other things too. It should cause too many conflicts in my life.

Women, hitherto in the ideal type career, also experience problems in combining family and research. One of them tells us that now, with family and children, she accepts that research advances more slowly. 'But it is not fun when somebody else has the results before you get them and you were the one that started on it. It is difficult to handle everything during a period of life when you ought to qualify yourself. But somehow you want your children and at the same time you are in your career'.

Several of the women teach a great deal and enjoy teaching. Many have administrative tasks as well and, in consequence, have little time for research. The academy's low esteem of teaching — and also administration at the department level — in combination with a sense of responsibility has consequences for a scientist's career. If one applies for a professorship, teaching and administration is not much valued; only research is really valued. The stories of women suggest that women more often than men are caught in this trap and teach themselves away from the career. Many of the women were able to begin their doctoral studies or obtained teaching positions after their PhDs because there was a need for teachers at the universities and they often won these positions because they were good teachers. So the possibility of teaching does give the women positions at the university but at the same time, in many cases, debars them from a research career.

> All had to teach a lot but some of them liked research and did not bother much about their teaching duties and in my opinion you could not do so. If you have assumed the responsibility for something you have to do it properly.

This statement from one of the physicists is in accordance with the theory of different rationalities women and men acquire through upbringing and work, rationalities which then continue to influence the acting of women and men (Ve, 1995 and this volume).

Once women have started to teach themselves away from the career it is difficult to come back. Age seems to be a big problem. Talk about age rules is common. It can be comments such as 'You have to be young and bright', 'When you are 30, you are already old, very old', 'If you would like to go to Cern you could not be more than 25', 'You cannot be older than 32–35 when you apply for money' or 'The industry does not want people over 35 years of age'. Age can be a problem for the career. If you do not intend to make a career and do not take the straight road, you can be seen as too old for fulfilling a proper career. You can be too old because you have had children and taken care of your family or you can teach too much. Being young seems to be more important now than 10–15 years ago, consistent with the growing cult of youth in western society. It is evident that age is more of a problem for women than for men because women usually assume responsibility for the family.

Perhaps women do not want to have those ideal academic careers? We find many statements like the following.

> I have never applied for a professorship / . . . / and the reason is that I do not think I should be happy with it.

> I think many women do not want to go to the top where you always have to fight and struggle and the workload is enormous.

One reason women do not want this type of career is because they dislike the way you have to work. They do not like the competitive culture. 'Publish, publish and publish and not have time for anything but work', one woman says. Another reason is that women want time for their children and other things as well, and a third reason is that they do not know if they are the right persons for this type of career. 'I was not sure I was clever enough for it', says one of the older women and another tells us that women step aside when things are getting difficult. The climate and the sharp elbows you have to have suit men better. Other women hint at similar things: 'You do not fight for yourself. You are not used to asserting yourself. It is not that you are discriminated against. You do not boast of what you have done'.

'Publish, publish and publish': that is very important for a career and it has been shown that women scientists publish less than male scientists and that the difference increases over time but emerges only gradually. Cole and Singer (1991) found that this publication pattern can be explained by small differences in the way women and men are treated and in the way they react to different events during the development of their career. If men have a greater chance to gain a position and if women step aside when things are getting difficult, differences between men and women start to build up. Although the differences between men and women are small and women scientists often state that personally they have not experienced any discrimination, the processes are cumulative and the result considerable.

The atmosphere is competitive and there is competition between different departments or universities but also inside departments. There is a difference in attitude between women and men concerning cooperation and competition, says a young scientist. She wants to compete with her knowledge in her speciality, but she disapproves of the personal competition in the workplace. Women talk to each other about problems with research grants or about their research: 'We do not compete with each other. But the boys do. It is my disappointment. I do not like it. Now they have been to the US and got it from there . . . There they compete, they do not cooperate'. Another woman describes the competitive culture like this: 'You have to be the biggest, the best and the most beautiful. It is hard and sometimes this competitive culture is not so productive, I suppose'. 'A lot of rubbish is produced', according to a chemist.

Many of the women chemists and physicists criticize the work culture in science. Combining a responsibility for teaching and students with research in a competitive surrounding is a problem. The threat of getting too old is a background against which these problems should be seen. The women still like research and want to do a good job but they question if essential research thrives in this competitive work culture. One woman says, 'I do not have the need for a career in that way. I want to be somebody who does something that is good'. Another says, 'If I had gone on with nuclear physics (instead of environmental physics) it would have been much easier to make a so called career'. The main problem for the women scientists though concerns the difficulty of combining family and children with research and we will now look at this problem in more detail.

Family and Science

Is it really worthwhile to keep on when it is so heavy combining everything? It is alright for a while but then you start wondering if it really works or if you are crazy.

These are words from a physicist, preoccupied with the problems of combining family and science. She is not alone. Thoughts around children and family engage most of the women. Almost all the women have children, one has as many as four. In many ways the women scientists of today have the same problems as the older ones in our former study. In studies about women scientists women's double responsibilities are often evident (Benckert and Staberg, 1992). This is in contrast to many autobiographical records by top women scientists where difficulties of personal life are ironed out (Rose, 1994, p. 15).

In an international perspective it is important to look at the conditions for working women. Through the scientists' stories you can follow how childcare in Sweden changes, how public childcare is built up, the maternity leave period increases and paternity leave is introduced (see also Elgqvist-Saltzman, this volume). In the 1950s and 1960s the women either employed au pair girls, or they found a private day mother. Slowly things changed. The public sector expanded including the number of child care centres. Towards the end of the 1970s parents could find day care centres, although perhaps not for the youngest children. Almost all the women have worked full time except for the maternity leave period, but some worked periodically part time or stayed at home an extra year. During this period they often studied.

Many of the scientists had support from a grandmother or another relative, some regularly for many years and others in acute situations. They have also had friends to help them. 'The network is crucial', says a physicist whose sister in law took care of the children for several years. 'They had practically two mothers, almost three with my twin sister as well. So this was a real network'.

What about the fathers, often scientists? Do they contribute or do they perhaps share the responsibility? Several of the older women say they had to do everything themselves. 'You did not share the burdens in those times', says one informant. 'I went home at four o'clock each day and then I worked in the evening, preparing lessons and so on while my husband was still here at the department. It is different now. Now women demand help from their husbands'. But another, born in the 1930s says that they have shared — in principle. 'My husband is very particular about being progressive. And compared to many others he is. But in my opinion I have done most of the care work. Because for men it is always the job in first hand, for women it is often the family. When he was in the last phase of his PhD it was very important and he was not to be disturbed and I had to do everything. But when I was in the same situation I still had to do everything'. The opinion of many women is that men can 'shut out the problems with home and children' while women always feel guilty.

Sharing is in many cases some kind of strictly organized shift work:

For many years my husband and I organized like this: Friday we both went home early, then I had Monday and Wednesday; these were my days. This meant that I left home one hour earlier in the morning, that is I took them to the day care centre. Then the evening was mine; I could do experiments as late as I wanted. And then he had Tuesday and Thursday.

The sharing seems to be hard, but can also be rewarding. The couple's relatively free jobs and the intellectual sharing are mentioned by several women. Almost none, however, believes conditions to be equal, but if you want to stay in a research career you cannot give up:

> It takes time. It usually takes time for women. I think that usually women achieve tenure later in their career than men. And it depends a little on the fact that they usually manage to have a couple of children along the way. So for me, it is a question of perseverance.

A special problem is caused by the now almost obligatory postdoctoral period. Unless you have decided not to have children this is a problem. Not many of the women we have spoken to have been postdoctoral students. Indeed some took their PhDs at a time when a postdoctoral period was not common, but several say that it was impossible because of the responsibility for children. A woman who did a postdoctoral period with her husband now has ambiguous thoughts. She found it most stimulating but also thinks it might hurt the children. She suggests that postdoctoral work is more and more valued and gets support from a relatively young woman, who says that in the ideal career 'you take your doctor's degree before 30 and then go on to postdoctoral study for a couple of years if you have any chance of advancement'. This woman argues that this is not possible for mothers of small children: 'Now they urge the research students to manage in four years. In my time it could easily take ten years. Then you had children. Now they usually have not'. This new pattern is followed by two younger scientists, who both have done postdoctorates and some years of research financed by the research council, before they had children. This is not an easy path either. Time works against women when they postpone having children. The young women clearly see the pattern but still hope. Listen to our youngest:

> The biggest problem is that women and men do not share the time for the care of their children. It is not only the fault of the man, I must say. It is about creating a relation and feeling that you do it together. These are our children, now we take care of them together and are loyal to each other. But I do not know if it will work. I believe and hope so.

The women clearly position themselves as 'others' in the science world when they look upon their lives as parents. As women with children they have to struggle harder than male scientists, with or without children. As scientists women are caught in a dilemma. The model for a scientist is a man and as women they strive to be good scientists, that is non-women, at the same time as they are very much aware of their womanhood.

Resistance?

'I have never met any resistance', say several of the women, and then they start telling resistance stories. Many of them, however, frankly say that they have met resistance and can also tell explicit stories. What do the stories of the women look like and at what stage of the women's lives do they happen?

Resistance is not obvious at the beginning. Few remember any resistance towards them as research students. Those who do were a little older than average and, as you are supposed to be 'young and bright', a woman of 35 years can be seen as 'an old vixen'. Rather, the women tell about the stimulating time as research students. Many chemists from different universities also tell how they enjoyed the good climate and the laboratory work. Often they went as research students to conferences or made stimulating contacts with foreign researchers in other ways. To be a young woman had advantages. 'There is a special buzz in a big hall when a blond Swedish woman gives a lecture but this interest rapidly ends when you start to compete with men', says an informant. It is when the competition starts, competition over money and jobs, that we find the problems.

In the beginning of their careers many were not prepared for the values and strategies ruling in the academic world. A woman who had been very successful as a research student and even had her own research money, gained tenure immediately after her examination. She was prepared to teach and took on a great burden, sometimes the ultimate responsibility for the department and her research suffered:

> And if I accuse him (the professor and former supervisor) of anything it is that he did not explain the rules of the game for me. I believed what they told me. That teaching gives merits and that administration at a high level achieves merits. Sure. But I did not know that you should gain the merits 'with the elbows', through your research.

This is to withhold information, one of the 'ruling techniques'. These techniques or strategies described in Ås (1982) are used by members of a dominant group toward members within the dominated group, e.g. men against women. This woman, cited above, believes that men but not women are directed towards research and career by their elders:

> On the other hand he [the professor] has never supported women as he has men. He had a capacity to bring forward crown princes and followers. And the way they were supported was that they did not have to teach and they were given different privileges. It never happened to a woman here. And little by little I learnt to see the pattern.

'Power and money lead to problems' says a very successful woman. It is the women who fight for a place in the world of science who meet the strongest resistance. Resistance towards women becomes obvious in connection with certain paid positions, especially research positions. Women born in the 1930s tell about professors who said 'you should realize that you are taking the bread from a wage owner' or 'could you not stay at home and have a scientific saloon instead?' or 'you really ought to stay at home with your family'.

Today open remarks are rare and resistance more subtle. We are told about a masculine culture where women can encounter difficulties. One woman, administrating part time, says reluctantly that she has some problems with men's ways at meetings on faculty level. She becomes invisible, and the only reason she can find is that she is a woman. To make somebody invisible is another ruling technique. Some also talk about the difficulty of playing the men's power game and that it is 'easier not to go into a clinch with them'.

The culture at meetings where women can be made invisible or ridiculed exists at department level and continues in the research councils. To ridicule is yet another ruling technique. Some of the older scientists have experience of the powerful committees of the research councils where women are few and not always wanted. One of them remembers a committee where she was the only woman in a group of 16. 'I had to swallow a lot in that group', she says. Once, when there was a vacancy, she wanted to vote in another well qualified woman. The reaction was: 'But we shall really not have any bloody women's rule here'. Two women out of 16 were seen as a takeover. In this group our scientist learned never to put forward any suggestions herself, but always to go through a man. The difficulties for women in achieving positions of power in the scientific community echo the lives of the women in our former study. There is a 'corruption of friendship in the academy', according to one informant:

> I think that many women fare badly there. They do not understand the game behind their backs. I can hear the same person say one day that we must describe the professorship broadly, broadly enough with these and these things. And then I know that he has a pal up his sleeve, but next time in another context the same person maintains that we must describe the post so narrowly, so narrowly, then he has another pal representing this narrowness and in this game women are losers.

Of course even male scientists can suffer from this 'friendship corruption', but women are more vulnerable, just because they are women and thereby 'others'. When the open resistance disappears as no longer politically correct, the informal obstacles become more visible. Today, as earlier, the culture can be an informal obstacle to women's participation in scientific work. Although many women position themselves both before and after their doctorate as having equal possibilities with men, they are simultaneously aware of the masculine environment as a negative factor. Professionally the women have to relate to men. Men relate to men since they have the power and the dominant positions and if women want their share of power and influence they also have to relate to men. We can say that as a minority they strive to become integrated and not differ from the norm for a scientist, just as Thomas (1990) has described the minority position of women students of physics.

Towards a Better Future?

In our stories of women's entry into science, their careers and their struggles, we have shown both consistencies and new trends. Women make their way into science, more so in chemistry than in physics but it is a slow march. Men take more responsibility for their children today, but women still do most of the unpaid care work. The open resistance disappears but informal resistance is still there. The competitive science culture fits men better than women. It is difficult to combine responsibility for children and a career in a competitive culture. Women also stand back in this culture because they do not assert themselves and they do not boast of what they have done and they do not know the game well enough to be winners. Many of them are not sure if they want to participate in this competition. They want instead to do something new and good. An interesting question is if women with their knowledge and experience of reproductive work can change this culture, if they can be disturbing elements of the prevailing order in a positive way, as Jane Roland Martin interprets Virginia Woolf's view of women's education and work (Martin, 1994).

Needless to say we are not talking about 'women scientists' in general but of some Swedish women scientists, working in the academy. On the other hand through other studies we have been able to show similarities with women at least from the UK and from the US, influential countries for Swedish science. We want to stress that our informants all think that work in chemistry and physics is essential, interesting and enjoyable even if there are problems. We have focused on problems since it is the problems that must be made visible in order to make change possible.

But what about the famous Swedish equity between women and men? The Government's equity policy in Sweden is known to be tougher than in most other countries due to pressure not least from women politicians. It also concerns the academy but the gendered structure of the academy is not easy to break down. In the latest equity bill from spring 1996 the Government proposed 30 professorships for competent women as a small step in order to come to terms with the enormous dominance of male professors, a kind of affirmative action. The proposal received much criticism in the form of an exaggerated fear of a lowered standard in the academy. Our informants are also doubtful of this measure and fear that such professorships will be considered second class. Affirmative actions have always been looked upon with suspicion in Sweden, even by women. The Parliament, however, decided to accept the bill. As another result of the bill the research councils now have to consider gender questions. Even if we are aware of the strength of the gender system in our opinion a step forward has been taken.

Sylvia Benckert and Else-Marie Staberg

References

Ås, B. (1982) *Kvinnor Tillsammans: Handbok i Frigörelse* (*Women of all Countries: Handbook of Liberation*), Stockholm: Gidlund.

Benckert, S. and Staberg, E.-M. (1992) *Forskning med Förhinder* (*Research with Hindrance*), Stockholm: Almqvist and Wiksell.

Benckert, S. and Staberg, E.-M. (1994) *Kvinnliga Fysiker och Kemister* (*Women Chemists and Physicists*) *1900–89: Hur Många och Inom Vilka Områden?* (Kvinnovetenskapligt forums rapportserie, nr 5), Umeå: Umeå universitet, Kvinnovetenskapligt forum.

Cole, J.R. and Singer, B. (1991) 'A theory of limited differences: Explaining the productivity puzzle in science', in Zuckerman, H., Cole, J.R. and Bruer, J.T. (eds) *The Outer Circle: Women in the Scientific Community*, New Haven: Yale University Press.

Elgqvist-Saltzman, I. (1992) 'Straight roads and winding tracks: Swedish educational policy from a gender perspective', *Gender and Education*, **4**, 1, 2, pp. 41–56.

Martin, Roland, J. (1994) *Changing the Educational Landscape: Philosophy, Women and Curriculum*, London and New York: Routledge.

Rose, H. (1994) *Love, Power and Knowledge: Towards a Feminist Transformation of the Sciences*, Cambridge: Polity Press.

Thomas, K. (1990) *Gender and Subject in Higher Education*, Buckingham: SRHE and Open University Press.

Traweek, S. (1988) *Beamtimes and Lifetimes: The World of High Energy Physicists*, Cambridge, Massachusetts: Harvard University Press.

Ve, H. (1995) 'On gender and equality in schools in late modernity', in Reisby, K. and Schmack, K. (eds) *What can Curriculum Studies and Pedagogy Learn from Sociology Today*, (*Didaktiske Studier*, Volume 16), Copenhagen: Royal Danish School of Educational Studies.

11 Women's Education, Career and Family in China in an Intergenerational Perspective

Grace Mak

Introduction

Reports of national governments and international agencies such as those under the umbrella of the United Nations typically present women's status in statistics. This reveals a conception of women as a uniform group, characterized by their physical distinction from men. The complexities of women's situations and how women arrive at such situations are conveniently ignored. Feminist studies of women and development challenge the anonymity imposed on women. Not only has development meant different things for men and women, its consequences vary as to women's social class and/or geographical backgrounds (Boserup, 1970; Chinchilla, 1977; Smock, 1982; Rogers, 1980).

In this chapter I pursue the notion of diversity among women. I argue that women's situations share as large a degree of variety as similarity. The situations result from a number of factors. In this study I examine how the factors of education and politics superimpose on women's gender roles to affect women's subsequent career and family lives in the People's Republic of China. The problem is tackled at different levels. First, I study how individual women made meaning of events that took place during the course of their lives. Then I compare the experiences of a sample of women from the same generation to see if and when individual accounts had so much in common that they merged into a common experience shared by a generation. Next, I put together collective profiles of women from three generations to see if and how they changed over time. This multilayered analysis is set in the context of sweeping reforms in education and employment for women in China. An in-depth probe into the experiences of individual women and how each woman explained their experience will reveal both the uniqueness as well as collective nature of such experiences. It will help us understand the benefits as well as limitations of reforms on women, and thus offer an alternative to assessing policy effectiveness other than the simplified statistical summary prevalent in government reports.

The Relevance of the Life-history Approach to the Present Study

A study built on the experiences of individuals raises the question of whose voice we are listening to (Thompson, 1978). If we rely on the official voice, the women in this study would be among the thousands who exemplify the Chinese slogan 'women hold up half the sky'. Voices from individual women may illustrate the reality from more angles and more authentically. Choosing to understand the world as perceived by the actors justifies the employment of interviewing as a means of data collection. Next, we want to understand the extent women were able to take advantage of the opening up of opportunities in education and the labour market in relation to their domestic obligations at different phases of their life course. Thus we need to design the interview in such a way that information elicited from it will engender a reconstruction of a woman's experience over time. The life-history approach has been chosen for this purpose. The inspiration came from Inga Elgqvist-Saltzman, who in her work (1986a and b, 1988) argued that educational reforms based on rational efficiency models fail to address the complex interplay between gender roles and labour market demands in women's reality, and that human sensibility has to be taken into account in order for reforms to be effective. The life-histories of all respondents in my sample combined yielded similarities and differences among individuals and among generations. The life-histories of individuals may, however, be woven into a collective life-history of a generation (Bertaux, 1990).

To pursue this goal I took life histories from a sample of three generations of women who lived through different kinds of changes in the Chinese political and economic systems and in education. The data were collected from open-ended interviews. In each interview I charted each woman's life history. In my study life histories consist of patterns of each woman's education, marriage, reproduction and employment. I developed a linear chart to represent highlights in each woman's life history. The chart illustrates when a woman attended school, married, gave birth to children, and joined the work force. Though appearing in linear form on paper, the events affected a woman's life cycle in a back and forth manner. As each woman recollected her past in an interview session, I noted major happenings in the course of her life on a life-line. The rest of the interview data substantiate and explain the charts, and reveal the women's perceptions about change.

I conducted the interviews in Beijing in 1988. Mine was a snowball sample comprising 31 women. They were in the neighbourhood of 60, 45, and 30 years of age at the time. I interviewed 11 women in the age 60 group, and 10 each in the age 45 and 30 groups. They were born in the 1920s, the late 1930s and early 1940s, and the 1950s respectively. They had all completed higher education. One group (11 women) attended university in the 1940s before the Communist Revolution; the second group (10 women) went to university in the late 1950s and early 1960s, and the third group (10 women) completed their education in the 1970s and early 1980s. The women were all professionals, most being college teachers and secondary school teachers. A few were vice-principal, education reporter, party cadre for education, or nurse. They were mostly in what are perceived as 'female' professions. Only one woman, an engineer, was in a 'traditionally male' profession. They were all married and living with their husbands. Except for a few in the older group, whose children were married and lived apart, they were living with their children.

It is necessary to give readers a brief historical background to the study. Before 1949, China was under the rule of the corporatist Nationalist Party. Higher education was characteristically a preserve of well-to-do males. Women's representation was extremely meagre. The country was torn by civil war between the Nationalists and the Communists, and the economy was in bad shape. An agrarian economy with nascent industrialization precluded widespread employment in the cities. Besides, society's confinement of women's space to the household reduced the effect of education on women's employment prospect. Sweeping change came with the Communist victory in 1949. The new government was committed to raising the status of women. It encouraged women to enrol in schools and join the work force after graduation. Women's participation was given a spur during the Great Leap Forward campaign in 1958, when the nation was engaged in efforts to boost agricultural output and the number of industrial plants, educational institutions and related facilities such as child care centres. However, with the failure of the campaign all fronts of the economy contracted. A period of restoration followed, but not for too long. In 1966, the Cultural Revolution broke out. It was a dark period in contemporary Chinese history. Irrational party faction wars marked those 10 years. Innocent people and practices had political labels imposed upon them and were condemned. From roughly 1976 onwards, the country took a more pragmatic turn. It is against this background that the stories of the women in this study were told.

The Routes of Women from Three Generations in China

All the women in this study managed to combine family and career. In this sense they constitute a successful demonstration of a state policy that encourages women's participation in education and the economy. In this section we examine what personal costs women paid for coping with the demands on them as producers and reproducers.

The Transition from School to Work

The life-lines show that regardless of generation, all the women I studied joined the work force after graduation from university. The age of graduation varied. The life-lines of the women educated before 1949 show a greater diversity in age of entry to university than those who went to university after

1960. They entered at younger ages, and within a great age range, from 15 to 20. There was greater uniformity among those who entered university in the late 1950s and early 1960s. After the Communist Revolution, the education system was under central state control and, at least in the cities, there was fixed age of starting primary school. With the exception of Du, who came from the countryside, where children often started school late, and was 22 when she reached college, they entered college at the ages of 18 or 19. Thus they mostly graduated in their early 20s. Diversity crept back among the women who attended university during or after the Cultural Revolution. Most of their childhood and adolescent years had been disrupted. University was a remote dream. Except for two (Hong and Jin), higher education was inaccessible until the national college and university entrance exam was reinstated in 1977. Many of the women in this study who entered university after 1977 had passed the standard age of 18 or 19, thus they graduated late. The life-lines show that, in spite of individual difference, there was a pattern in each cohort of women here which was largely shaped by external events.

While the life-lines illustrate a smooth transition from school to work, the process was more frustrating for the older group of women. Many reported having found work of sorts, but often had to settle for low paid jobs that did not promise much of a future. Only after 1949 did they manage to land professional jobs, thanks to a policy of centralized government placement which was not overtly discriminatory. In contrast, the two younger groups of women met less discouragement in initial employment. For by their time, the central job allocation system had been firmly in place. School leavers were as a rule allocated to work places.

Marriage

With few exceptions, marriage took place after completion of education. The women in this study married late by Chinese standards. In China the average age at first marriage of women was 18.4 in the 1940s, 19 in the 1950s, 19.8 in the 1960s, 21.6 in the 1970s, and 23 in the 1980s (Zhu, 1985, p. 12). The urban average has always been higher than the rural average (ibid., Banister, 1987, p. 156). The life-lines here show that most of the women who attended university in the 1940s married in their mid to late 20s. In a society which expected married women to assume full, traditional responsibilities as wives and mothers, marriage and pursuing a university education was incompatible. Completion of education at this level would necessarily have a deterrent effect on marriage. Typically, the women in the older group had worked for a few years before marriage. The women who attended university around 1960 tended to graduate at the age of 22 or 23, work for a few years, then marry in their mid to late 20s. The women who attended university in the 1970s also married rather late, but within a relatively narrow age range, from 25 to 29. Usually marriage took place immediately or shortly after graduation. The Cultural Revolution meant that they were denied university until after age 20. They were in their mid to late 20s by graduation. Some of them reported that before entering university, they already had a close boyfriend. Because of the regulation prohibiting student marriage, they had to wait until after graduation.

Thus, the marriage ages of the women in this study acted independently of the rising national trend. It remained similar for the women from the 1940s to the 1980s. Higher education has kept these women from early marriage. The link between the two is particularly clear among the women who attended university after 1949, when student marriage was not tolerated. Mid to late 20s remained a typical age bracket of marriage for the women regardless of the age at which they graduated. This suggests that higher education always delays marriage and that it has not changed.

Fertility

The women's life-lines show a direct link between age of marriage and age of having the first child. Because of late marriage, most of the women had their first child within two years after marriage. A few had their first child three or four years after marriage. The pattern was similar among the three generations. The only exceptions were two women who graduated in the 1960s. They had their first child six and eight years, respectively, after marriage. Political upheavals appeared to be part of the reason for the delay. For several years after marriage, they lived apart from their husbands and did not have children until they were together.

Another characteristic of these women was low fertility. Their fertility rates stood in sharp contrast to the national rates. The average fertility of women in China were 5.44 in the 1940s, 5.87 in the 1950s, 5.68 in the 1960s, 4.01 in the 1970s, and 2.24 in the 1980s (Zhu 1985, pp. 12–13; Guojia, 1987, p. 29). The fertility pattern in this study confirms evidence from another study which shows that the higher the level of mother's education, the lower their fertility (Banister, 1987, p. 142). The three generations differed only in minor ways. Most of the women who attended university in the 1940s had one to three children. One of them explained that she was so busy with work that she dared not consider having a second child. Others pointed out that unlike most less educated Chinese, intellectuals did not desire many children. Only two women in this group had four and five children respectively. They had the most children of any of the women in the entire study here, but they still had fewer children than the national average.

Individual difference narrowed among the women who attended university around 1960. Half of them had each one child, the rest had two. Apart from the fact that intellectuals were open about having fewer children, their low fertility was related to career demands, economic restraints and political instability. What two women reported was typical in this group. One woman said that:

> I only have one child. . . . children demand a lot of time. Our wages are very low, and we are too busy with work. We don't have the time or energy to raise many children.

Another woman recalled that:

> I have one child because I married late. I was busy with my work then . . . Having one child was tough enough. It was during the Cultural Revolution, life was rough.

The women who attended university in the 1970s also had low fertility, but for a different reason. They each had one child. This was a direct result of legislation. In 1979 the one-child per couple policy was introduced which aimed at curtailing population growth. None of these women expressed strong discontent with the policy, and they attributed a more open attitude in this regard to their education and urban residence. In sum, the three generations of women in this study resembled each other in low fertility, which was largely affected by their education and work force participation. However, political and economic considerations, which varied according to the times, also contributed to their low fertility.

Women's Coping Strategies

How did the women in this study balance professional and domestic roles? The housework situation was crucial. It differed for the three groups of women. The older group were the most fortunate. The most exhausting phase of their lives, when as mothers of young children they had to work full-time, coincided with a lenient government policy on the hiring of domestic helpers. Therefore, for most of the time, housework did not impose too heavy a load. Nevertheless, they still had to care for the family and manage the house. As one of them said:

> Female comrades' burdens are particularly heavy. Even when you have a maid, you still have to tell her what food to buy. You have to plan family finance, to take care of clothing, to knit sweaters and to sew clothes. This is all female comrades' work.

During the Cultural Revolution, hiring domestic help was condemned as 'capitalist'. The women in this study who attended university in the late 1950s and early 1960s had young children at this time. They had to make do with whatever help was available. For example:

> After my child was born, my situation was very bad. Whenever I look back on those days, I burst into tears. My wages were low. I was ill. I did not have housing. I stayed at the place of a lady who used to be a maid. My husband

lived in (College) in Beijing. I woke up early every morning to face a busy day. I nursed the baby, then went to work. At noon I ate in the mess hall and immediately after went home to nurse the baby. After work, I had supper in the mess hall, then went home to nurse the baby. In the evening I went to school again to mark the students' assignments, and did not go home until 8 or 9 pm.

Another woman recalled similar hardship:

During the Cultural Revolution life was very rough. The minute you were informed, you had to roll up your blanket at once and leave for labour camp in rural areas. Once my maternity leave was over, I had to go to the rural areas. I left the baby with her grandma. I was not transferred back to my teaching post in Beijing until the baby reached the age of 2. When her grandma was ill and hospitalized, I did not know what to do with the baby. I had to work during the day and take part in political meetings in the evening. The nursery refused to take her. The only solution was to leave her at the home of a housewife. My daughter was 11 years old when she came home to live with me and my husband.

To these women, child birth highlighted their difficulty in combining work at home with work for a wage. Motherhood rather than wifehood caused them most stress. However, intellectual status (i.e. being educated) was the ultimate source of their suffering. The problem was aggravated when they were poor and when state-provided child care facilities had shrunk. That they went on with work meant that they had to make huge sacrifices in family life. Like the women who attended university in pre-Liberation China, they stayed in the work force. However, this was only possible at the expense of their family life.

The situation had improved when the women who attended university in the 1970s reached child bearing age. The ban on hiring maids had been lifted. But being relatively junior in their professions, these women usually could not afford a maid. A few were able to do so because they had additional income from moonlighting or support from their parents. Of the women I studied in this age group, only one had a full-time maid. The others had to rely on elderly relatives or to leave their babies at the homes of housewives. Their children were sent to day nurseries when they reached age 2 or 3.

Therefore, while all three generations of women remained in the work force, they managed their household situations differently. Since professional women were torn between demands from work and family, husbands had to help out. What was the nature of such help? Many of the women who attended university around 1960 and in the 1970s at first gave the impression that husband and wife shared the housework, but what they revealed later indicated that women still shouldered most of the housework and that there was a sex role division of labour. For example, a woman who attended university in the late 1950s reported a division of labour in the home which emerged time and again in the other interviews in this study.

What clothing the children need, what to buy for them is all my responsibility. The meals are my responsibility. He [her husband] buys food and I cook it. It's almost like the male being responsible for the work outside and the female inside.

A woman who went to university in the late 1970s reported similarly. At first she said that she and her husband shared housework:

My husband and I share the housework. The one who comes home first does the work. Most couples are like this, because female comrades have a job too.

Then she hastily added that:

Of course, I have a heavier share. Generally I cook and clean up the place, and he does the laundry. Probably he does grocery shopping more often than I do.

These descriptions do not quite support the women's statement that 'the two of us share the housework'. Rather, they show that housework was heavier for wives. The sex role division of housework was also rigid. Caring and cooking remained largely women's work; light duties, e.g. washing machine laundry, and tasks outside the home, such as grocery shopping, were men's work. Such a division sounds like a modern version of the traditional Chinese saying which sets boundaries for males and females: 'men are responsible for affairs outside the home and females for affairs inside it'.

Even though husbands did less housework, some of them complained. As one woman who attended university around 1960 said:

Sometimes male intellectuals hope their wives will do all the housework so that life is easier for them and they can concentrate on their careers. But we [educated women] do not want to give up our careers either. My husband certainly feels his work is affected. He is upset about it, but then there is no alternative.

A woman who attended university in the late 1970s reported a similar conflict.

My husband helps a little, but once he has to do a bit more he is unhappy. I think most Chinese men are like that. Model husbands? There may be a few, but too few. In intellectual families men at least help a bit — buy food etc. . . . They are actually unwilling to do it, but they have to.

Therefore, progress for these women in schooling and employment has not been matched by parallel progress in the domestic sphere. When a wife does most of the housework and her husband helps to some extent, she is appreciative; but when he takes up even the lesser share of housework, he complains. Educational attainment and a career have not fundamentally changed the traditional expectations of wives. On the other hand, these women, to some extent, had internalized these values. That they seemed thankful when husbands helped reveals that they accepted being assigned a secondary status.

Status at Work

Given the unequal distribution of family responsibilities, how did the women in this study, who usually had similar qualifications as their husbands, fare in the workplace? They generally felt that there was no discrimination in promotion. The perceptions differed little in this regard among the generations. Only two women who attended university in the late 1970s were vaguely aware of discrimination. They said earlier in the interviews that they were not discriminated against at work, but revealed later that 'yes, male doctors are favoured in promotion' or 'when our bank sends staff abroad for training, it considers male colleagues first'. Even so, they pointed it out as a general phenomenon and seemed reluctant to associate it with their personal situation. The equality that the women in this study readily pointed to referred solely to entry to the work force. Where comparison between husband and wife could be made, these women were inferior to their husbands in job ranking; or, if husband and wife had the same ranking at the time of interview, she had been promoted later than he was. Two reasons accounted for it. First, the husband had more credentials. Few husbands in this study started with higher qualifications than their wives. However, some of them obtained a second degree at some point in their professional lives. Their wives did not have a second degree, or they earned it at a later time. Second, when a husband and wife had equal credentials throughout, the husband tended to be promoted earlier. Preference for men in the work world mostly led by male bosses must have largely accounted for this. As far as our study is concerned, uneven housework division was also responsible for it. Its effect at the household level explained how eventually it would lead to disparate career futures for husband and wife. The observations of a woman who attended university in the 1970s illustrate this point.

> Our split arises mainly from housework. He doesn't do any work at home, but tells his friends that he does this and that. If occasionally he does a little housework, it's because he can't avoid it, but he's unwilling. Well, I don't want to do it either, but I have to . . . He thinks because I am female, I have to do housework . . . That's why I say that in China it is very difficult to be a good female intellectual. Many of my classmates have become like housewives. They cook and wash clothes everyday [after work]. All they aim at in the workplace is to get by. They do not expect to have a successful career.

Ironically, although most of the women in the study rated themselves on an equal footing with their husbands, some of them had internalized the idea of male superiority in society. For example, while resenting her husband's chauvinism at home, a woman who went to university in the 1940s said:

> I do not want to make my husband do a lot of work at home. It will make him a good-for-nothing. After all men are more important in society.

Another woman, who went to university in the 1970s, was bitter about the load forced on her at home.

> I have to do housework. If I just concentrate on my career and neglect my family, society will exert pressure on me. When I attended university I was among the competent students. Once I had a child, I lagged behind my former classmates. They have published articles and even books. They are mostly men. My husband helps a bit, but if you ask him to do a little more housework, he is unhappy. I think most Chinese men are like him.

Yet later this woman said:

> I hope my husband is stronger than me in his career and gets promoted earlier than me, so as to compensate for my loss in this aspect . . . I don't want to sacrifice my career, but I must not proceed too fast, for one of us must take care of our family.

Thus, the degree to which presence in the work force represents an upward move in women's status begs more careful investigation.

Conclusion

The life stories of the women in my study demonstrate that for almost over a half century in China, change in access to opportunities in the public sphere for women as a group was evident in areas that public policy can reach. This was reflected in the new situations for women brought about by structural change in the political and economic contexts. However, in areas where public policy cannot readily penetrate, such as gender relations in the family, the benefits from expanded access to education and to paid work were less clear. The fundamental nature of gender roles, which are rooted in the socio-cultural context, persists in the family, and in a less conspicuous way, in the workplace. The mismatch between the results of reform in public and private spheres rendered the assessment of policy effectiveness a multidimensional issue. The life-lines and in-depth interviewing offer a fresh perspective to understanding the complexities in pushing for a qualitative shift in gender roles. They enable us to see the intersections of different influences on women's realities: those that affect women as a group (e.g. gender-based division of labour), and those that distinguish one subgroup of women from the rest (e.g. higher education). Therefore, while the women in this study formed a collective profile to some extent, they were different in some aspects from the majority of women in China. This combination of similarity and difference is also found among different generations of women, and among individual women. The data from the study reveal the contradictions between the measurable status of women and the perpetuation of patriarchy at work and in the family. Each life story, while unique, is also common. The personal is also collective. Together they present an eloquent plea for an alternative approach to assessing policy effectiveness.

References

BANISTER, J. (1987) *China's Changing Population*, Stanford: Stanford University Press.

BERTAUX, D. (1990) 'Oral history approaches to an international social movement', in OYEN, E. (ed.) *Comparative Methodology*, London: Sage.

BOSERUP, E. (1970) *Women's Role in Economic Development*, New York: St Martin.

CHINCHILLA, N.S. (1977) 'Industrialization, monopoly capitalism, and women's work in Guatemala', *Signs*, **3**, pp. 38–56.

ELGQVIST-SALTZMAN, I. (1986a) 'Swedish educational reforms: Women's life stories, what can they tell about a rational reform era?', Paper presented at the conference of the American Educational Research Association in 1986.

ELGQVIST-SALTZMAN, I. (1986b) *The Life-history Approach — A Tool in Establishing North–South Education Research Cooperation?*, Umeå, Sweden: Umeå Universitet, Pedagogiska Institutionen, Arbetsrapport nr. 32.

ELGQVIST-SALTZMAN, I. (1988) 'Educational Reforms: Women's Life Patterns; a Swedish case study', *Higher Education*, **17**, pp. 491–504.

GUOJIA TONGJIJU SHEHUI TONGJISI (SOCIAL STATISTICS SECTION, STATE STATISTICAL BUREAU) (1987) *Zhongguo Shehui Tongji Ziliao* (Social Statistics of China), Beijing: Zhongguo tongji chubanshe.

ROGERS, B. (1980) *The Domestication of Women*, London: Tavistock.

SMOCK, A.C. (1982) 'Sex differences in educational opportunities and labor force participation in six countries', in ALTBACH, P., ARNOVE, R. and KELLY, G. (eds) *comparative Education*, New York: Macmillan.

THOMPSON, P. (1978) *The Voice of the Past*, Oxford: Oxford University Press.

ZHU, C. (1985) 'Social development and the female population in China', *Renkou Xuekan* (Population Studies) **3**, pp. 1–7.

12   Doppler Effects: Female Frequencies in Higher Education

Kerstin W. Shands

That which you are, that only can you read (Bloom, 1975, p. 96)

Contexts

Dipping my pen in the ink of epistemology as I begin to formulate this essay, I suddenly notice other, peripherally placed sources out of which different patterns rise. As I study the charts of pedagogic theory, episodes and memories from my own life and those of other women I have known begin to unfold. I remember my grandmother. When she was young, her dream was to become a teacher. Her brothers would be receiving education in engineering or accounting or some such field; for her, the dream was to be accepted at the teachers' seminary. She had prepared for the entrance exam (I believe the brothers helped procure the books) — and she had been accepted! My great-grandmother, however, seems not to have been at all cognizant of these plans. When she found out, her response was to fling the books into the fire. Girls were not to waste time on books, they were to marry: this was the incontestable bottom line.

For me, this episode is a personal heritage. But it also points to a particular link between ontology and epistemology in women's lives. In this essay, I examine some of the ways in which women's educational possibilities and women's ways of knowing differ from those of men and what consequences this might have for higher education. My perspective will be informed both by thoughts of women inside or outside — welcomed into or excluded from — higher education, and by my own experiences as a woman travelling from passionate undergraduate classrooms of lively debate to the more disembodied and abstract, self-reflexive and self-ironic, postgraduate sphere of theoretical 'sophistication.' My reflections, which will shuttle between American and Swedish contexts, will be influenced by readings in women's psychology, feminist theory, and university pedagogics.

If we want to improve our teaching, it is crucial to study how university students learn. What different stages do they go through during their years of higher education — and beyond? William Perry's 1970's map of the typical epistemological 'Pilgrim's Progress . . . Slough of Despond and all' which found that 'every student . . . spoke from some place or "position" on this journey' (1988, p. 150), weeded out the few answers it culled from women students, so it tells us nothing as to whether there were gender differences to the pilgrims' ways of learning. A hypothesis in feminist theory, however, is that the process of learning itself is gendered, that is, linked to what it means to be a man or a woman in patriarchal society.

We may of course have divergent views on what that means. However, I argue that whatever the differences are, they will affect men's and women's learning. There are both obvious and 'invisible' aspects that influence women's epistemological development, consciously or unconsciously. For example, most women I know have been exposed to some form of harassment, ranging from rape to more 'harmless' ways of invading women's spaces and keeping women in their place. The idea that women could subject men to similar behaviour is unthinkable outside comedies of sex role reversal.

The message conveyed by various shades of harassment is that women are objects, spaces to be invaded. But the notion that women are objects to be gazed at by male subjects is fatal when transferred to a situation of learning and scholarship. If women are objects, they belong to the same category as the scientific objects classified by male scientists, and for women to cross over to being scientific subjects is not necessarily effortless. This binary hierarchism of subject–object may affect women's pursuit of knowledge in negative and obstructive ways whether or not an individual woman has been harassed. A majority of women are not harassed; a majority of men do not harass. However, the defensive awareness of the unpalatable possibility may put internalized, although 'invisible,' restraints on women academics. Furthermore, it is important to recognize that sexual harassment — whose key characteristic is that it is *unwanted* — constitutes a form of misuse of male power.

Due to proclivities or contexts, then, many women do take somewhat different paths on their journeys toward insight and learning. My central theses in this essay will be that epistemological and psychological development is inextricably linked in both men and women, and that this development is to some extent gender related. Traditionally, a masculine model has been applied to both genders, to the detriment of both. I believe that we must look more closely at women's developmental processes and determine how they differ from those of men, as well as how those differences affect women's *and* men's ways of knowing. We know that women's ways of knowing are affected by academic androcentricity. But how is the academy affected by women's ways of knowing? Or, should it be? I will submit that not only do women lose out from the monopoly of super-rational and objectivist, nationalistic and universalistic, scientific ideals of classical Aristotelian logic: men's scholarly achievements, too, will be impoverished if they are too masculinist, i.e. if they exclude an openness to learning about women's experiences of, attitudes toward, and methods of learning. Whenever it remains deaf to female frequencies, there is a closed quality to the masculinist perspective in academic scholarship, since it thinks that its work is exhaustive and comprehensive — 'universal' — it is uninterested in listening to other voices such as feminist ones.

Perhaps these voices could be compared to doppler effects? The doppler effect involves 'the apparent change of frequency of sound waves or light waves, varying with the relative velocity of the source and the observer: if the source and observer are drawing closer, the frequency is increased' (*Webster's Dictionary*). The sounds of women in the academy could be conveyed metaphorically in terms of doppler effects, with female (or feminist) frequencies appearing more shrill the closer they come to the academic center point, and distorted as they move away from that center — sound stretching out to become oblique and increasingly unhearable. In *Women's Ways of Knowing: The Development of Self, Voice, and Mind*, Belenky, Clinchy, Goldberger and Tarule (1986) make a distinction between what they call separate and connected knowing. While the voices of separate knowing, favored by the academy, are eminently hearable, the voices of connected knowing are less audible — because we are not tuned in to their frequencies.

Experience

An appeal to 'women's experience' as unquestionably linked to pedagogical development may seem an unproblematic fusion of ontology with epistemology, and it does represent an unavoidable dilemma in feminist pedagogy pointing to the essentialist–constructionist debates in feminist theory. While in the initial stages of the most recent wave of feminism an appeal to experience seemed indispensable, poststructuralist feminism has questioned commonsensical ideas of 'experience' along with concepts such as 'identity,' 'truth,' and 'politics' as based on a metaphysics of presence. If, as Diana Fuss has put it, 'the appeal to experience, as the ultimate test of all knowledge, merely subtends the subject in its fantasy of autonomy and control,' then it is easy to see why feminist theory in the earlier stage saw experience as particularly empowering, since autonomy and control was precisely what women most seemed to lack. Experience, in classical, Aristotelian thinking seen as 'the doorway to the apprehension of essence' and consequently 'understood as a real and immediate presence and therefore a reliable means of knowing' (Fuss, 1989, p. 114), is a dangerous measuring-rod since it creates an inside/outside metaphor. Yet, however displaceable and fleeting, experience is difficult to keep outside of feminist pedagogy. Perhaps experience needs to be continually posited, yet continually questioned. In this vein, we could call it experience-in-flux.

Looking at 'women's experience' with Pierre Bourdieu's concept of habitus, i.e. certain dispositions of thought, expression and behavior, one might argue that women, in sharing certain economic and social circumstances, share a habitus — a term I find rich in associations: it suggests place (to inhabit, a habitat), habit (inclination, tendency, routine, proclivity, disposition), as well as fashion, i.e. wearing a particular dress or habit. One acquires a habitus through practical experience of a certain field, writes Toril Moi, who explains field, another of Bourdieu's key terms, as a social structure — or battlefield — characterized by competition. The goal for the players in this *espace de jeu* (Bourdieu's term) is to gain a maximum of power over the field and over legitimation, i.e. the accepted — although not openly acknowledged — praxis of the field. Since any player must play by the rules or be rejected, a field also has a censuring function which Bourdieu connects with what he calls symbolic violence, the unarticulated violence that keeps certain classes or groups in place. Such censuring functions within the field of the academy has much to do, I think, with the weaving of a heavy, womanly habitus of silence and service. At the same time, however, silence and service are *positive* elements in high-quality learning and teaching that men, in particular, need to (re)learn.

Classrooms: Dialogue, Silence, Listening

Perhaps it should not come as a surprise that women graduate students distrust their intellectual capacity more often than men and feel less at home in the academy. During my years in graduate school, I observed how male seminar leaders habitually — although quite unconsciously, I'm sure — turned to their male graduate students in gestures of affirmation and recognition so subtle as to go virtually unnoticed, but which function to reinforce male students' sense of worth at the same time as it diminishes that of women graduate students, whose achievements are more often ignored or 'forgotten' — made invisible (see also Almlöv, 1997).

While women have always been active participants in the creation and maintenance of culture, religion and society, the official injunction from the days of St Paul has been that they remain silent. Not surprisingly, silence seems to echo throughout women's writings, formally and thematically, as suggested by titles such as Tillie Olsen's (1965) *Silences*. In women's writings, silence becomes sonority and sorority. In reflections on women's attitudes to learning and culture and of culture's attitude to women and learning, it is interesting to see human world-making as taking place through ongoing conversations with others. Culture is produced collectively and dialectically through our participation in a never-ending dialogue with the world. If we think of culture this way, the dimensions of women's oppression becomes even more clear — or more audible — as does the importance of the imagery of listening, hearing and silence, in feminist epistemology. It is with a marginal and anomic sphere of silence, cut off from the conversation of culture, that Woman has been identified. In not *fully* receiving the female frequencies, in denying women full participation in culture-producing conversation, the academy is still denying women full humanity.

There is now ample research documenting women's sense of not being heard and of not gaining respect for what they have in fact achieved as well as their difficulties in recognizing their own achievements and acting assertively and authoritatively on that basis. There are two 'worlds' in terms of how we use language in public: roughly speaking, men talk and women listen. Perhaps, as Marguerite Duras suggests, men need to learn how to be silent, so that they can hear more:

> Yes, these prating men were up to their old tricks during May '68. They are the ones who started to speak, to speak alone and for everyone else, on behalf of everyone else, as they put it. They immediately forced women and extremists to keep silent. They activated the old language, enlisted the aid of the old way of theorizing, in order to relate, to recount, to explain this new situation: May '68. (cited in Eagleton, 1991)

Perhaps many of us need to learn how to *super-listen*. People who believe that they already know how to listen may possess vast, underutilized dimensions of hearing unknown to themselves. Improving our listening, according to pioneering music therapy, helps remove psychological blockages and makes the energy flux to the brain and the nervous system flow more freely, opening doors to inner worlds. It is only when we have come quite far in this development that we are able to hear silence.

Female Frequencies

As has been suggested here, women take slightly different routes to learning. At a certain time in their lives, for example, many women pass through a particular stage of communion or attentive love that I call symbiotic friendship, a passage which I believe is of both epistemological and psychological importance. In symbiotic friendship, one merges into a total sharing of the trifling and the sublime. Were they to last forever, symbiotic friendships would no doubt constitute a cosy form of stagnation. However, I would argue that the *passage* through this stage of profound mutuality can be extremely empowering to women, since, through the incessant dialogue, women do eventually find their own voices, grow out of an unquestioned dependence on authorities and begin to move toward an acceptance of ambiguity, plurality and paradox, all of which is of vast significance for learning.

In its final stages, moreover, symbiotic friendship might offer a chance of a deeper acquaintance of one's shadow. Towards the end of a symbiotic friendship, one might take a great dislike to certain personality traits exhibited by one's friend — traits which one might do well to look for within oneself. For individuation to occur, the shadow must be recognized, not denied or repressed. The conscious and the unconscious must cooperate. Potentially, then, this stage of symbiotic friendship might offer insights into less pleasant levels of one's self but an exploration of which is of utmost significance for one's epistemological development as well.

Symbiotic friendships also pose a threat to growth in their powerful checking mechanisms which react to differentiation, since they demand merging, not distancing. This problem can be seen in the light of the affiliation vs. achievement conflict much discussed in feminist theory. Success, for many women, is linked to loss: women feel that they cannot achieve success without in some way being punished or having to pay for it. Harriet Goldhor Lerner (1989) writes that 'feelings of depression and anxiety, as well as self-sacrificing and self-sabotaging behaviors, are common ways that women apologize for their competence and success on the one hand, or ensure the lack of it on the other' (p. 172). For many women, then, achievement and success can be highly anxiety-provoking, since in patriarchal society the two units, affiliation and achievement, are set up as dichotomous parts of an insoluble equation. One relationship that is central to women's way of knowing is the mother–daughter relationship. Many of our mothers were housewives who gave up their career aspirations in order to be the best mothers and wives they could be — and they were phenomenal, powerhouses of domestic zeal. As we, the daughters, stand before doors of opportunity not open to our mothers, we feel a vague sense of guilt for moving into areas they could not explore, finding levels of fulfilment denied them, all of which seems to deny our affiliation with them. Tillie Olsen (1965) writes: 'How many of us who are writers have mothers, grandmothers, of limited education; awkward, not at home, with the written word, however eloquent they may be with the spoken one? Born a generation or two before, we might have been they' (p. 208).

Other central relationships, in which the affiliation–achievement equation might appear equally daunting, are those with lovers, husbands, and children. If you gain affiliation, you will not reach real achievement, this equation says, or, alternatively, if you choose achievement, you will lose out on what is most important in life: you will miss out on the deepest satisfaction a woman can know. Feeding into this equation are both obvious and subtle stipulations and heritages. Many women still have Ellen Key's admonitions in *The Renaissance of Motherhood* (1970) in their heads: 'During the child's first seven years, years that determine its whole life, its educator cannot well fulfil her mission without having a daily opportunity to observe the child's nature, in order by consistent action to influence it, encouraging certain tendencies and restraining others. This alone precludes the mother's working outside the home' (p. 133). The conflicts and difficulties in combining motherhood and work outside the home are, still, constantly reiterated in women's magazines, those publications so despised by men but whose articles, in my view, in traditional and radical ways, reveal much about where the real dilemmas for contemporary women lie. Since men seem not to need articles entitled 'will fatherhood jeopardize your career?' they can afford to sneer at the advice proffered in the women's press.

Looking back, I realize that it took me years to reach what seemed then like the heroic decision to complete my dissertation while opting for pregnancy and motherhood at the same time. More than anything, I wanted a baby. Conceivably less conscious, my desire to pursue graduate studies was, as it turned out, equally strong. Apparently irreconcilable, the two impulses were exasperated by the double doppler effects of both biological and career clocks. In a surreal dream I remember from this time, I was glancing at my watch when suddenly, to my utter surprise, I noticed that the hands of the watch were moving faster and faster until they jumped out of the watch and fluttered away, like butterflies! Why, then, was this such a difficult decision? Probably in part because I was still in a dualistic stage, viewing alternatives dichotomously, but also because society itself was — and still is — in a dualistic stage as regards this dilemma. Moreover, I was living in America, where the difficulties of combining scholarship and maternity appear to be even greater than in Sweden. To a large extent, I had realistically assessed the costs of being flex time doctoral student and daytime mother of a super-high-energy toddler. Of course, despite the exhaustion, I was right about the rewards.

Doppler Effects

I made a metaphorical use of the doppler effect above. Doppler effects have to do with the faculty of hearing, and can thus be linked to a central imagery in feminist epistemology which persistently refers to hearing, listening, gaining a voice of one's own and being heard. While the voice of Western masculinist philosophy has been droning on and on, enveloping (or drowning) any outside voices, the voice of feminine or feminist discourse has barely been heard above the excessive volume of patriarchy, neither to the dominant voice nor to itself, appearing a mere irritant coming from an imprisoned interior, a kind of tinnitus or reverberation which becomes all the more clamorous in silence. Metaphorically speaking, our old analogue system of broadcasting needs to be replaced by a digital system allowing both for superior sound quality although using up less energy *and* for a larger number of co-existing channels, as well as, due to the improved reception, increased mobility on the part of the listeners.

The question has been raised in feminist theory whether there are significant differences between masculine and feminine ways of seeing, hearing and knowing, differences we might detect in or impose on our employment of metaphors (such as hardware and software, hard sciences and soft humanities). Descriptions of men's ways of knowing — or *proving* that they know — have traditionally been riddled with battle metaphors. Up to the Renaissance, rhetoric was a principal subject, oratory constituting a fundamental paradigm for both verbal and written presentations, with written material being merely viewed as a support for the listener's attention. The very words 'disputation,' 'opponent,' 'defense' (of one's dissertation) reveal an antagonistic, territorial, possessive and conflictual attitude to scholarly exchange. Feminist critics have written about how most of us have been trained in traditions of critical one-upmanship, traditions feminist scholars need not adopt. I would even suggest that the usual academic persiflage and self-irony not infrequently camouflage, albeit in elegantly amiable ways, inhibited antagonistic and competitive impulses. Harold Bloom's (1973) way of describing intergenerational rivalries and competition among male artists in *The Anxiety of Influence* could be applied to the masculine academic establishment as well. Bloom perceives a battle for comeuppance fought by the ambitious sons affirming their independence from and superiority over the great fathers of literature. This sceptical stance could be related to what Belenky et al. (1986) have called separate knowing, a mode of knowing fundamentally adversarial in form. It is also a self-suppressive form of knowing: the self of the scientist is cleaned out of the picture.

Women scholars are sometimes accused of having poor self-confidence, of not being assertive enough or standing up for themselves, a notion which — whether correct or not — could be related to women's greater empathy and wish to avoid unnecessarily hurting others. Scholars often tend toward one epistemological stance or another: differentiation, impersonality and distance, on the one hand, or mutuality, interdependence, empathy and participation, on the other. Empathy means entering into a different realm of thought and seeing things from another person's perspective. The more over-autonomous and superindividuated an individual is, the greater his or her difficulty in doing this. But empathy, defined as above, may be the greatest asset a person can have in terms of learning. Because isn't that what profound learning, as opposed to surface approaches, is all about: removing certain barriers and entering into *other* perspectives?

Remedies

When the social democrats came back to power in Sweden in the fall of 1994, they promised to attack the problem of inequality with renewed force. Carl Tham, Minister of Education, recommended some form of affirmative action at Swedish universities in order to appoint more women professors. One suggestion has been to create a position as professor for women who have applied for such a position and been rejected, despite the recognition of their competence. However, even though the effects of such a measure would be negligible, the number of such women being in reality quite small, only eight per cent of male university teachers are in favour of such an idea; instead, surveys show that a majority of men are against compensatory measures to increase equality — an attitude which reveals a total unawareness of how men themselves, all the time, are appointed to high positions through an unrecognized praxis of affirmative action which favours even the most mediocre male scholars (Wennerås and Wold, 1995). Men who have never lifted a finger to combat discrimination against women blanch at the very possibility that they themselves might be discriminated against.

So how can we achieve the changes necessary to create a radically new kind of university where women and men are equals? To begin with, teacher

training should address the issue of women's ways of learning more specifically and challenge androcentric assumptions. It has been said that if we pro-
ceed at the pace we have had so far, it will take around eight hundred years to
achieve full equality in higher education. Is affirmative action an option? Would
men do well to adopt more 'feminine' ways of knowing? My answer to both
questions is yes — but with decided reservations. As to the idea of affirmative
action, society seems to have found nothing wrong with it so far: men, after
all, have been favored by preferential treatment of themselves for as long as
we can remember — and they still are saluting friendships with each other
sported through informal, old-boys networks and intradepartmental buddyships.
So why not introduce some affirmative action on behalf of women? By all
means. However, we must keep in mind that affirmative action can only be a
temporary measure, necessary only for as long as the present inequality persists. Yet, I see dangers in focusing too much on the pros and cons of affirmative action, since such a discussion can veil more pressing issues, such as
whether or not women applying for academic positions are evaluated in fair
ways and in accordance with the principles for evaluation that already exist.
The whole discussion around affirmative action may obscure academic power
plays and reaffirm myths of meritocracy. My point is that if basic biases are
done away with, affirmative action may prove entirely unnecessary. Thus,
even before we consider affirmative action, we must examine whether men
and women scholars are really and truly given the same chance at all the
echelons of the educational pyramid. A recent study in Sweden shows that this
is still far from the case: in medicine, there is a broad, easy lane for men where
one out of four arrive at research positions, and a narrow, difficult one for
women, where one out of twenty arrive at such a position. In other words, it is
easier for mediocre male scholars to obtain research positions than for women
of excellence, according to Christine Wennerås and Agnes Wold. Pierre Bourdieu's theories may shed a light on this situation. In his view, the educational
system is one of the main factors in the reproduction of symbolic violence.
Since women lack what he calls social capital to a larger extent than men do,
they need to compensate by accumulating even more educational capital if
they want to advance in their careers.

Women's knowledge has historically pertained to areas that have been
suppressed in our rationalistic Western world, such as the knowledge of
medicinal herbs. Today, certain aspects of women's ways of knowing may
constitute remedial strategies in a male-dominated academic world. If women's
ways of knowing involve different, super-listening rather than battle-oriented
ways of approaching knowledge, they may very well coincide with what alternative methods in pedagogy point to as highly efficient ways of acquiring knowledge. In that case, Swedish education, still incongruously marked both by a
hierarchical order initially modelled on the armed forces and the church on the
one hand and by the organization of the industrial society with its conveyor
belts on the other — impersonal and rationalistic assembly-line-arrangements
that are outdated and inefficient, even anti-functional, when applied to learning

processes — might do well to learn from women's approaches to learning, although without idealizing or glorifying such approaches.

However, a celebration of 'feminine' ways of knowing can be a dangerous tightrope walking on the borderline to essentializing ideologies which traditionally have no particular interest in furthering women's entry into the male ivory towers. This is why we cannot fall wholesale into the potential trap of essentializing womanlore. It is not a reason that needs to be jettisoned, after all, but the kind of reason that is severed from feeling.

The low percentages of women higher up the academic ladder is not a phenomenon that can be isolated from the total context which includes the situation of women students on the lower levels as well as, even more generally, the situation of women in our society. Women in Sweden and America are in many ways still outside what Gayatri Spivak has called 'the teaching machine', an androcentric educational system which favors masculine interests and ways of learning. In my discussion of symbiotic friendship, however, I suggested that one of its important aspects, from a developmental perspective, is a recognizing, even a welcoming, of one's shadow. In Sweden and America, women have passionately aspired to get into the academy, a passion that has not yet, as it were, been entirely reciprocated by the academy. As a concluding thought I would like to suggest that masculinist Western science would do well to greet — even to lovingly embrace — the shadow of *its* symbiotic friendship: before higher education can be whole, the 'shadow' of Woman must be incorporated into it. Academic frequencies need to be modulated in order for its female voices to be transmitted and received.

References

ALMLÖV, C. (August, 1997). 'Female and male politeness strategies: A study of interaction in advanced research seminars.' Conference paper: The Promised Land: The gendered nature of higher education. Lidingö: Sweden.

BELENKY, M.F., CLINCHY, B.M., GOLDBERGER, N.R. and J.M. TARULE (1986) *Women's Ways of Knowing: The Development of Self, Voice, and Mind*, New York: Basic Books.

BLOOM, H. (1975) *Kabbalah and Criticism*, New York: Seabury.

BLOOM, H. (1973) *The Anxiety of Influence*, New York: Oxford University Press.

EAGLETON, M. (1991) 'Introduction', in EAGLETON, M. (ed.) *Feminist Literary Criticism*, London and New York: Longman (pp. 1–23).

FUSS, D. (1989) 'Essentialism in the classroom', *Essentially Speaking: Feminism, Nature and Difference*, New York: Routledge (pp. 113–19).

KEY, E. (1970) *The Renaissance of Motherhood*, New York and London: GP Putnam's Sons, (Translated by Anna E B Fries). Originally Published in 1914.

LERNER, H.G. (1989) 'Work and success inhibitions', *Women in Therapy*, New York: Harper & Row, (pp. 171–99).

MOI, T. (1994) 'Att Erövra Bourdieu' *Kvinnovetenskaplig Tidskrift*, **1**, pp. 3–25.

OLSEN, T. (1965) *Silences*, New York: Laurel.

PERRY, W. (1988) 'Different worlds in the same classroom', in RAMSDEN, P. (ed.) *Improving Learning: New Perspectives*, London: Kogan Page, (pp. 145–61).

Wennerås, C. and Wold, A. (1995) 'Därför Forskar Inte Kvinnor: Undersöking Visar att Män med Låg eller Obevisad Kompetens Får Deras Forskningstjänster,' *Dagens Nyheter 22*, January, A4.

Part III

Towards the 21st Century

Introduction

This final section reminds us, above all else, of the need for complexity in our analyses as we head towards the 21st century. Both Lyn Yates and Joan Eveline ask us to examine very carefully the categories we use when we write about girls and women in education.

While constructing 'girls' as a disadvantaged group has had important policy results in schools, it can also be seen now to have limited them by seeing them as a homogenous group, often as victims — a claim vigorously disputed by many young women today. Class and ethnicity fracture the category 'girls': while some need significant support, others also claim considerable advantage. Importantly Joan Eveline reminds us that white girls and women often experience advantage undreamed of by indigenous men.

Should we then discard the categories and strategies of modernity? Both Yates and Eveline ask us to undertake a more difficult task: to keep a creative tension between the confrontational strategies of modernity and the ironies and deconstructions of post modernity. At times we can position women as a group, in relation to sexual harassment policies for example. At other times we must be aware of difference, between girls and women of different classes, ethnic groups and religious beliefs.

Kasja Ohrlander's essay, at times tongue-in-cheek, at times more serious, returns us to a theme alluded to throughout the book. How can women's voice be heard within the academy? If women disrupt familiar narratives are they seen as contentious, impertinent, unfeminine? As both Yates and Eveline point out, approaches to a 'girl's way of knowing' can be criticized as reinstating unwanted stereotyping, as being essentialist. This is a different issue, however, than that of hearing women's voices in an environment familiar with the male voice.

We still need to be contentious, impertinent, indeed, at times pugnacious, as we head into the future, while remembering that girls and women are in Yates' words 'complex beings actively constructing a complicated world'.

13 Constructing and Deconstructing 'Girls' as a Category of Concern

Lyn Yates

Since the 1970s, many countries have initiated projects of reform for girls and women in education. Now, at the turn of the century, the media and education policy-makers are beginning to raise new questions about what has taken place. Have the aims of the original reforms been achieved? Have feminist agendas 'gone too far'? Is it boys who now deserve special attention? Should economic agendas replace social concerns in the development of education policy?

In one version of the new questions, we are told that the concerns of women in the 1970s with equal rights and access to education were important, but have now been won, and that young women today are impatient with continued attempts to reform education on their behalf. Women are now successful in education, young women are independent and able to stand up for themselves, and they object to programmes which continue to set them up as a disadvantaged group who are in need of special programmes and protection. Another contemporary account of the debate between generations of women sees almost the opposite dynamic. Here media stories feature well-known older feminists complaining that current campaigns, especially about sexual harassment, are going too far, that the new generation of young feminists is puritanical and vindictive, that young women now pounce on men for the slightest joke or well-intentioned gesture, and subject them to legal processes in which it is up to them to prove their innocence. These women, the articles say, are making life impossible for men, and are feeding a backlash which is beginning to be widely felt.

The debates that are set up in this way are, of course, highly exaggerated. But they do touch on some of the key developments that have taken place in relation to girls, women and education over the last two decades, and they highlight some questions concerning directions for future action:

- In many countries, including Australia, there have been some undoubted achievements of access and retention for girls in education. How are we to acknowledge these successes of girls? Can we do so without accepting that it is really boys who are now the disadvantaged group?

- In setting up special programmes for girls, or procedures to deal with sexual harassment, do we reinforce a view of women as victims, do we perpetuate the relations and subjectivity we are trying to address? Is this what young women are rejecting when they say they do not want feminist reforms in schools?
- How do we acknowledge, and work with, difference among girls and women?
- What is the political and cultural context for girls at school at the turn of the century? How are issues framed for girls when gender reform is not a new issue, but one associated with the mothers' and teachers' generation? How are reform agendas affected by broader changes in the shape of schooling and policy-making?

These questions form the background of this chapter, which is an attempt to revisit developments of gender reform in the last decades of the twentieth century.

Education and Gender Reforms in the Late Twentieth Century

In Australia, we could now tell the story of what took place in these last decades of the twentieth century in a number of different ways (see, for example, Kenway, Willis and Junor, 1995; Yates, 1993a, 1993b; Yates and Leder, 1996). Emphasizing the achievements of feminist reformers, we could note the existence of legislation that enshrines rights of equal access and that outlaws sexual harassment and intimidation; we could cite the considerable resources that have been devoted to this area by governments, the policies and action plans that have been and continue to be enacted; we could refer to the steadily increased retention of girls at school and their increased entry to higher education; their greater participation in senior mathematics subjects; and their increasing success in the final examinations of schooling. The campaigns to persuade girls and their parents that 'Maths multiplies your chances' have had some effect, both on perceptions and on actual patterns of participation in this area.

Or we could tell a more pessimistic story: that, although governments sponsored many programmes and policies 'tagged' for girls and women, these seem relatively marginal in the conduct of education as a whole, and also that the special programmes have been a source of many backlash complaints that there is too much attention to girls and not enough to boys. We could note that mathematics and science have been increasingly promoted as the only measure of what is important knowledge, and could consider the effects of this on women's work and lives. And we could observe that the outcomes of schooling as measured by pay, unpaid labour, and postgraduate patterns show a much smaller degree of improvement for women than one might expect from their improved school success.

The stories we tell, the ways we evaluate what has happened, the contemporary media debates, frequently assume a 'givenness' about girls, women and education as a project of reform, that this has a clear and self-evident character. But a feature of the last decades of the twentieth century has been a shaping and reshaping of what the project of reform related to gender and education has been about. There has been some rethinking of what it means to take 'girls' as a category for attention in education; and also some change in the visions, the types of changes that are emphasized at particular points.

To some extent the different constructions I will outline in this chapter are a linear development: they chart some changes over time in Australian reform policies for the education of girls, which were in turn influenced by changing frameworks and findings of feminist research. But each way of taking up these questions remains an issue for some parts of the debate at the turn of the century. In my discussion then, I will try to show the different constructions not just as a story of progress to an ever more adequate conception. One thing that poststructuralist theorizing of recent years has brought with it is an awareness of how *any* constructions necessarily pick out some interests and silence others, and I will be attempting to show what was important, what was picked out by earlier emphases, as well as what is silenced in later approaches. In the final part of the chapter I will turn to some of the questions now being raised about the future of education reform in the gender area.

Confronting 'Girls' as an Object of Education Reform

First Construction: Girls as Disadvantaged; Girls as 'Equally Human'

In the mid 1970s Australian policy-makers discovered (or rediscovered) the education of girls as a concern for schooling (for details see Yates, 1993a). 'Being a girl', a national report declared, constituted a disadvantage in Australian schools. Girls got a poor deal out of schooling, in that they ended up with a more restricted, lower status, less powerful, and more poorly paid range of higher education and of jobs. The problem, policy-makers declared, was that schools were promoting and reinforcing sex differences, when what they should be doing was treating all students, girls and boys, as equally human; giving all of them similar and wide-ranging careers and subject-choice advice, and learning to see gender or sex difference as something of no consequence for education. This process for 'the elimination of sexism' in schools was often associated with a critique of single-sex schooling, and the promotion of coeducation. The task was to de-emphasize gender, so grouping children by sex was not seen as a good thing. 'Sexism' was seen to mean 'treating girls differently from boys'.

Girls here were able to be constructed as a category for attention in education by reference to some traditional concerns of education policy-making:

patterns of outcome and achievement. But this construction was achievable only because of a second and newer achievement by the Women's Movement: that there was a case to be answered if girls and women were not in the same positions of success, power and public prominence as men. As the 1975 Australian Schools Commission Report, *Girls, School and Society* (p. 8) put it:

> An observer not raised with our cultural assumptions would be struck by the fact that one half of the population was assigned by birth to activities which, whatever their private gratifications and social importance, carried no economic reward, little public status, and very limited access to public power.

So, this era *constructed* girls as a category of concern for education in a way that they had not been previously. It was not that the patterns of girls' success and outcomes of education in this period were worse than they had been previously, quite the reverse. What was being asserted was that sex-differentiated patterns of outcomes were not desirable; and that social factors, especially schools, were the underpinnings of women's difference and inequality. 'Girls' were being treated here as a category that made sense (in some senses, that is, as a unitary category) — but it was a category whose prime use was critique. As learners, girls were being constructed as something of a 'black box': if curriculum and careers advice were made non-sexist, it was assumed a different type of girl would be produced.

Subsequent feminist research found much to criticize about this first construction of 'girls' as a category for education. They noted the lack of attention to differences among girls. In terms of strategies, teachers soon found that the emphasis on messages (curriculum) rather than learners and learning processes, was somewhat lacking. The new kits about 'non-traditional' careers for girls did not instantly win a host of converts. The construction of girls here was neither sensitive to difference, nor to the subjectivity of girls.

But the legacy of this initial construction is powerfully present in the framing of gender debates at the turn of the century. The legacy of debates about 'disadvantage' which compare statistics about a category 'girls' with a category 'boys' are now being used in arguments to regard 'boys' rather than 'girls' as the disadvantaged group. To some extent this new debate selectively picks out the evidence of relative success and exaggerates the changes that have been achieved for girls. Though girls have improved their participation and success in mathematics, boys continue to take and succeed in these subjects and fields in higher numbers; although girls stay at school in larger numbers and are a majority of undergraduates, the meaning of this has changed, as 'women's work' of nursing and teaching has been brought fully into the higher education sector, and as higher education becomes a mass rather than elite achievement (Yates and Leder, 1996). Arguments can still be mounted that school results continue to indicate a 'disadvantaging' of girls (Foster, 1994); or that school 'outcomes' in the sense of future career, income, power have by no means been turned around (Kenway, Willis and Junor, 1995; Yates and Leder,

1996). Nevertheless, increasingly, we have to acknowledge that some forms of discrimination against girls have been addressed; that there have been some changes in patterns of success; and that issues about success and about who is losing at school require attention to *which* girls and *which* boys. This does not mean that a focus on gender is irrelevant: both Teese et al. (1995) and Davy (1995) show gender and class as significantly interactive effects in achievement patterns, not only for girls but also for boys.

This initial reform construction of girls and sexism has also influenced how the generation of students two decades later now see their world (Yates and McLeod, 1996; Kenway and Willis, 1993; Kenway et al., 1993). Young people at the end of the century now widely understand that 'sexism' means treating males and females differently, or having stereotypes according to sex, and many believe, because equal access is now enshrined in legislation, and because the cruder forms of exclusion have been amended, that gender is no longer an issue. Yet research studies continue to show that students interact with each other and with schooling as gendered and not as neutral, genderless beings: for example, in the significance of appearance for girls (Yates and Macleod, 1996; Burns, 1993); in the necessity for boys through their subject-choices and appearance to show themselves decisively as 'not girls' (Teese et al., 1995; Davies, 1989); and in their aspirations and expectations in relation to a culture in which public institutions (politics, employment) and domestic life are still significantly structured by gender.

Second Construction: 'Girl-friendly'; Girls as 'Other'

By the mid 1980s in Australia, the education of girls was still seen as a problem, but the diagnosis was different. The outcomes of schooling for girls in terms of jobs and tertiary fields of study were seen to be as bad as ever. But the reform agendas now identified the source of the problem as not simply due to girls' restricted access to types of study, or to poor careers advice (though, despite a lot of funding to change the latter, how much it had actually changed at school level was debatable). The problem was now seen to be that the *processes of schooling* were oriented to boys. Girls' learning styles and the dynamics of who did the talking in the coeducation classroom had not been sufficiently taken account of. Instead of teachers being asked to de-emphasize gender and sex stereotypes, they were asked to become more *gender-sensitive*; to be 'girl-friendly'; to be 'sexually inclusive'. Now coeducation was criticized, and single-sex grouping took on a new popularity (for girls, though not necessarily for boys).

This was a period in which researchers spent a lot of time trying to identify patterns of difference in relation to girls as compared with boys. Some of this research involved the counting and mapping of classroom dynamics; of who was using the space in the playground, and so on. There were also investigations of girls' preferred learning styles as compared with boys, and attempts to identify things that teachers or schools did that might work for boys but were turning girls off. Many people were influenced by Carol Gilligan's (and related) work on girls' psychology, and the emphasis on caring and relationship. Researchers investigated gender preferences in assessment by essay as compared with short-answer test; preferences for discussion-based learning compared with individualized problem-solving; and the fact that a teacher's joking might be enjoyed by the boys as friendly banter, but alienate the girls who saw it as a form of sarcasm, and so on.

This second construction still treats girls as a unitary category, and indeed intensifies this tendency. Girls are seen as people who do things in certain ways; who react to situations in certain ways; who feel comfortable in some situations and not in others. Girls are not seen as diverse, or as complex beings actively constructing a complicated world. Subsequent feminist theory has widely criticized such 'essentialist' views of 'women's voice' or 'women's ways of knowing'.

But what is sometimes forgotten here is that, in its origins and in its practical, political effects, this second construction of 'girls' as a category for education was also a *deconstruction*. It worked theoretically and concretely to undermine the existing construction of the universal abstract subject: to undermine assumptions that there is a single form of good pedagogy for all students, or that any (gendered) individual can stand for any other in representations in texts. This is not necessarily an essentialist perspective, though it is often used that way. It can be, and was in its origins, a way of beginning to look with new eyes at what should be included as the content of subjects; at whose interests were being served by current ways of organizing schools, and current teaching methods. But, of course, differences among girls were silenced by these approaches.

As a construction of agendas for education, this second approach also brought a new emphasis on the *processes* of schooling (not just outcomes) as matters of concern in themselves. This issue is being taken up in new ways at the turn of the century, in a claim that there has now been too much attention to maximizing girls' learning environments, and too little to the needs of boys. But it is also being taken up in stronger concerns about sexual harassment and bullying as issues for education, issues which victimize boys as well as girls, and which have a strong gendered component even in same sex harassment.

Third Construction/Deconstruction: 'Girls' as Diverse; 'Girls' as Active Subjects

By the late 1980s, the policy-makers were talking about *difference*. Being a girl did not take just one form. It was up to teachers to be sensitive to the multiple differences of race, ethnicity, class, rurality, and to teach appropriately to these. In terms of outcomes of schooling there had now been some changes in relation to the inequalities identified earlier, though also some continuities. Many more girls now went on to university (though there had been a considerable redefinition of what 'university' was by this time — it now included nursing and primary teacher education). They had increased too their proportional representation in fields like medicine and law (though not in engineering, agriculture, economics). Women's pay relative to men had improved over the 1970s and 1980s, to be around 80 per cent for full time-work (much less when part-time and over-time were included), but then from the mid-1980s it remained static or slightly declined (Australian Bureau of Statistics, 1993).

In Australia, prior to developing the new *National Policy for the Education of Girls in Australian Schools* in 1987, the Schools Commissioners went around to different schools and listened to what girls themselves had to say about schooling and their own needs. The policy stressed the different forms that 'being a girl in an Australian school' took: differences of ethnicity, of class, or urban or rural setting, and so on. The policy incorporated some of the earlier frameworks in some of its planks, reiterating the rights of girls to expect equal treatment through their school system and its resources. But it emphasized very much that teachers should be sensitive to the (diverse) specificity of the girls they teach: that they should teach in an 'inclusive' way that is sensitive to different cultural and class formations; and that school should offer an 'appropriate' curriculum, one in which they found their own experiences represented. Feminist researchers too were now significantly concerned with differences among girls and with a growing debate about racism in feminism.

As a *construction* of girls as an issue, there is a shift here in two ways. Girls are now seen as necessarily diverse: gender will mean different things in different contexts; the category 'girls' is beginning to be deconstructed. And girls are now constructed (to some extent) as themselves 'knowing subjects': people who can be consulted, not just researched.

The legacies posed by these ways of addressing girls as an object of reform are twofold: one concerns the practical politics of certain forms of contemporary feminist theory; the second concerns generational change and the subjectivity of students formed in a context where certain feminist issues and reforms are part of the status quo.

Feminist theory in the 1980s and 1990s has been much concerned with debates about the political implications of deconstructing women (for example, Modleski, 1991; Hirsch and Fox Keller, 1991). In terms of education policy and practices in Australia, as I have argued elsewhere (Yates, 1993b, 1993c), the problem is that policies which talk of being inclusive to differences of all types often lack a practical force. In promotion procedures, all teachers claim they are 'inclusive' in their teaching styles; in terms of strategy the concerns with difference can be enacted as a liberal belief in 'individual' differences or as a patronizing stereotyping of problems faced by girls of particular ethnic backgrounds.

In terms of the subjectivity of girls at the turn of the century, issues about girls' rights to be formally treated as 'equally human' have now broadly been established. Many girls reject the idea that they are in need of special protection or special nurturing.

Fourth Construction/Deconstruction: Power, Sex and Gender

By the mid 1990s, in Australia at least, the education of girls is still being seen as an area for reform by policy-makers, though boys are increasingly being added to policies and becoming the subject of new reports and initiatives. Girls' retention to the end of school is now around 10 per cent higher than that of boys; their results in year 12 (the final year of schooling in Australia) are broadly better than those of boys; and they are a clear majority of undergraduates. Despite this, they are still under-represented in postgraduate study, in some prestigious areas of study and employment, and in patterns of pay beyond education. The focus of the reform agenda for girls at this stage emphasizes *eliminating sex-based harassment* in schools and working more on reforms for the girls who have been *benefiting least* from school. In terms of general strategy, where earlier reports drew attention in turn to 'non-sexist' curriculum and de-emphasizing gender in pedagogy; then to 'girl-friendly schooling' and attention to girls' learning styles; then to differentiated 'inclusive' practices which were sensitive to other differences as well as gender; the new emphasis is *the construction of gender* (Curriculum Corporation, 1993).

In principle at least, this approach takes up but reworks concerns of the earlier stages: it de-essentializes, and assumes that students are not stereotyped examples of 'a girl' and 'a boy', but diverse and conflicting subjects, but it also assumes that the cultural shaping of what femininity and masculinity mean, their 'discursive construction' do make gender a meaningful category from which to understand and work with different individual students. The strategy recommended under the *Australian Action Plan for the Education of Girls 1993–7* was that from the beginning of school, students should be taught to see and reflect on gender practices, values and desires, and to deconstruct these. At the same time, more attention is being given to how girls have responded to reform practices, what criticisms and resistances they have to these, what is important to them.

Constructing Agendas of Reform

To this point I have tried to show, rather schematically, that we have seen some quite different types of frameworks and assumptions in how policy-makers, school reformers, and feminist theorists have addressed the education of girls. Other countries have not necessarily been through these shifts in quite the same order as Australia, nor given certain developments the same degree of emphasis. In many countries, the emphasis is still primarily on securing equal rights and access; in some places there has been a strong interest in girls' learning styles; and in others gender has been very much a subsidiary interest to concerns about race. And, for researchers and teachers, the different emphases I have outlined do not necessarily replace each other; they often exist simultaneously. I am not trying to go through the shifts in policy or changing paradigms of research to draw up a typology to explain why a particular paradigm or politics is the superior one. I have extracted them as different conceptions of research and reform to draw attention to what has been important about the questions and visions dominating *each* approach (as well as what has been limited about them).

First, consider how girls as learners, as subjects, as students, have been conceived in these developments. In the first stage of reform, the subjectivity of girls was not highly theorized and the vision of reform was oriented to some androgyny: the inculcation of a similar range of skills and ambitions for girls and boys. There was also much more emphasis on making girls more like boys than on adding to or reforming boys. It is common today for researchers to criticize both the 'black box' conception of the learner that was implicit in this strategy, and the conservativeness of the end-point of reform (equal access to what was currently considered valuable). But this conception of girls and of reform was widely understood and politically powerful, and should not be easily given away. The case being made was that if there are skills and attributes which are powerful and socially valuable, then it is an ongoing and legitimate issue if there are structured differences in the extent to which different groups get access to these.

These matters are now an issue in a new way because to some extent they have been taken over as the basis for the 'what about the boys?' debate. To some extent too the social inequality rationale for attention to what happens to girls in school has been lost and muddied as a result of girls' increasing participation and success within school. The case for more attention to boys is being made today in terms of politically powerful facts and figures about boys' lesser retention rates in school; their higher delinquency and suicide rates; and their declining (relative) performance in year 12 assessment. In terms of backlash arguments then it can seem that the case for girls' programmes is purely 'ideological'.

It is not that there is nothing to be addressed in relation to boys, but, in relation to girls, it is important now to revive clearly and specifically the ways in which women and girls *are* socially unequal, to not allow the discussion to be dominated by taking up year 12 results as the only indicator of what happens, and to note that the outcomes of schooling for girls and boys, including the outcomes of equivalent schooling results, continues to show patterns of difference. In other words, we need to be clear that although girls are successful in many areas at school, the 'facts and figures' continue to show that the outcomes of schooling for women are unequal: in terms of some areas of prestigious study, postgraduate entry, and earnings relative to certification.

Strategies based on 'rights' and entitlements to be treated 'equally' are also still important as practical politics within the processes of schooling, notwithstanding the sophisticated theoretical critiques of these assumptions. Recently in Australia for example there has been enthusiasm for the idea of getting very young children to 'deconstruct' their gendered behaviour in the ways they treat each other (for example, Davies, 1993; Alloway, 1995). However, I would argue that working with the much simpler approach that children should learn that each is entitled to the same (equal) time at the computer is not only more achievable, but is as strategically valuable in confronting and raising to consciousness existing patterns of gendered inequality as the attempts to do some intellectual deconstructions of this — a process that is difficult enough to achieve with university students (see the various contributions in Luke and Gore, 1993; also see Macleod, 1993).

In the second stage of Australian reform I described earlier, and in a range of research projects, the emphasis turned to girls as learners. It is common now for approaches and research associated with 'girl's ways of knowing' to be criticized and disowned, to be seen as reinstating stereotyping and essentialism. But what was and is important about this interest was the issue of how we might begin to see new things in what happens in the classroom; how we might begin to conceive of practices with new eyes. What was important about the work of Gilligan and Martin and others was not that they developed a template that applied to all girls, whatever their class, or culture, but that they showed what an approach which began with girls, or which took girls seriously might look like (see also Martin, 1994 and Yates, 1988 and Shands, this volume).

The approach to the education of girls that was set in train here was the need for more empirical research about how girls (and boys) actually thought and acted, but this empirical enterprise had to go hand in hand with broader theoretical thinking about education and its concepts, and about women in society. It is true that in practice this approach to girls and their education often did trample over the experiences of some girls (not all of them liked communal and discussion-based learning; not all of them felt silenced in the mixed-sex classroom). But it also provided an important challenge to taken-for-granted practices of teaching and assessment which had contributed to women's inequality.

The third type of construction of 'girls' attempted to take seriously difference among girls, to be sensitive to, and to work with, their different background experiences and values; and to represent different types of girls and women in the curriculum. The strength of this way of thinking about girls is that it begins to de-essentialize girls as a group; its weakness is that it is harder to say what the rhetoric of this strategy means as practice. Ironically, the focus on differences of ethnicity, race and class within gender projects can, in the ways they are taken up as practice, actually weaken rather than extend the politics of reform for girls, can reinstate stereotyped and deficit visions of particular groups of girls (Tsolidis, 1993). So here, for the future, the challenge is to find ways to understand differences among groups of girls as more than simply individual ones; but not to turn this into stereotyped classifications which limit the ways that girls from particular ethnic or class backgrounds are taught.

In the latest stage of Australian policy, there is some attempt to both reinstate 'gender' and attention to sex-based experiences of girls as a group, but also to acknowledge difference and the constructed nature of the experiences in question. So, on the one hand, the new policy attention to 'sex-based' harassment acknowledges that patterns of exclusion and inequality within school are not merely matters of random individual differences, they are patterned in ways which relate to how femininity and masculinity are constructed within contemporary discourse, to broader patterns of power. Now students as well as teachers are to be encouraged to identify how such constructions of gender work.

The challenge with this approach for the future is encapsulated in those media debates I referred to at the beginning of the paper. How do we engage students to see gender at work in the world when they see this as an old issue which is not of interest to them? How do we set up processes which address harassment without perpetuating stereotypes and assumptions of all girls as fragile and in need of protection and all boys as potential rapists, which is likely to draw the hostility of many in both camps?

The attitudes of young women that the press caricature do need to be taken seriously. When they reject programmes of reform designed for them, they are insisting that they have a voice and a potency and do not want to be perpetually constituted as victims. The fact that we who have worked for 20 years on a particular issue think that we have a more powerful understanding of it does not mean that the appropriate strategy is necessarily to attempt to directly transfer what is in our heads into the heads of those we teach. But equally, the point of schooling is that students are taught something, and we are right to be concerned about what that something is.

Over recent years, girls have been both constructed and deconstructed as an object of research, policy-making and practice in education, and it is important that we go on doing so. Constructing 'the education of girls' as a field of concern raised important questions about the social and educational purposes that frame schooling. Deconstructing 'the education of girls' as a field for concern helps to raise questions about the form in which governments attend to this area (the huge stress on science and careers, notwithstanding a shift in actual jobs to the service sector; the failure to significantly change the status of unpaid work as an object of study). Deconstruction is useful too in reflecting on our own projects as truths and emanations of power, and to put in perspective the responses girls give to these.

Schooling is an institution where students are selected and channelled, and where students are taught things. Over the past 20 years there has been widespread upheaval in the world about the roles of women and men, the structure of jobs, and what is to count as valuable knowledge and skill in the world. Just as schooling and its social and political context is not static nor unidimensional, so there is not just one framework or set of issues or model practice for addressing girls and their education. What I have been trying to do in this chapter is to say that we do need to keep addressing the assumptions inherent in the ways we take up 'girls' as an issue because we need to keep thinking about the changing political, economic and educational policy contexts of our work, and to consider the specific effects of taking up 'girls' as an object of reform in particular ways, in particular national contexts and at particular points in time.

References

AUSTRALIAN BUREAU OF STATISTICS (1993) *Women in Australia,* Canberra: ABS.

ALLOWAY, N. (1995) 'Surveillance or personal empowerment?: Macro- and micro-politics of gender and schooling', in *Proceedings of the Promoting Gender Equity Conference,* Canberra: ACT Department of Education.

BURNS, R. (1993) 'Health, fitness and female subjectivity', in YATES, L. (ed.) *Feminism and Education,* Melbourne Studies in Education 1993: La Trobe University Press.

CURRICULUM CORPORATION (1993) *Action Plan for Girls in Australian Schools 1993–7,* Canberra: Curriculum Corporation.

DAVIES, B. (1989) *Frogs and Snails and Feminist Tales: Pre-school Children and Gender,* Sydney: Allen and Unwin.

DAVIES, B. (1993) *Shards of Glass: Children Reading and Writing beyond Gendered Identities,* Sydney: Allen and Unwin.

DAVY, V. (1995) 'Reaching for consensus on gender equity: The NSW experience', in *Proceedings of the Promoting Gender Equity Conference,* Canberra: ACT Department of Education.

FOSTER, V. (1994) 'What about the boys?' Presumptive equality, and the obfuscation of concerns about theory, research, policy, resources and curriculum in the education of girls and boys', AARE Conference Paper, Newcastle.

HIRSCH, M. and FOX KELLER, E. (1991) *Conflicts in Feminism,* New York: Routledge.

KENWAY, J. and WILLIS, S. (1993) *Telling Tales: Girls and Schools Changing their Ways,* Canberra: Department of Employment, Education and Training.

KENWAY, J., WILLIS, S., BLACKMORE, J. and RENNIE, L. (1993) 'Learning from girls: What can girls teach feminist teachers?', in YATES, L. (ed.) *Feminism and Education,* Melbourne Studies in Education 1993: La Trobe University Press.

KENWAY, J., WILLIS, S. and JUNOR, A. (1995) *Critical Visions: Curriculum and Policy Rewriting the Future,* Canberra: Department of Employment, Education and Training.

LUKE, C. and GORE, J. (1993) *Feminisms and Critical Pedagogy,* New York: Routledge.

MACLEOD, J. (1993) 'Impossible fictions? Utopian visions of feminist educational research', in YATES, L. (ed.) *Feminism and Education,* Melbourne Studies in Education 1993: La Trobe University Press.

MARTIN, J.R. (1994) 'Methodological essentialism, false difference and other dangerous traps', *Signs,* **19,** 3, pp. 630–57.

MODLESKI, T. (1991) *Feminism without Women: Culture and Criticism in a 'Post-feminist' Age,* New York: Routledge.

SCHOOLS COMMISSION (1975) *Girls, School and Society,* Canberra: Report of a Study Group to the Schools Commission.

SCHOOLS COMMISSION (1987) *A National Policy for the Education of Girls in Australian Schools,* Canberra: Schools.

TEESE, R., DAVIES, M., CHARLTON, M. and POLESEL, J. (1995) *Who Wins at School? Girls and Boys in Australian Secondary Education*, Melbourne: Melbourne University Department of Education Policy and Management.

TSOLIDIS, G. (1993) 'Difference and identity: A feminist debate indicating directions for the development of a transformative curriculum', in YATES, L. (ed.) *Feminism and Education*, Melbourne Studies in Education 1993: La Trobe University Press.

YATES, L. (1988) 'Does "all students" include girls?', *Australian Education Researcher*, **15**, 1, pp. 41–57.

YATES, L. (1993a) *The Education of Girls: Policy, Practice and the Question of Gender*, Melbourne: ACER.

YATES, L. (1993b) 'Feminism and Australian state policy: Some questions for the 1990s', in ARNOT, M. and WEILER, K. (eds) *Feminism and Social Justice in Education*, London: Falmer Press.

YATES, L. (1993c) 'What happens when feminism is an agenda of the state?', *Discourse*, **14**, 1, pp. 17–29.

YATES, L. and LEDER, G.C. (1996) *Student Pathways: A Review and Overview of National Databases on Gender Equity*, Canberra: ACT Department of Education.

YATES, L. and MACLEOD, J. (1996) *Can We Find Out about Girls and Boys Today, or Must We Just Talk about Ourselves?*, New York: AERA.

14 On the (Im)possibility of Being Impertinent, Contentious, Feminist and Feminine

Kajsa Ohrlander

When, as a woman, I set out to write an article about my own contentious or provocative research — yes, well, the problems start to pile up right at the start.

Let me first make clear that I am never contentious. It is not that I do not want to be, it is just that I disagree with how the term is used. Contentiousness is often looked upon as a personality trait or mark of bad behaviour. But this just avoids the crux of the matter — that contentiousness always occurs in relation to something or someone. There have to be at least two persons for one of them to be quarrelsome, and then it is the little guy who appears contentious in the eyes of the big guy. The father accuses his son of being impertinent when the boy remarks that he does not like the food on his plate. The teacher accuses the schoolboy of impertinence when he struggles to explain himself. Contentiousness has often been looked upon as a term of abuse in the past, belonging in the same order of things as authoritarianism, masculine methods of child-raising, (military) hierarchies, and the top dog–underdog dichotomy — labels used by men about men. But insubordination has also been associated with healthy freedom-loving masculinity, with the demands on the schoolboy to achieve male independence. Rousseau transformed little Emile's contentious behaviour into a democratic principle of self-expression. The would-be ferocious bite of the wolf was transformed into the care-free youngster's mischievous teasing.

It would be a mistake to look upon contentiousness as having to do only with men. For all intents and purposes the concept does seem incompatible with femininity — which makes it even more difficult for me as a woman to call my research contentious or to say that I as a researcher make it a point of honour to be quarrelsome. Rebellious women are not beautiful; they are not conciliatory, nor are they supportive, nor sweet, nor gentle, nor appealing; they are just not nice at all. A contentious feminine woman is a linguistic impossibility.

But if we think about contentiousness as it is attributed to men, i.e. with thinking and speaking one's own mind, with the driving urge to ask new questions, to explore new paths — yes, well, then we have transformed contentiousness into a principle of democratic liberation. Contentiousness becomes a virtue; for research, a necessity.

But this does not solve my problem as a woman, as a female researcher at the Stockholm Institute of Education. For a woman's femininity alone will not give her access to unfettered and independent research. For a woman to think freely, to ask inopportune questions, to explore new paths is to do battle with her femininity. It is manly to think free, bold and independent thoughts. The woman who tries to do the same is often treated with scepticism — both by herself and by others, or else she becomes a feminist — in which case she is looked upon as unfeminine, aggressive, in other words, as masculine. To be critical of the male privilege that is still rampant today in most intellectual fields is also to show a lack of femininity. It is to strike at the very centre of the image of the warm and affective woman which has been our ticket to the male intellectual arenas in the public sphere. It is unfeminine to assert that men have acquired their privileged position more often than not by virtue of their gender rather than of their competence. To assert that the male's privileged position in the academic world has been handed down through centuries of a discriminatory gender quota system is, in all its immodesty, a masculine assertion.

Writing this makes me out to be an unfeminine female researcher. And although what I write here could be taken at one level in jest, a light touch to the debate, what I am actually doing is opening the door to a profoundly serious, I would even go as far as to say scientific, discussion with the academic community. I use myself as an example in order to show how linguistic qualifiers and gender discourses are perforated with a multitude of contradictions and conflicts that I as a woman am forced to learn to live with, whether it means embodying them, repressing them, rebutting them or consciously suffering from them. Putting into words what has otherwise gone unsaid serves to demonstrate the relationship between knowledge and myself as a woman and it is to assert that the problem I describe is scientifically relevant. My aim is to help reshape the Institute's insensitivity to gender into an awareness of gender as an empowerment problem. I am taking part in a speech act, participating in a linguistic interplay, posing new questions.

Unfeminine Feminist Research

Feminist research today, both in Sweden and in the world beyond, is more free, more unfeminine and more creative than what is considered compatible with the feminine norms and the masculine power structures that apply in the field of education in general and the Institute's research and education in particular. In contrast to the almost non-existent role it plays at my Institute, feminist research today is at the cutting edge of creative research in many other fields of endeavour. It has shaken the very core of the self-understanding and concepts of philosophy; it has redrawn the boundaries of historical periods and reformulated historical interpretations of economic and political processes; it has recast concepts like liberalism, freedom, solidarity, society, state, citizen;

it has taken the lead in formulating thought-provoking deconstructions and in opening up post-structuralist approaches has unmapped bold new paths. It not only contests the tenets of established ways but also finds new ways of looking at the history of music, literature and art. It claims that gender is a world-wide economic, social and cultural sorting mechanism which appears in a thousand and one forms. Feminist research has become one of the most important means for women to gain access to the power that knowledge wields. Feminist research is seldom read by men.

Women who have battled their way into the bastions of brotherhood, by which term the academic world can still be described today, have followed a tortuous but crucial path. The journey has been tortuous because the path is flanked by masculine power structures, but also because the language and the rules of the game have been imposed on knowledge by masculinity. It is a question of physical and linguistic masculinity that has dominated education and culture, of the female gender's entrapment in the phallic, authoritarian knowledge structure, but also of such occurrences as the mundane yet disturbing presence of the female form in a seminar room appropriated by men. It is concerned with the brotherhood's own invisible logic which causes men to refer almost exclusively to other men. And of course because the power structure is masculine, pronouncements by men are judged to be more weighty and relevant, even for women.

When women researchers who have become feminists set themselves the task of transcending given definitions of femininity and ask bold new questions, they are engaging in a social project that is of the utmost importance: they are helping to turn women into people, helping women to gain access to language; they are preparing a space for language and they are creating a public domain for the silenced and invisible worlds of women, for women's conflicts and experiences. In so doing they risk still being looked upon as so disruptive and threatening that they jeopardize their good relations with men. Today there are few who would call these women bearded ladies or asexual monsters, as some men at the beginning of this century called women who advocated full citizenship and the right to vote. But a reintroduction of the old de-sexualizing stamp of inferiority lies just around the corner. Paradoxically, feminist researchers challenge the very foundations of femininity — woman as non-subject, as an object of knowledge and control. They create for women a new subjective meaning that is not the traditional one; an own perspective that breaks down the barriers erected by those who would keep vital truths secret. Thus they also contribute to penetrating, liberating and changing the meanings and differences between the feminine and the masculine.

For male control over knowledge about women's female existence is concerned in the last analysis with male control over sexuality, children, property and love. A concept of woman came into being as the bearer of 'otherness', of the private, of the body, love, ethics, underwear and house-cleaning, i.e. of the personal meaning of life. For men as well as women, this is the meaning that is based on feelings, caring and the desire of men to be looked upon as 'private' individuals. Thus dichotomies like masculine–feminine, public–private, rational–irrational, high–low have also contributed to conceptualizing this division as a natural phenomenon. That women are different has become a law of nature and is incorporated into how men define nature — since it is the white male who has elevated himself to the position of master of the universe, conqueror, the one who defines the very meaning of meaning.

The Questions that I Pose as a Woman, Researcher and Unique Subject

When I began work on my dissertation in the beginning of the 1980s, the last thing I wanted to be was contentious. Embarrassingly enough, I was not even a feminist at that time. But I did want to be proactive, fascinating, courageous — to take up a position other than the one usually adopted by educational researchers at that time. Above all I did not want to join the ranks of submissive research workers who solved the educational problems of the National School Board, The National Board of Health and Welfare, or the Swedish government. I wanted to infuse new life into the conventional thought patterns I saw all around me — where Basil Bernstein's 'codes' and Dahllöf-Lundgren's 'frame factors' were what radicalness had to offer. I was obsessed by the idea of unmasking the ideological prattle of pompous truth-prophets. And although many laid claim to the truth, the turnover of 'true' ideas was more rapid than ever. The incompatibility of all the ideas about children that I encountered at child-health centres, nursery schools and at my job is what inspired my formulation of the initial aim of my doctoral thesis — to study how ideas such as these developed and changed through history.

All those historically changing images and discussions of children made me aware of my deep embeddedness in my own time and its ways of thinking. History is indeed a wonderful tool for understanding the present. The wild child, the virtuous child, the child as a flower or plant, the Darwinian child with abilities like a prehistorical lizard, the child as a power-threat, the child as innocent, beyond every suspicion, the child as 'the other', 'the strange' the child as an area of discovery and scientific inventions, the 'needy' child — this endlessly changing set of images of children's needs, normality, healthiness, all those also endlessly changing ideals and norms worked like dynamite for a new self-understanding. All these new knowledges meant to begin with a sort of liberation, and in a very new sense of liberation as a woman. Because this was indeed an area where as a woman I was under pressure, living within a sometimes visible and sometimes invisible control over my thinking and making, where the needs of the child were defined by science, the different professionals and in relation to the Swedish state and the future. This discovery of a very basic historical relativity meant that I was able to take new positions, to stand aside, begin to reflect over these as truths.

This was merely a beginning. A bunch of questions popped into my head as to how, why and from where all those ideas came: what was the purpose? To understand I needed a deeper contextualizing.

Armed with a battery of advisory pamphlets on medical child care and child-raising practices, I set off to find their origin. It turned out that these mass produced medical pamphlets originated at the time when the Swedish welfare state was under construction at the beginning of this century. The journey took me through a territory peopled by poverty, ideas, utopias, visions of the good life, the rational controlled society and the 'new man'. It was quite simply the breakthrough of modernity in the social sphere in Sweden, a decade into the new century.

All of the rules and regulations about intervals for breast-feeding, meal-time schedules, the child's need to be kissed and caressed, comforted and punished, to be read to, the importance of the clock and so on — all aimed at prevention, at creating a hygienic lifestyle and populace, at using children to stave off social problems, to build up strength and power for the future.

The question of whether or not children should be allowed to play with their mother's nipples after breast-feeding was in point of fact concerned with how to curb criminality, poverty and the threat of socialism. Toughening practices, cold baths and vigorous rub-downs were exercises in withstanding adversity, learning subjection to the dictates of time, the regularity of the clock, the father's will. For industries to bloom and the economy to flourish the virtues of endurance, obedience, self-discipline and strength of character had to be inculcated in the rising generation.

The result was a challenge to 'virtue's image of itself' which says that scientific knowledge through professionals such as doctors, child-care workers and teachers, always aims towards what is best for the child. Here it was revealed that both the professional experts and the scientific community were co-actors in directing the harsh light of modernity on to children — that it was less a question of virtue than of a monumental social construction.

My questions hardly reflected the 'normal' stance of a doctoral candidate. On the contrary, I had taken a giant step away from the normal modes of academic behaviour. I had asked questions that came from within myself as a mother, privately, outside of the institutions that were subjecting me to all kinds of influences. At the same time I was a postgraduate student and had a place within the walls of the institution. In addition there was my Marxian analysis of the state which I had brought with me from the leftist movement of the 1970s.

By relating the background to my doctoral thesis, I am also saying that my questions were posed in a particular historical present, in a particular unique situation and that the 'I' who asks such questions is a person, a woman, a subject, a co-creator. I make no claim to be a better person or to have a patent on truth — nor to be a neuter, a neutral, an ungendered researcher. Today my early research seems much less inopportune than it did when I started. It has generally become much easier to talk about the political aspects of the welfare state (see Ohrlander, 1992, 1995, 1996).

Feminism as an Educational Challenge

To incorporate research on gender and education into the internal life of the Stockholm Institute of Education is not only to set in motion a project for the emancipation and liberation of women and girls through education. It is also to participate in a process of testing and recreating that has to do with post modernism, post positivism, post structuralism. Feminist educational research is a major force for critical analysis and reappraisal. In this process the researcher directs attention towards the structures and concepts that entrench authority and power. In this sense feminist research serves as a spearhead in the work of giving meaning to what would otherwise be empty slogans like 'the reflective practitioner', research-directed teacher training institutions, the reflective approach. Reflective practitioners are, after all, supposed to reflect on their own activity, the positions they hold, their construction of their own identity. For a nursery school worker or a grammar school teacher to be able to reflect on these matters requires, besides freedom of thought, not least access to the ongoing discussion and the reflective texts that are produced within the domain of education research.

The reflective researcher studies, for example, how conceptions of 'the one correct view' on children's needs came into being, in what context this idea first appeared, with what view of children in mind, what gender, what class, what racial identity, what changes this idea has undergone with time — and how various interests, power relations, economic and political processes have been created around this 'one correct view' of the child. What is being studied here is hardly the innocent or disinterested way in which institutions, professions and research have constituted themselves. Post-structuralist research has questioned the belief in universalism, 'the grand narrative' of progress, prosperity and an all-pervading good that is waiting to be discovered and realized — beyond the historical present and changes through time, beyond human concepts and consciousness. Instead, what is brought to the fore is the changeability and complexity of how we identify what is good, just and true, that we ourselves are part and parcel of the process of formulating the idea of the good school, the good pupil, the good home, the good parent — how deeply involved we are in all of this and how these ideas in turn are incorporated into a whole range of power relations, silences and acts of concealment.

Feminist educational research poses a challenge by asking questions about where we stand with our knowledge in relation to the gendered educational culture in living out our lives as women, as feminized human beings. How do we create ourselves in relation to our external forms — our breasts, our stomachs, our eroticized deviant bodies. How should the school teacher dress — so as not to be unfeminine and hidden from view but at the same time to make herself unfeminine so as to be rational, methodical, a no-body? How does one become both a body and a no-body?

What does the school do with the young girl's body and mind? How does the girl choose between the demand to think of others and to create/present herself, to perform before others and to experience deep feelings that are in themselves in conflict with the acting style as such? Words, bodies, identities are placed high on the agenda in feminist research.

The Feminizing of the School — Whose Problem Is It?

Feminist educational research has revealed how the school's systemized linguistic and social power relations have been largely determined by men. Girls and women teachers, with their identities rooted in otherness, in the private, the objectified have been split off and stamped as 'second-rate'. While boys are given generous room to develop a certain measure of unfettered boisterousness and their own masculine subjectivity, girls have been rewarded for being obedient and conforming. Men teachers are rewarded and acclaimed for reproducing the power relations of society, for exercising authority and promoting a hegemonic view of knowledge.

Today, however, in Sweden there is a movement in the schools towards pluralism, knowledge construction and a diversified and explorative method of work, which is in the process of replacing masculine power relations.

Against the background of the concern today about the feminizing of the school, the concern about there being too few 'masculine' role models that could promote the development of a healthy gender identity in boys can be seen more as a concern about the dissolution of the old dualistic structure — a concern about gender dichotomies being disrupted. A change towards an explorative school, with inquisitive students and teachers, will lay the foundation for more flexible and versatile gender identities. Both girls and boys, female and male teachers can construct their own knowledge using themselves as subject. In this less constricted arrangement there will be less need for role models that discriminate between masculinity and femininity (see Ve and Berge, this volume).

When concepts of masculinity and femininity are examined from the perspective of educational history, it becomes clear how gender categories have undergone steady change. We have witnessed in earlier times a far more dramatic feminizing of the school than is the case today.

From where we stand today, there are few who wish we had foregone the feminizing of the school that took place at the turn of this century. At that time there was a tremendous upheaval in Sweden in which the former militaristic state underwent transformation towards a more democratic and, as one could say, more feminine state as femininity was understood at that time. Almost no area of life remained unaffected by the transformation — not only schools and teaching. Where children in orphanages were once dressed in uniforms and awoken to the tune of the reveille, drills and military exercises, they now came to be cared for in small, individualized children's homes run by women. Authoritarian and impersonal relationships in the former poor relief system were replaced by compassion, individualization and scientific rationality. The masculine master — subject relationship of the church, the sovereignty of the head of the household, corporal punishment in the family were all abolished. 'Liberalism' was often associated with femininity whereas conservatism was associated with masculinity. Women philanthropists, socially committed women, women teachers in private girls' schools fought for the new, the modern, together with liberal and modernized men whereas priests, the military men of power, often defended the old system. Women reform educators such as Anna Sandström, Ann Sörenssen, Anna Whitlock, Sofi Almquist and others criticized the old school, the boys' grammar school, for its heavy hand, meaningless drill and formalized education. Men gymnastic instructors with their militaristically inspired sports instruction opposed the feminizing of gymnastics as represented by the influx of women instructors. One of the women gymnastics instructors in Stockholm, Elin Falck, was a pioneer in this transformation in that she introduced a more gentle and harmonic system of movements to replace the more rigid and militaristic programme.

Education — A Submissive Subject?

One of the reasons feminism finds it difficult to make inroads in education is probably because the field of education — despite a temporary interruption at the beginning of the 1970s — has hardly been in a position to challenge the prevailing state of affairs. The responsible and politicized mandate given to state-centred teacher training and educational research does not seem to encourage open inquisitiveness and bold thinking. But perhaps this also has something to do with the culture of submissiveness and collusion that many see as characterizing not only Sweden but also Swedish women. It has not been difficult in Sweden to shape womankind — with their tacit consent — in accordance with 'the rhetoric of virtue' and turn women into a kind of service facility. More women work outside the home in Sweden than anywhere else in the world — an enviable situation you might think. But women are generally employed in positions that continue to turn them into pliant, solicitous, angels of mercy to whom real people can come for succour, nourishment and consolation. Swedish women, in exchange for a social contract — admittedly not without some fringe benefits — have agreed to continue bearing the responsibility for their home, their children, their father-in-law's prostate problem at the same time as they take responsibility in their unpaid professional lives for children, the aged, the weak, the distressed. And when these non-people, through education or the like, begin to develop a self-identity and make their own demands for satisfaction, decent salaries, power — that is when the mighty masculine network begins to writhe in pain, that is when the talk centres on all the many new problems that confront us, about sectors that are a drain on the economy, about how funds cannot be stretched any further. It is then that money is transferred from these creatures, these women, to the real people, to men. We see this going on today — transferrals from the women's spheres of care, school and child-care to private capital accumulation, golden handshakes and the private or privatized sectors of the economy.

Kajsa Ohrlander

I believe it is crucial that women, not least of all within the educational system, allow our thoughts to soar high, that we critically reappraise the whole array of normalities and benefits that go into shaping our femininity. To study to be a teacher, to educate coming generations of teachers and to conduct research on education has to mean reflecting on the power aspects of knowledge, on institutionalized processes of creation and on our own subject's genesis. Teacher training must entail the risk of contentiousness, insubordination and a lack of femininity.

Acknowledgment

This article was first published in 'Against the Current: Provocative Research at the Stockholm Institute of Education', 1997.

References

BURNS, R. (1993) *Health, fitness and female subjectivity: what is happening in school health and physical education?* In YATES, L. (ed.) Melbourne: La Trobe University Press.

ELGQVIST-SALTZMAN, I. (1992) 'Gravel in the Machinery or the Hub of the Wheel?' in EDUARDS, M. et al. (eds) *Rethinking Change: Current Swedish Feminist Research*, Stockholm: Uppsala.

GUSTAFSSON, C. (1994) *Ramfaktorteoretiskt tänkande pedagogiska perspektiv: en vänbok till Urban Dahllöf*, Uppsala: Pedagogiska Institutionen.

MARTIN, J.R. (1985) *Reclaiming a Conversation: The Ideal of the Educated Woman*, New Haven: Yale University Press.

NILSSON-GTANGNEBIEN, J. and SÖDERSTRÖM, S. (1995) *The emergence of a female occupation and physical education from a genus perspective.* Paper presented at a course in Feminism's theory of knowledge and pedagogy, Stockholm: Institute of Education (Swedish).

OHRLANDER, K. (1992) In the children's and nation's interest: Social reformation policies from 1903 to 1930, Stockholm: Almqvist & Wiksell (Swedish).

OHRLANDER, K. (1995a) Modernising femininity: outmoded masculinity, in Arkiv för studier i arbetarrörelsens historia, nr 63–4 (Swedish).

OHRLANDER, K. (1995b) From Philanthrophy to Social Work Conference Paper Sköndalsinstitutet 9–10 October 1995 (Swedish).

ROSE, H. (1994) *Love, Power and Knowledge: Towards a Feminist Transition of the Sciences*, Cambridge: Polity Press.

SOU: 1995: 110. *The will to know and the will to understand: Gender, power and the scientific challenge posed by women in higher education*, Stockholm: Utbildningsdepartementet (Swedish).

ULLMAN, A. (1994) 'Outfitted with a hat and civil courage: women as school principals at the turn of the century', *Praxis* nr 3–4. Research report from a project by OHRLANDER, K., TROTZIG, E. and ULLMAN, A. Female radicals and educational innovators from the bourgeois class at the turn of the century (Swedish).

YATES, L. (1996) Understanding boys' issues: what sort of challenge is it? Paper presented at the AERA Annual Conference, New York, April 1996.

15 Naming Male Advantage: A Feminist Theorist Looks to the Future

Joan Eveline

Concerns about gender equity entered education as the result (direct and indirect) of feminist intervention. Translated into policy these claims frequently meant a focus on the disadvantages of girls and women in schools and higher education. Currently, the focus on just *who* education disadvantages is shifting rapidly. In many corners of the globe talk of 'male disadvantage' now occupies centre stage, while the spectre of 'female advantage' hovers at the margins. So why is it difficult to find the topic of 'male advantage' specified as a problem?

As with power, the most entrenched manifestations of advantage are the most difficult to talk about. Theorists as far apart in concerns as Karl Marx, Adrienne Rich and Michel Foucault have argued that people tolerate power on condition that it mask most parts of itself. A similar discussion of advantage, as concept and practice, is overdue. This book participates in that project. My contribution uses examples from education, feminist politics and indigenous politics in Australia, to sound out some ideas about how educationists might use the notion of male advantage. Can the seemingly general concept 'male advantage' deal with the complications of race and class?

The examples embrace a broad notion of education, including the de-normalizing elements of Aboriginal films. Feminist educationists confronting the challenges of the new millennium, I conclude, will need to deploy both the oppositional politics and the postmodern ironies entailed in the concept of 'male advantage'.

Are Women Empowered through Education?

Feminism and education have a long association. More than two centuries ago Mary Wollstonecraft pointed out the disastrous consequences that Rousseau's gendered educational model would have on girls, women and future societies. Since then feminist theorists and activists alike have viewed education ambiguously: as a producer of women's oppression in its conventional mode, and as an essential component of women's development if its masculinist practices are challenged.

Throughout industrializing countries, women began by fighting for inclusion in existing institutions, often finding innovative ways of educating their daughters along the way (Elgqvist-Saltzman, this volume). While some sought to reform girls' education, others turned their attention to secondary and tertiary sectors (Mackinnon, Chapter 2). With notable exceptions in certain technologies and sciences, we enter a new millennium with women infiltrating most areas of higher education, as students at least.

In Australia, women enrolled in law and medicine now roughly equal the numbers of men, and female undergraduates in the arts and humanities usually outnumber males. In curricula reform, gender is now more likely to be taught as a topic for discussion and critique (Yates, this volume). In tertiary education feminist scholarship has achieved a high degree of respectability in fields from philosophy to technology, and many universities now have women's studies programmes (although these are still fledgling and often marginal). Undergraduate numbers, in fact, promote the idea that women are now advantaged over men in higher education (Maslen, 1995). Yet talk of 'men's disadvantage' ignores the fact that the recipients of power and privilege in the commanding heights of tertiary institutions are, at more than 10:1, men. A study of the upper tiers of Australian higher education in 1992, for example, found only two women amongst the 33 vice-chancellors, 2 per cent of deputy vice-chancellors were women, and they were 7 per cent of professors (that they are 18 per cent of senior lecturers rules out the argument that they have not been around so long) (Luke, 1993, p. 61).

Manifestations of male advantage are as visible today as in the past, but they are nonetheless resilient to being discussed. Whereas gender is now frequently regarded as irrelevant, it is still gender that dominates women's chances. A condition which haunts girls throughout their school lives and pursues women into the highest of office, is the practice of being 'known' by their sex, and in fact *as* sex. When US President Clinton appointed Madeleine Albright Secretary of State, for example, he felt obliged to mention that her gender was of no concern. 'Gender', he said, 'had nothing to do with her getting the job . . . And I hope she will be an inspiration to young women all across the country, all over our world' (*Weekend Australian*, 1996). Clinton made no similar mention of gender when he gave other top posts to men. Was Clinton reassuring the populace that Albright has avoided 'becoming a man' in her sortie onto male terrain, or do his allusions mean that she is certainly not a regular 'woman'? Emotions and tensions clearly increase whenever a woman moves close to the upper terrain of prestige (Mackinnon, this volume).

The marking out of male territory is not only a condition of, and conditional upon, the 'othering' of women. It is also a crucial element in the normalizing of male privilege. Whether on building sites, in school playgrounds or technology labs, men and boys protect their domains through the 'regulatory device of the "male gaze" and its vocal accompaniments' (Brook, 1994, p. 53). In schools girls may be given a place, but they often experience difficulty finding a space within territory staked out for and by boys (Foster, this volume). Contemporary corridors of power, by contrast, are not necessarily designed to protect men's space from women; rather, as Pringle and Watson (1992, p. 57) suggest, public institutions conduct their affairs 'as if men's interests were the only ones that exist'. Yet they are equally effective in marginalizing women by shaping that exclusion as normal.

Limiting Women

For the feminist with a practical orientation academic feminist theory can seem increasingly out of touch with women's everyday experiences. As Hester Eisenstein (1991, p. 97) remarked in her comparison of feminism in Australia and the United States:

> I keep getting a sense of a lack of fit between feminist theory in its many complex academic varieties, with the lived experience of women in a period of moving and miraculous transformation for some women and increasing oppression and violence for others.

More recently, Barbara Pocock (1997, p. 2) made a similar point:

> The preoccupations of feminist theorists sometimes strike one as esoteric and remote from contemporary political debates and more immediate events shaping women's lives, as if there were a tendency to over-theorise.

Both Eisenstein and Pocock are referring to deconstructivist theory — feminist critiques of how we use the political and analytical categories 'women' and 'gender'. How important have these latter criticisms been? Is recent theory so irrelevant to practical feminist politics?

For more than a decade feminist theorists have been diligently unbraiding the complexity of the category 'women', the uses to which it is put, and the differences it conceals. The difficulties they warn against have profound ramifications for research and scholarship, suggesting we be suspicious of the category on at least three counts:

1 It can be used to essentialize women (the idea that biology determines women's past and future, Spelman, 1988);
2 It has a tendency to universalize (concealing differences between women — Lorde, 1984; Huggins, 1994); and
3 It pays lack of attention to context (how the meanings accorded the term change across histories and cultures — Riley, 1988).

Yet on close analysis these deconstructions challenge us to be cautious about the terms and concepts we use, not fearful of acting. Denise Riley (1988), for example, argues that feminists should remain alert to how the category 'women' is used politically, contesting its noxious use in some instances and manipulating it for the benefit of women in others. Taking the use of the category 'women' into the heart of liberal feminist concerns about affirmative action, Carol Bacchi (1996) embraces Riley's position. Feminists should use the universal 'women' in reforms such as affirmative action with care, she argues, since it has been deployed to both advance and retard women's cause in different national contexts. Her text pays less attention to the category 'men', however, and does little to review the question of advantage.

One frequent generalization conflates 'women' with the concept of 'gender'. Employers and teachers in universities and schools often explain the situations of women and girls by their gender alone — 'women are more interested in teaching than research' (Castleman et al., 1994), or 'girls are quiet and well-behaved' (Berge, this volume). Such descriptions of girls and women *construct* and *contain* girls and women at the same time as they deny differences between them. They resonate with the commonsense view that gender is a reflection of some innate biological essence which cements a commonality between women. Simone De Beauvoir (1952, p. 295) moved us beyond biology when she argued five decades ago that 'One is not born, but rather becomes, a woman'. Throughout literature, philosophy, politics and western culture, she argued, women are constructed as a peculiarity, the sexed Other to universal, ungendered 'man'. But while de Beauvoir showed us 'woman' as a unit of social construction, she also left us a legacy of turning our feminist attention towards the 'second sex', a legacy which subsequently came under challenge on the grounds that it left 'man' as the standard of measure.

The Deconstruction of 'Man'

By the end of the 1980s, feminist theory had gone beyond problematizing the category 'women'. There was a growing recognition that equity policies failed to problematize the male norms against which women were being assessed (MacKinnon, 1989), and that a focus on women alone frequently meant identifying 'women' as 'the problem' (Ferguson, 1993). Leaving 'men' out of the analysis meant that masculinism remained central but veiled, and doubly powerful (Cockburn, 1991; Pocock, 1997). Feminist and pro-feminist scholars were beginning to deconstruct our uses of 'man' and 'men' (Cockburn, 1985; Hearn et al., 1989; Connell, 1987). Collinson and Hearn (1994) noted that men and masculinity are conflated with leadership, authority and power:

> Men are not named as men . . . Men are both talked about and ignored, rendered simultaneously explicit and implicit. They are frequently the centre of discourse but they are rarely the focus of interrogation.

Showing how 'men' have been taken as the standard case, therefore, is necessary when investigating what is happening to 'women'. It allows connections to be made between, say, current anxieties about the prospects of boys, and the 'crisis' in middle-class masculinity attending the notion that patriarchal authority is 'leaking away' (Weiner et al., this volume).

Placing 'men' under scrutiny, however, is a strategy deserving of caution. For a start, it is not simply 'men' who exclude, marginalize and problematize 'women'. The anti-women proclivities of some women are evident in the decision-making of Margaret Thatcher in Britain, for example, and in Australia, in the scathing criticisms of 'women' and feminism by one of Australia's most senior academics, Dame Leonie Kramer (Eisenstein, 1991, pp. 19–20; Eveline, 1996). Categorizing 'men' as a universal problem in and of themselves, therefore, is subject to the traps that attend the naming of 'women' (Ferguson, 1993). For the sake of a more accurate analysis we need to take not only men and the production of masculinism into account, but also the asymmetrical locations and allocations of advantage.

Politics

A search of the feminist literature on gender equity reveals a significant omission. In 12 books I took from my shelves, chosen because they indexed 'equality', only one indexed 'men', 'advantages of'. Ten out of these twelve books included 'patriarchy', ten itemized 'difference', seven had 'inequality' and a similar number referred to 'discrimination'. Five indexed 'equal opportunity', and just two had 'male privilege'. The processes that advantage men may be pervasively familiar, and the workings of these processes are challenged in feminist literature. Yet the conceptual category 'male advantage' has not become common, unlike talk of patriarchy, equality or difference, or indeed 'disadvantage'. Nor have feminist microscopes focused on the semantics of the advantage–disadvantage dualism and how they meaningfully situate women. Why have theorists, including feminists, ignored this dualism?

One clue to how talk about advantage is repressed can be found in the responses of Australian feminist policymakers, at the National Women's Electoral Lobby conference in 1992. As one of those who helped formulate policy for the 21st century, I queried why we always used 'women's disadvantage' to justify claims on the state. Why, I asked, don't we criticize 'men's advantage'? Some delegates incorporated the idea as a strategy worth trying. A number of equal opportunity practitioners in industry, government and education, however, spoke of the backlash they would face if they attempted to focus on 'men' or 'men's advantage' as a problem. As one affirmative action training consultant said:

> My heart drops to my boots when you say we need to focus on men as advantaged over women, because I know that means I'd be in for a fight. It's too confrontational, it would put men offside and leave us without the political support we need.

Such responses encapsulate the contradictions and compromises for women whose task it is to pursue gender equity in businesses, bureaucracies and education. The ability to meet their targets is marshalled around inadequate resources and against criticism from right and left, set within a web of allegiances and alliances with those (mainly men) who exercise policy-making power.

Another group of feminists worried that the strategy would lead to the institutional death of existing equity procedures. Political theorist Marian Sawer voices this reaction succinctly:

> The first rule of democratic politics is never to be seen to be taking anything away from anyone . . . Hence equal opportunity policies are sold because they give opportunities to women and benefit everyone, rather than because they take away male advantages.

The fear expressed here is that equal opportunity procedures will be quashed or ignored if women's claims go beyond liberal assimilationism.

In drawing attention to the practical limitations of highlighting male advantage, the women who expressed the above concerns are being realistic about how disruptive such a move would be. But causing disruption is not unknown to feminism. As a major force for change this century, the big success story of the second-wave women's movement has been not only the degree to which it has raised awareness that inequality between women and men is illegitimate, but also the expectations of many women that they can do something about that inequality. The question for the women's movement certainly, but also for policymakers given the task of combating gender inequities, is whether it is possible to turn the hierarchy of advantage/disadvantage on its head, and flesh out the ways that men gain when advantage is relegated to 'hidden text'.

When the concept of 'male advantage' remains unspoken the silence makes gender inequality seem normal. Breaking that silence is no easy task, however. Britt-Marie Berge's chapter in this book exemplifies how attempts to de-normalize the links between 'males' and 'advantage' in schools shows teachers, women and men, actively regenerating that advantage.

Leaving the behaviour of men and boys out of our accounts of educational decision-making, Eleanor Ramsay argues (1995, p. 177), continues 'to normalize both the behaviour and its effects'. Yet a failure to focus simultaneously on how, as women, teachers and feminists, we are also within the body of power that produces advantage can lead us to miss important clues to institutional processes.

The Colour of Gender and the Gender of Colour

A shift from a woman-centred analysis to a focus on men, women and gender politics is indispensable for an analysis of gender equity strategy. Yet in its simple version it leaves the colour of gender, and thus the complexity and contradictions of male advantage, out of the frame. There has recently been much questioning of this colour-blindness, with a growing body of post-colonial writing suggesting that white, middle-class feminism asserts a cultural domination, or hegemony, over other women (Spivak, 1987; Hooks, 1984).

There are few white feminists who can easily face up to charges of racism. Nonetheless, such challenges have propelled feminist theory away from a simple view of gender, or gender and class, to a more wide-reaching examination of the constellation of power dimensions comprising gender, racism and sexuality (Lorde, 1984; Eisenstein, 1994). In tune with women of colour in other countries, indigenous writers in Australia (Sykes, 1975; O'Shane, 1976; Huggins, 1994) mounted significant critiques of the ethnocentricity of white feminists. Joined by the critical voices of migrant women they pointed out that the ideal of the 'Australian woman', on which policies were based, masks an Anglo-Celtic norm (Kilic, 1994).

In what follows I describe two approaches taken by Aboriginal women to de-normalize white ethnocentricity: the first, as I see it, incorporates the modernist, oppositional methods that white feminists in Australia used in their claims for education against the state; the second deploys post-modernist irony and resistance to entertain — and educate — both Aboriginals and non-Aboriginals on the topic of women's lives.

In the 1970s and 1980s, indigenous women demonstrated that the racist heritage of white policies, and white feminists, left their needs out or rendered them invisible. The approach they took was vigorously to confront the racism of non-Aboriginal women: in print, at conferences, in theatres of education, industrial relations and law.

Their most dramatic challenge was a critique of the Women's Electoral Lobby's six-point plan, a catalogue of claims on behalf of 'women', which was used to lobby governments (and which feminists filtering into government agencies implemented) (Eisenstein, 1991). On each of the six points stated indigenous women showed that the claim was antithetical to their needs. On the issue of equal opportunity in education, for example, both Sykes (1975) and O'Shane (1976) argued that Aboriginal men needed these supports as much as women, white or indigenous, since Aboriginal women are more likely to stay on at school, and to go into higher education, than indigenous men are. The narrow focus on gender, they argued, was even more damaging to indigenous culture as a whole — it obscured the cultural genocide against indigenous Australians that resulted from European-based education (O'Shane, 1976). Finding no common ground on any of the six goals of the liberal women's movement in Australia, these critiques challenged the very foundations on which white feminism had constructed its claims for 'full' citizenship for 'women'. In their claims about education, indigenous women were thus educating non-indigenous feminists, and educationists more widely, about the normalization of white, Anglo ethnicity.

The educative thrust of hybridized Aboriginality uses post-modern as well as post-colonial techniques. Hybrid Aboriginal culture has its roots in the near-annihilation of Aboriginal people and community. Ironically, the tragedy of the 'stolen generations' — the shameful taking away of Aboriginal children until the late 1960s and placing them into white adoption or foster care — meant that a small minority of indigenous people gained a degree of Anglo-celtic educational capital. Some have used the knowledge they gained about 'whitey' culture to enable a different, more nuanced confrontation with that culture. Turning to art and politics the approach taken frequently manages to show that 'white' is a colour too (Frankenburg, 1993).

In looking at the work of one of those artists, film-maker Tracey Moffatt, my aim is to juxtapose it with the more confrontational of Aboriginal women's claims for educational equity, and to ask what the two together might indicate about a theory of male advantage for the future.

Tracey Moffatt's films show the multiple ironies in the lives of indigenous women in both pastoral and urban settings. *Night Cries* (1989) reflects the changing power relations between a white 'mother' and an Aboriginal 'daughter'. The film evokes the complex of love, duty and desire for escape that is universally emblematic of mother/daughter relationships. Throughout the film neither woman speaks, and communication occurs through physical, often gentle, touch. One compelling scene, however, chills the white audience: the daughter laughs triumphantly as she cracks a whip outside the house, while inside the aged, crumbling body of the mother convulses with each lash.

The message here is not simply about Aboriginal anger, since it establishes that Aboriginal people are wise to, and wise about, 'whiteys'. Nor is it solely an analysis of the destructive force of racism, because the power of gender is never absent from the women's interactions.

One of the features of the film that many reviewers see as incongruous is the role of Aboriginal songwriter Jimmy Little, who plays himself (Jayamanne, 1993). Yet if we thread gender into the analysis of racial oppression we can see that the pasting on of Little's presence across the interactions of the women is always a signal that racism and sexism cannot be prised apart. Unlike the women, the film's assimilated Aboriginal man has the ability to mimic, and surpass, his white educators in appropriately normalized voice: the Christian missionaries into whose 'protection' so many Aboriginal children were placed have never achieved the popular success in white culture that Jimmy Little's Christian hit song, 'Telephone to Glory' did. There is only one time when Little's hybrid voice is silenced. As if in a dim memory, the young Aboriginal girl sobs inconsolably, despite the mother's sorrowing comfort, after she is sexually harassed by her indigenous playmates, two young boys. Across this universal primal scene — the grief of the mother and daughter at the daughter's realization of sexual vulnerability — Moffatt shows the cheerful figure of Jimmy Little. Silently, he mimes the Elvis Presley hit, 'Love Me Tender', while his face takes on an inappropriate, and sinister, smile.

While the colour of gender constructs the lives of the film's women differently, the gender of colour is a constant companion. My suggestion that Moffatt targets the intermeshing of racism and sexism gains weight from the casting of

Marcia Langton — renowned academic, indigenous activist, and feminist — in the part of the grown-up daughter.

The film is breathtakingly 'educative' in its imagery of Aboriginal survival, in the knowingness about Whites that has ensured regeneration in the face of near-annihilation and tragedy, and in the complicated and contradictory questions and answers to which it alludes.

My purpose here has been to examine the links — but also tensions — between a direct confrontation with white culture (the oppositional strategy of political activists such as Marcia Langton) and the post-modern resistance of Tracey Moffatt's films (which also, for a specific purpose, use Marcia Langton's undoubtedly complex powers). Both modes of address challenge and de-normalize white ethnocentrism. Both are necessary components of reform.

What then can we conclude about the concept of 'male advantage' from these examples of women confronting power in their lives, and using it in their activism and cultural productions? Can we account for how women are implicated in the reproduction of male advantage? How should we understand the agency women marshal from *within* the complexities of race and gender? Does this analysis herald workable clues for educational futures?

For a start, a complex and fluid concept of male advantage would include a focus on power and asymmetry, just as useful accounts of gender and 'race' do. It would mean emphasizing the politics of advantage as well as disadvantage, and being able to stand up and name *who* is being advantaged in what context. It would also mean turning our eyes towards how those advantages are normalized by mundane practices, as Britt-Marie Berge shows in this book.

Second, an understanding of the politics of categorizing would mean recognizing that direct comparisons of 'disadvantage' or 'advantage' cannot be made on the basis of gender or ethnic origin unless the prior structuring which orders 'men' and 'women', or 'Whites' and 'colours' hierarchically is taken into account. In educational terms, we would need to acknowledge that 'girls' disadvantage' and 'boys' disadvantage' are categories comprising two quite different relations of power, privilege and cultural anxiety; they demand educational strategies that can compensate for these differences in structural advantage. Simultaneously, it would mean watching for the effects of our categories, to ensure that dominant cultural norms are troubled by our claims in the same way as gender is, and not shored up by those claims.

Third, we must start from an embodied account of gender which recognizes how constructions of femininity and masculinity not only shape women's bodies as inferior, but deny the diverse ways in which women and girls are anything but passive victims in a patriarchal system. Instead of a view of women as outsiders we need the post-modern visions of Tracey Moffatt's films, and of Robin Burns' research on the gendering effects of discourses of sport and health. We need to remind ourselves that we are never totally outside the body of power. In other words, that we shape our diverse subjectivities and reshape our institutions from within the parameters of gender and male advantage.

Fourth, we need to know that the politics of advantage is always a transformative site of struggle — a fluid, contradictory project. Women need to mount both modernist, oppositional critiques, as indigenous and white feminists have done in Australia, as well as post-modernist resistances which unsettle the stability of any single image of advantage and agency, as Tracey Moffatt's films do. In education this means paying attention to who is accorded what space for movement and growth. It also means being watchful as to whether educational systems are teaching girls to be 'good' and 'nice', and failing to teach them how to challenge impertinently the adequacy of those systems (as Ohrlander suggests).

Finally, this raises the question of how much education itself is a producer of advantage. The advantaging practices in which educational institutions engage are stitched together in diffuse reiterations of power and privilege. As the chapters in this book show, women change education and its outcomes. Yet we must remain alert to the ways in which the hierarchical organization of educational institutions are complicit with the transnational ordering of class (Coulter, this volume), to whether grading practices privilege certain forms of knowledge over others, and to what extent the values they profess are culturally hegemonic. Our response to these questions can be as simple as asking just who our schooling system is teaching to nurture, as many chapters do in this book. And this entails naming the ways in which current practices advantage those who grow up to be most like 'men'.

References

BACCHI, C. (1996) *The Politics of Affirmative Action: 'Women', Equality and Category Politics*, London: Sage.

BROOK, B. (1994) 'Femininity and culture', in PRITCHARD HUGHES, K. (ed.) *Contemporary Australian Feminism*, Melbourne: Longman Cheshire, pp. 52–78.

BURTON, C. (1991) *The Promise and the Price: The Struggle for Equal Opportunity in Women's Employment*, Sydney: Allen and Unwin.

CASTLEMAN, T., ALLEN, M., BASTALICH, W. and WRIGHT, P. (1994) *Limited Access: Women's Disadvantage in Higher Education Employment*, South Melbourne: NTEU.

COCKBURN, C. (1985) *Machinery of Dominance: Women, Men and Technical Know-how*, London: Pluto Press.

COCKBURN, C. (1991) *In the Way of Women: Men's Resistance to Sex Equality in Organizations*, London: Macmillan.

COLLINSON, D. and HEARN, J. (1994) 'Naming men as men: Implications for work organization and management', in *Gender, Work and Organization*, **1**, 1, pp. 2–22.

CONNELL, R.W. (1987) *Gender and Power: Society, the Person and Sexual Politics*, Cambridge: Polity Press.

DE BEAUVOIR, S. (1952) *The Second Sex*, PARSHLEY, H.M. (trans.), Harmondsworth, UK: Penguin Books.

EISENSTEIN, Z. (1988) *The Female Body and the Law*, Berkeley and Los Angeles: University of California Press.

EISENSTEIN, H. (1991) *Gender Shock: Practising Feminism on Two Continent*, Sydney: Allen and Unwin.

EISENSTEIN, Z. (1994) *The Color of Gender: Reimaging Democracy*, Berkeley and London: University of California Press.

ELGQVIST-SALTZMAN, I. (1992) 'Gravel in the machinery or hub of the wheel?', in EDUARDS, M.L., ELGQVIST-SALTZMAN, I., LUNDGREN, E., SJÖBLAD, C., SUNDIN, E. and WIKANDER, U. (eds) *Rethinking Change: Current Swedish Feminist Research*, Uppsala, Sweden: HSFR.

EVELINE, J. (1994) 'The politics of advantage', *Australian Feminist Studies*, **19**, Autumn, pp. 129–54.

EVELINE, J. (1996) 'The worry of going limp: Are you keeping up in senior management?', *Australian Feminist Studies*, **11**, 3, pp. 65–79.

FERGUSON, K. (1993) *The Man Question: Visions of Subjectivity in Feminist Theory*, Berkeley: University of California Press.

FRANKENBURG, R. (1993) *The Social Construction of Whiteness: White Women, Race Matters*, Minneapolis: University of Minnesota Press.

GATENS, M. (1991) *Feminism and Philosophy: Perspectives on Difference and Equality*, London: Polity Press.

HEARN, J., SHEPPARD, D.L., TANCRED-SHERIFF, P. and BURRELL, G. (1989) *The Sexuality of Organization*, London: Sage.

HOOKS, B. (1984) *Aint I a Woman?: Black Women and Feminism*, Boston: South End Press.

HUGGINS, J. (1994) 'A contemporary view of Aboriginal women's relationship to the white women's movement', in GRIEVE, N. and BURNS, A. (eds) *Australian Women: Contemporary Feminist Thought*, Melbourne: Oxford University Press, pp. 70–9.

JAYAMANNE, L. (1993) 'Love me tender, love me true, lever let me go . . . : A Sri Lankan reading of Tracey Moffatt's night cries — a rural tragedy', in GUNEW, S. and YEATMAN, A. (eds) *Feminism and the Politics of Difference*, St Leonards, NSW: Allen and Unwin, pp. 73–84.

KILIC, K. (1994) 'Who is an Australian woman?', in HUGHES, K.P. (ed.) *Contemporary Australian Feminism*, Melbourne: Longman Cheshire, pp. 11–29.

LORDE, A. (1984) *Sister Outsider: Essays and Speeches*, New York: The Crossing Press.

LUKE, C. (1993) 'Women in higher education: Gendered discourse and cultural power', in BAKER, D. and FOGARTY, M. (eds) *A Gendered Culture: Educational Management in the Nineties*, Melbourne: Victoria University of Technology, pp. 55–74.

MACKINNON, C.A. (1989) *Toward a Feminist Theory of the State*, Cambridge, Massachusetts: Harvard University Press.

MASLEN, G. (1995) 'Gender roles swapped: Report finds uni men "disadvantaged"', *Campus Review*, **5**, 12, March 30–April 5.

O'SHANE, P. (1976) 'Is there any relevance in the women's movement for Aboriginal women?', *Refractory Girl*, **12**, September, pp. 31–5.

PETTMAN, J. (1992) *Living in the Margins*, Sydney: Allen and Unwin.

POCOCK, B. (1997) 'Gender in the field of industrial relations: What are we missing?', Paper presented at AIRAANZ Conference, Brisbane, 3 January–2 February.

POINER, G. and WILLS, S. (1991) *The Gifthorse: A Critical Look at Equal Employment Opportunity in Australia*, Sydney: Allen and Unwin.

PRINGLE, R. and WATSON, S. (1992) '"Women's interests" and the post-structuralist state', in BARRETT, M. and PHILLIPS, A. (eds) *Destabilizing Theory: Contemporary Feminist Debates*, London: Polity, pp. 53–73.

Joan Eveline

Ramsay, E. (1995) 'Management, gender and language — Or who is hiding behind the glass ceiling and why can't we see them?', in Limerick, B. and Lingard, B. (eds) *Gender and Changing Educational Management*, Sydney: Hodder Headline, pp. 174–86.

Riley, D. (1988) *Am I That Name? Feminism and the Category of 'Women' in History*, London: Macmillan Press.

Spelman, E.V. (1988) *Inessential Woman: Problems of Exclusion in Feminist Thought*, Boston: Beacon Press.

Spivak, G.C. (1987) *In Other Worlds: Essays in Cultural Politics*, New York: Methuen.

Sykes, R. (1975) 'Black women in Australia', in Mercer, J. (ed.) *The Other Half*, Victoria: Penguin Books.

The Weekend Australian. (1996) 'Albright appointment signals Clinton's new style', 7–8 December, p. 1.

Walter, C. and Young, B. (1997) 'Gender bias in Alberta social studies 30 examinations: Cause and effect', *Canadian Social Studies: The History and Social Science Teacher*, **31**, 2, pp. 83–6 and 89.

Weis, L. (1990) *Working Class Without Work: High School Students in a De-industrializing Economy*, New York: Routledge.

Notes on Contributors

Madeleine Arnot is a university lecturer in the Faculty of Education and a Fellow of Jesus College, Cambridge. Recent publications include: *Gender Equality and Educational Reforms* with M. David and G. Weiner; *Feminism and Social Justice: International Perspectives* (edited with K. Weiler, Falmer Press). Forthcoming books are: *Gender and Educational Performance* (OFSTED) and *Closing the Gender Gap* with M. David and G. Weiner (Polity Press). Dr Arnot currently holds a Leverhulme Research Fellowship to extend a European Project on gender and citizenship and is working on *Project Arianne: Broadening Adolescent Masculinity*.

Sylvia Benckert is an Associate Professor in Physics at Umeå University in Sweden. She teaches physics and has been working in the field of gender and science. She is now working with Else-Marie Staberg on a project about women chemists and physicists in Sweden.

Britt-Marie Berge is a senior lecturer in the Department of Education at Umeå University, Sweden. Her 1992 dissertation was entitled *Craft Teachers as Spearheads for an Equal Society? A Study of Female and Male Future Craft Teachers and of the School Subject Craft in Swedish Compulsory School*. Currently, her main field of research is the construction and (re)construction of complex gender relations in compulsory school classrooms. Of special interest are those classrooms where teachers are developing gender equity pedagogy: what happens to gender relations when teachers try to change prevailing patterns?

Robin Burns has worked in experimental psychology, anthropology, the diplomatic service, comparative education, peace education, social education, public health and women's studies, from her position within the Graduate School of Education at La Trobe University, Melbourne, Australia. Her current major interest is in people and wilderness manifested in two projects: writing a book on women in Antarctica, and investigating the ways in which scientists, conducting their research in remote environments, interact and construct knowledge based on their fieldwork. This has taken her so far to Antarctica and the Namib Desert. In 1996 the culmination of her peace education work was published (co-authored with Robert Aspeslagh), *Three decades of peace education around the world*, Garland, New York, USA.

Rebecca Priegert Coulter is Associate Dean of the Faculty of Education, University of Western Ontario, London, Ontario, Canada. Her teaching and research interests lie in the areas of gender and education, the history of education, and the politics of educational restructuring. She has been actively involved in the Canadian women's movement and in the struggle to defend public education.

Miriam David is Professor and Dean of Research at the London Institute. Formerly she was Professor and Director of the Social Sciences Research Centre at South Bank University. She has an international reputation for her research into family, gender, education and social policy. Her most recent publication is *Educational Reforms and Gender Equality in Education,* 1996 EOC (with Arnot and Weiner). She is also co-editor with Dr Dulcie Groves of the *Journal of Social Policy.*

Inga Elgqvist-Saltzman is Professor of Educational Science. For many years she was affiliated with the Department of Education at Umeå University, Sweden, and held a post as Fellow in Behavioural Research on Sex Equality set up by the Swedish Council for Research in the Humanities and Sciences 1986–1992. Since retirement she has been linked to Teacher Training at the University of Kalmar where she is undertaking research on early women students and the cultural heritage of teacher training. Her publications in the area of gender and education include contemporary as well as historical studies. Her innovative life line perspective methodology, was presented in *Gender and Education in a Life Perspective* (co-editor Gunilla Bjerén, Avebury, 1994).

Joan Eveline lectures in organizational and labour studies at the University of Western Australia, after eleven years in Women's Studies at Murdoch University, Western Australia and Flinders University, South Australia. As a postdoctoral fellow at the Research School of Social Sciences, Australian National University, Canberra, she wrote on organizational resistance to affirmative action, with the *Reshaping Australian Institutions Program.* Her research on men's advantage and women's work has canvassed management, mining, politics, citizenship and tertiary education.

Victoria Foster is a Visiting Scholar in the Faculty of Education at the University of Canberra, Australia. Her research interests and publications focus on interdisciplinary gender studies related to philosophy of education, curriculum development and praxis and the emerging field of civics and citizenship education. She is currently working on a book entitled *Space Invaders: Barriers to Equality in the Schooling of Girls* to be published by Allen and Unwin in the Contemporary Issues in Education series. She works as a consultant in professional development activities in gender and education.

Alison Mackinnon is Professor of History and Gender Studies at the University of South Australia. She is also Director of the Institute for Social Research. She has published widely on the history of women's higher education and the links between higher education and changing patterns of family formation. Her most recent publication *Love and Freedom: professional women and the reshaping of personal life* (Cambridge University Press, 1997) won a major Australian award for literary and cultural criticism. With Moira Gatens she edited *Gender and Institutions: welfare, work and citizenship* (forthcoming in 1998 from Cambridge University Press), an anthology of feminist critique of institutional design theory.

Grace Mak is Associate Professor at the Chinese University of Hong Kong. She teaches courses in Comparative Education and Sociology of Education. She has published on education in China and Hong Kong and has been a consultant to education and community development projects in China. She is editor of *Women, Education and Development in Asia* (New York: Garland, 1996) and co-editor of *Higher Education in Asia: An International Handbook and Reference Guide* (Westport, CT, 1997)

Kajsa Ohrlander is a senior lecturer and coordinator at the Centre for Child and Youth Research, in Stockholm Institute of Education, Sweden. Her academic writing has been wholly focused on Sweden and mainly concerned with historical analyses of power-relations children's politics and women's politics. She is currently working on a project called 'Concepts of children's needs and gender equality — discursive transformations within the 1960–70's Swedish reform politics'. In April 1998 she is arranging a conference in Stockholm with a similar topic 'Safe children and free women' where the status of women in Sweden will be critically analyzed. She is building up a women's studies program in education in the Stockholm Institute of Education. This is her first article in English.

Alison Prentice is a Professor at the Ontario Institute for Studies in Education of the University of Toronto and an adjunct professor at the University of Victoria, British Columbia, Canada. Her early research in the history of education focused on elementary schooling and teachers; more recently she has explored the history of women's work in higher education. She has published articles and books in the fields of educational and women's history, most recently the second edition of the co-authored text, *Canadian Women: A History* (1996) and a co-edited essay collection entitled *Creating Historical Memory: English — Canadian Women and the Work of History* (1997).

Kerstin W. Shands is an Assistant Professor of English literature at Stockholm University and an editor for *Kvinnovetenskaplig Tidskrift*. She has been a visiting scholar at Columbia University, New York, and a postdoctoral research associate at the University of Kansas at Lawrence. Among her books are *Escaping the Castle of Patriarchy: Patterns of Development in the Novels of Gail Godwin* (Uppsala, 1990), and *The Repair of the World: The Novels of Marge Piercy* (Greenwood, 1994). She is currently at work on a study of spatial metaphors in feminist texts (to be published by Greenwood Press).

Else-Marie Staberg is a senior lecturer in Education. Her 1992 thesis focused on gender and science education in Swedish lower secondary schools. She is working on a study of science education in secondary schools and on another, with Sylvia Benckert, on Swedish women chemists and physicists. She is currently Director for the Centre for Women's Studies at Umeå University, Sweden.

Gaby Weiner is Professor of Educational Research at South Bank University, London, United Kingdom and Visiting Professor at Umeå University, Sweden. Involved with social justice issues since the 1970s, she has published widely on a range of topics, in particular relating to equal opportunities and gender. She has written and edited a number of books, research reports and articles, and is currently co-editor (with Lyn Yates and Kathleen Weiler) of the Open University Press series *Feminist Educational Thinking*. Her most recent publications are *Feminisms in Education: an introduction* (1994), *Equal Opportunities in Colleges and Universities*, 1995, (with M. Farish, J. McPake and J. Powney) and *Higher Education and Equality: a guide*, 1997, (with J. Powney and S. Hamilton).

Hildur Ve is Professor of Sociology at the Institute of Sociology, Bergen University, Norway. Her research interests include a feminist perspective on family sociology and sociology of education with particular emphasis on class and gender differences in socialization, citizenship and gender, and gender differences in primary school. She has published widely in these areas.

Lyn Yates is Associate Professor of Education at La Trobe University, Melbourne, Australia. She is author of *The Education of Girls: Policy Research and the Question of Gender* (ACER, 1993) and editor of the collection *Feminism and Education* (La Trobe University Press, 1993).

Index